THE INDONESIAN ECONOMY SINCE 1965

First published 1978 in Great Britain by
FRANK CASS AND COMPANY LIMITED
Gainsborough House, Gainsborough Road,
London, E11 1RS, England

and in the United States of America by
FRANK CASS AND COMPANY LIMITED
c/o Biblio Distribution Centre
81 Adams Drive, P.O. Box 327 Totowa, New Jersey 07511

British Library Cataloguing in Publication Data

Palmer, Ingrid
The Indonesian economy since 1965.
1. Indonesia—Economic conditions—1945–
I. Title
330.9'598'03 HC447

ISBN 0-7146-3088-8

Printed in Great Britain by
T. J. Press (Padstow) Ltd., Padstow, Cornwall

THE INDONESIAN ECONOMY SINCE 1965

A Case Study of Political Economy

INGRID PALMER

FRANK CASS

Contents

List of Tables

Preface

Numerous articles have been written on the economy of Indonesia since 1965, but as articles they have not been substantial enough to present a detailed overview of all sectors. Nor have they offered a framework of continuity from the past to the most recent developments. And yet this country, the fifth most populous in the world, merits such a study because it has received a disproportionate amount of attention from foreign capital and aid.

This study is presented in a form which describes the underlying structure of the mass-based economy and its problems, and goes on to show how the hectic economic activity after 1965 failed to come to terms with the real needs of the people. It divides the new Indonesian economy into endogenous and exogenous parts in order to highlight the gulf between 'growth' and 'development'.

An index was not included for several reasons. First, very few persons were named in the book as leading actors in the events recorded and those persons who were influential or who have written on the Indonesian economy in a useful manner are recorded in the Bibliography. Second, as can be seen from the Bibliography, as well as from the text, the book was written not only for academics but also for journalists and people in ordinary walks of life who are interested in Indonesia, and was therefore not intended as a formal textbook. Third, the titles of the chapters, the list of contents and the list of tables offer the reader a quick and ready guide to where individual subjects are discussed.

I have to thank Professor W. F. Wertheim for his many detailed comments on the manuscript which were of great help. The ideas, and any mistakes, remain my own. My thanks also go to Pat Triviere and Susan Simmonds who prepared the manuscript for publication.

Chapter 1

Introduction

The term 'political economy' is used in the title of this book to focus attention on the incessant interaction of political and economic life. To talk of 'the economy' alone is to imply that this aspect of life has a relentless, but objective, imperative of its own constrained by the limits of resources whose active dimensions are independent of non-economic or non-physical factors. More importantly, the awareness of political economy is an aid to identifying the sectoral flow of surpluses and their availability for re-investment. By awarding greater recognition to the dichotomy of private and social profit one is less inhibited when viewing the internal consistency of a strategy of overall development and of the feasibility of maintaining the momentum of its general thrust. To challenge the hegemony of mere economic analysis is to question why price distortions and market imperfections are so obsessionally seized upon by development economists when the viability of a strategy is suspect for far more obvious and significant reasons. It is to question why a system of thought which reduces human contribution to development either to profit-maximising entrepreneurship or to units of labour ever gained such popular currency. It is to question why a country should be obliged to aim at the outer edge of its national material production possibilities, with only passing reference to social and political possibilities.

We know, of course, that the expression 'the most efficient allocation of resources' is highly subjective to the prevailing distributions of income, assets and political power as well as to artificially created wants. And yet it is a response which is chanted with unfailing religious reverence by western economists. We all know the gross astigmatisms of theoreticians, yet the reverence continues.

Indonesia is such a huge archipelagian country with its full share of dualisms and pluralisms that there are as many optimal plans for it as there are places from which to view the country. For this reason any attempt to utilise the theory of comparative advantage will be damaging to some people's livelihoods and so to power balances. The theory as it was applied to East Pakistan jute exports intended to finance West Pakistan's industrialisation gave birth to Bangladesh. The same relation, pushed hard between Sumatra and Java, could produce a similar result for Indonesia. The theory of comparative advantage must always flounder in the issues of 'whose advantage?', and 'subject to which political feasibilities?'.

The other main theory which is worshipped as intellectual manna is that of equating economic opportunity costs at the margin. This theory states that if a resource can earn more in another employment its current employment has an opportunity cost and that its allocation is therefore sub-optimal. Apart from the fact that the market value of resources in alternative employments will vary for every distribution of income and wealth, it ignores the implications of one important factor of production always reproducing and multiplying itself in a manner largely independent of its economic return. This peculiar characteristic of labour has never been properly accommodated in the body of economic theory except in scarcely veiled suggestions that the working class should be prevented from breeding. This indifference to human needs, and the implicit assumption that human beings are there to serve the economy and that the economy is not there to serve the people, explains the strange omission in the literature of a term such as 'nutritional opportunity cost': that is to say, that a strategy being followed may have a higher cost in terms of malnutrition or undernutrition than alternative strategies. Likewise the absence of political and social opportunity costs; though less so because, whereas there is no known case of an economist starving some have been known to fall from power for causing political trouble, and they act as an example to others.

This study of Indonesia describes the intended and actual sectoral growth patterns since 1966 and the likely effect of both on overall development.

In designing this study there were found to be difficulties of bringing order to an analysis of the economic changes. For example, should there be separate chapters on foreign investment and domestic investment? If so, how does one record what is rehabilitation and what is expansion, a distinction which is so important?

It was finally decided that the separation of rehabilitation and expansion was the more valuable design for several reasons, chiefly:

1. With the emergence of so many major new characteristics of the economy the fortunes of the original mass endogenous (and indigenous) economy needed special treatment. Since it was in the rehabilitation process that labour-intensive mass livelihoods were

to be found rather than in new technological investment (whether domestic or foreign) the extent of real rehabilitation had to be recorded on its own.

2. Although the conflict of foreign investment versus domestic investment is dear to the hearts of both the international left and the Indonesian middle class it is seen differently by the majority of Indonesians. Given half a chance Indonesian investors would follow foreign investors into the same enclave industries, would also remit profits overseas, would do the same ecological damage, and would use the same capital-intensive technology. The effect therefore of *net* investment in *new* industries on the body of the economy would be the same for both domestic and foreign investments.
3. With the emergence of the *pribumi* (indigenous Indonesian ownership of capital) issue, of the obligatory joint venture, of the stock exchange and the transfer of shares in foreign enterprises the rivalry between foreign investors and the Indonesian middle class is being resolved politically and institutionally. From the point of view of the Indonesian masses foreign and domestic investors combine into the new ruling class. Since they have a common high consumption culture, and indeed almost a common language (English), the foreign investment issue is more accurately described as an alien techno-cultural investment issue. What is now foreign-owned is, in fact, kept hostage in the country for the benefit of the new middle class.
4. There remains, of course, the factor of economic nationalism and it has a bearing on the future managerial quality of post-1965 investments. Moreover, the transfer of title to capital from foreign hands to *pribumi* hands makes an interesting political study. Thus provision has been made to describe these changes in a later chapter after the rehabilitation and expansion issues have been covered.

Thirty years after independence the economic structure of Indonesia bears characteristics which are reminders of the last hundred years of colonial rule. Until the turn of this century colonial development was almost exclusively on Java with the aim of providing a cheap supply of dessert crops, such as coffee, tea, tobacco and spices as well as sugar. The Culture System (1830–1870) had obliged Javanese farmers to cultivate certain export commodities which were highly lucrative to the European-Indies trade, and had set the pattern of Java's present production. The fine allocation of land resources and attempts to raise crop yields led to a rapid increase in Java's population during the nineteenth century. Although enjoying only 12 per cent of cultivable land in Indonesia (not allowing for double-cropping), Java today carries 60 per cent of the population. Poverty surveys at the turn of the century ushered in the Ethical Policy of health, public works and canal irrigation for rice cultivation. But industry was disallowed because it would have threatened Dutch home-based industries. The twentieth century exploitation of Banka, Biliton, Sumatra and Sulawesi for tin, rubber and copra came too late to redress this cruel demographic imbalance. Today Java's population density averages out around 600 per square kilometre against Sumatra's 42, Kalimantan's 9, and Sulawesi's 48. Transmigration efforts go back to 1900 but they reached a peak of only 47,600 persons annually in the years 1938–1941. Between 1957 and 1962 they had regained a (gross) level of 22,000 persons annually (Jones, June 1966).

Even before the Second World War Java was struggling to feed itself on its great rice industry and after independence it became plain that this island was increasingly to fail to pay its way. The dualism of the economic structure of the country was accompanied by the dualism of urban and rural life styles, which was most marked in Java.

Another legacy of the colonial past which still imposes a heavy burden on the development process is the nature of political growth. Colonial government was like an authoritarian one-party system. Since its *raison d'être* was to extract primary produce at a low cost the rural administration had to be efficient. After independence the administration became heavily urbanised and intellectualised as the cargo cult mentality of the educated elite led it to measuring its distance from backwoods rural people. The continued extraction of primary produce at a low cost was done less efficiently after independence because this political growth caused economic and infrastructural erosion. The sector producing the economic lifeline to the new state was left to be politically serviced by a rural elite. It has become increasingly apparent that this political dualism leaves two voices speaking at cross purposes, and this latent conflict as well as that between national Moslem businessmen in urban areas and military leaders, has become one of the most important justifications for a study of the *political* economy. For many years in Indonesia these underlying fractures between rural and urban interests and between entrepreneurial and parasitic interests were camouflaged by the exciting rivalry between the army and the Communist party which so obsessed foreign observers. Unfortunately the only force which had any chance of reconciling rural and urban interests and of substituting something new for the economic and civil order of colonial days, namely the Communist party, has been withdrawn from the scene. By removing the Communist party the national economic elite and the military-bureaucratic complex have unveiled their mutually antagonistic interests. It is only by the recent entry of enriched military officers into the modern economic sector that some of that antagonism has been reconciled.

The means of entry as well as the sectoral interests of foreign aid and investment are further reason for a recognition of political economy. The extent of foreign aid since 1966 has been greater than was predicted by the donors. Compared with the attention awarded other developing countries the interest lavished on Indonesia by rich industrialised countries and by international agencies cannot be explained by the country's poverty. The terms on which foreign investment entered Indonesia, its choice of industry and its erosive effect on existing national industry, all indicate a bonanza for foreign investors, secured by preceding stabilisation and rehabilitation aid from the public international sector. The choices made by the foreign investors must always have more to do with optimising their interests than those of the recipient country.

The exploitation of resources in turn has determined the domestic distribution of income and wealth, both regionally and class-wise, setting up new parameters in the political economy. A minority of Indonesian nationals, especially a clique of Chinese, the military and the state oil company leadership, have found themselves in new powerful positions.

All these changes could not have occurred in the way and to the extent they did unless Indonesian political sovereignty was prostrate in 1966. Few would contest this. To understand how this came about and how low was the resistance of the national economy to the invasion of foreign funds the crisis of 1965/6 needs to be described.

Chapter 2

The Economic Crisis of 1965/6 and the Gamble Taken

Before describing the nature of the economic watershed it must be stated that the popular thesis that the events of 1965 were caused overwhelmingly by economic factors is erroneous. Newcomers to the Indonesian scene since 1965 have been so thoroughly propagandised by the economic verbiage of policies of stabilisation and rehabilitation that, without anyone saying as much in so many words, thay have frequently gained the impression that the political upheaval was necessary to save the economy. It would be more accurate to say that the economic extremities of the last few years of President Sukarno's rule lent cover of confusion to the long-desired liquidation of the left.

No special brief is held here for the Communist party of Indonesia. But it is imperative to point out that, on balance, political forces which encourage the more effective developmental use of resources were enormously diminished by the massacres and arrests that took place, while those which obstruct that use were commensurately strengthened. The Communist party was easily the most important agent of change threatening the duality of poverty and privilege. That rehabilitation of a kind ever took place in these circumstances must be put down to the massive inflow of aid. Moreover, the political upheavals that followed in 1965/6 could hardly be said to have facilitated remedies to the economic crisis. The ferocity of the military is evidence in itself that a non-economic crisis of severe proportions was occurring concurrently with economic decline. The massacre and imprisonment of the left could not have relieved the burden of military expenditure on the budget, which all were agreed was the major cause of inflation. The suspension and regression of land reform was not going to raise the effective use of resources in agriculture.

THE NATURE OF THE FINANCIAL CRISIS

Having said this the extent of economic paralysis can be described. At the time the single most eloquent statistic was the total debt of about

$2,300 million, of which about half was a Soviet and East European military debt. The immediate forecast, for 1966, was of foreign exchange earnings of $430 million (including oil) and minimum import requirements of $560 million; not to mention a debt servicing of $530 million. Rice import requirements were conservatively put at $30 million and imports of equipment, new materials and spare parts another $350 million (Panglaykim and Arndt, 1966). There were no reserves left, In fact, the only thing left in the national till were some bureaucratic fingers groping for any remaining dollars.

The shortage of imported raw materials had reputedly brought industrial production to less than 20 per cent of its capacity. Inflation was running at about 500 per cent a year with obvious further erosion of exports, and the Rupiah was many times over-valued. Transport and communications were in some disarray. It was later estimated that $140 millions were required to restore the railway system to its 1939 capacity. Lack of inter-island shipping was seriously affecting the movement of food such that while hunger oedema was spreading in Java stocks of maize (encouraged by the drive to substitute maize for rice in the declining diet) were rotting elsewhere in the archipelago, or being considered for export as 'surplus stocks'. The earlier drive towards outright self-sufficiency in rice had failed, and the higher (although of questionable human digestibility) protein content of maize had led the government to aim for domestic procurements of 302,000 tons of maize in 1964. In the event only 89,000 tons could be gathered. Even where shipping was available bank credit sometimes could not be obtained for the transportation of food.

In December 1965 foreign exchange commitments were no longer met. The Central Bank found itself unable to honour cash letters of credit and suspended payment on some foreign trade credit. The prognostication was bleak: the momentum of budget deficit expansion could not be restrained without extra resources, but the inflation that stemmed from it was eroding export earnings. At the same time foreign debt servicing was peaking.

While gross government expenditure had risen about seven times between 1961 and 1964 gross receipts had risen less than five times. Therefore, the deficit was increasing as a proportion of gross receipts. Income tax, though improving, never played a role comparable to that in developed countries. Even had confrontation towards Malaysia and all development expenditure been immediately halted, the narrowing of the gap between revenue and expenditure would have depended on some rationalisation of production incentives to raise the tax-bearing capacity of production.

The impact of inflation on exports and the lagged consequence for imports can clearly be seen in Table 2.1.

TABLE 2.1

Balance of Payments: 1960-6 ($U.S. millions)

	1960	1961	1962	1963	1964	1965 (to 30 June)	1966 estimate)
RECEIPTS							
1. exports (fob)	601	527	470	412	426	173	360
2. oil*	280	239	241	244	206	25	50
3. other	—	—	—	—	—	—	20
TOTAL	881	766	711	656	632	198	430
EXPENDITURE							
4. imports	749	1,056	737	602	590	230	450
5. invisibles (net)	316	231	222	282	272	125	170
6. debt service	**	**	**	**	**	**	530***
TOTAL	1,065	1,287	959	884	862	355	1,150
7. capital inflow	180	353	80	86	142	21	n.a.
8. deficit/surplus	—4†	—168	—168	—142	—88	—136	—720

Source: J. Panglaykim and H. W. Arndt, *The Indonesian Economy: Facing a New Era?* Rotterdam University Press, Rotterdam, 1966, p.14.

* Gross to 1964, net for 1965 and 1966.

** Included in item 5.

*** Before rescheduling. Also debt servicing would have been $270 million in 1967, $275 million in 1968, and then progressively to under $200 million.

† Corrected from the reference.

Even oil exports, emanating from an enclave industry with its own supply of foreign exchange for spare parts, declined sharply. By 1965 annual total exports were running at little more than one quarter of 1961 imports. Clearly development was not being supported by the expansion of foreign earnings. The process of deterioration in 1965 simply accelerated.

The situation could best be described by saying that the economy was locked into a downward spiral whose circumgyrations were becoming smaller and faster. Inflation had decreased incentives to produce for export and therefore the capacity to import. With a substantial proportion of government revenue coming from import duties and sales of excise taxes, the decline in imports of consumer goods and raw materials had weakened the tax-raising capacity more than if income tax had played the role it does in developed countries. Inflation, so largely caused by deficit financing, could not then be ameliorated by sudden reductions of the deficit. Yet holding down consumer prices by an injection of imports of consumer goods required foreign exchange which could not be generated by the economy. Furthermore, the very momentum of inflation was breeding new inflation by speculative withdrawal of goods from the market. Thus had persistent and increasing inflation closed the circle of cause and effect. The violence of the political changes that occurred later in 1965 aggravated this situation by causing postponement of production decisions and turning liquid assets into non-perishable commodities and raw materials which were then hoarded.

THE MIXED PERFORMANCE OF PRODUCTION

But to understand the inadequacies of the later stabilisation and rehabilitation programme and the first Five Year Plan (1969–74) it is necessary to describe the issues of production which lay behind the financial crisis of 1965. Inflation has been chronic in Indonesia since full sovereignty in 1949. Post-war reconstruction, the Korean War boom in tin and rubber, and the attempt to build a national economy added to the enlarging military budget to exert demand pressure on limited resources. Periodically the gradual impact of inflation was sharply rectified by devaluation or monetary reform. The role of the banks as deposits of savings and as lenders of funds weakened. In 1950 40 per cent of the money supply was in bank deposits, but by 1965 the figure was only 26 per cent. The informal credit market that expanded into the vacuum was highly susceptible to speculative forces, while the official monetary instruments were diminished in efficacy. But all these monetary events had different impacts according to the final markets of each sector of production. It might be surmised that the erosive effect of long-term inflation on purchasing power would lead to a shift towards production of more staple, low-grade foods and decline in inter-island and inter-province specialisation. This seems to have been the case with peanuts and soybeans, especially the latter which is a specialisation of East Java. But it is not possible to separate the influence of declining inter-island shipping. Moreover, as Tables 2.2 and 2.3 show, the shift towards cheaper sources of calories began in the mid-1950s when there was no suggestion of declining per capita purchasing power. It is more likely to have been governed by limitations of land in Java and in populated areas of the other islands. The decline in harvested areas of irrigated rice on Java, in particular, could hardly be explained by an economic analysis of inflation. The weakening irrigation systems are much more likely to have been the chief cause. The more erratic performance of rice acreage in Java and Madura can be attributed to fluctuating rice imports, which were heavily directed towards Java's cities, as well as to drought. A probable factor in maintaining the level of rice production was government purchase and distribution of rice. These procurements of rice were distributed in cities and towns to government employees of various kinds (including coolies) as part of their salaries but at a very low imported price. The measure constituted a very important redistribution of income and one which retained its real value during inflation. According to the National Social and Economic Surveys of 1963–4 and 1969–70 the poorest category of rural people could depend on government-distributed rice for almost ten per cent in 1963–4 but for only two per cent in 1969–70 (Susenas 1963–4 and 1969–70). The same data also indicate that while government rice distribution in 1963–4 was relatively (as proportions of total rice consumed), though not absolutely, egalitarian, by 1969–70 there was no pretence at even a relatively egalitarian distribution: absolute amounts of government-distributed rice rose very much faster with total *per capita* expenditure on rice in 1969–70. Whereas in 1963–4 the *per capita* quantity of government-distributed rice was 8.3 times greater in the highest than in the lowest expenditure class, in 1969–70 it was 34·8 times greater.

TABLE 2.2

Harvested Areas of Most Important Food Crops in Indonesia: 1953-64 (100 hectares)

	Irrigated paddy and gogorant-jah	*Non-irri-gated paddy*	*Total Paddy*	*Maize*	*Cas-sava*	*Sweet Potat-oes*	*Pea-nuts*	*Soy-beans*
1953	5380	1085	6465	1969	1042	325	292	457
1954	5469	1144	6613	2518	1071	285	324	525
1955	5517	1053	6570	2042	1077	279	298	515
1956	5701	1001	6702	2232	1125	384	317	502
1957	5748	1050	6798	2087	1221	404	341	525
1958	5914	1076	6990	2702	1341	449	331	594
1959	5936	1217	7153	2290	1456	394	364	612
1960	5975	1310	7285	2640	1417	393	377	651
1961	5534	1273	6807*	2462	1478	366	365	625
1962	5836	1447	7283	3175	1449	544	373	594
1963	5329	1402	6731	2559	1598	484	352	539
1964	5484	1496	6980	3646	1579	620	373	571

*Corrected from the references.

Sources: 1953-61: Sie Kwat Soen, (1968), *Prospects for Agricultural Development in Indonesia,* Centre for Agricultural Publishing and Documentation, Wageningen. 1962-64: *Statistical Pocketbook of Indonesia 1964-7,* Central Bureau of Statistics, Jakarta, pp. 92, 94.

TABLE 2.3

Total Indonesian Rice Imports and Harvested Areas of Principal Food Crops in Java and Madura: 1940, 1953-64 (1000 hectares)

	Total Rice Imports (1000 tons)	Irrigated paddy and gogor-antjah	Non-Irri-gated paddy	Total Paddy	Maize	Cassava	Sweet Pota-toes	Pea-nuts	Soy-beans
1940		3724	365	4089	1983	1041	209	251	418
1953		3768	249	4017	1499	868	216	240	422
1954		3897	260	4157	2000	866	174	270	478
1955		3925	264	4189	1578	876	176	253	462
1956		4076	224	4300	1702	899	260	264	447
1957		4069	242	4311	1556	987	277	289	462
1958		4124	265	4389	2106	1075	302	283	533
1959	608	4056	273	4329	1677	1188	258	300	531
1960	967	4006	314	4320	1929	1145	250	313	577
1961	684	3668	324	3992	1823	1142	213	294	541
1962	536	3707	384	4091	2352	1137	350	293	514
1963	487	3301	346	3647	1867	1276	285	282	462
1964	1085	3295	360	3655	2775	1255	418	296	477

Sources: 1940, 1953-62: Sie Kwat Soen, pp. 51-2; 1965-6: *Statistical Pocketbook of Indonesia 1964-7*, p.91.

When Dutch estate managers and technical advisers were expelled in 1957–8, the fortunes of the estate and peasant export sectors began to diverge. The decline in the former and its impact on the balance of payments is frequently used as illustration of the effect of inflation on export earnings. However, smallholders managed to maintain production levels and in some instances raised them, so that the quick conclusion that inflation was the main cause of a decline in export crops must be questioned. Table 2.4 suggests that the complaints about Sukarno's mis-management of the primary export sector were largely to do with trends in estate production whose former and remaining foreign owners were highly vocal. The pattern of estate and smallholder production was not to continue in the next decade.

Industrial production declined in the last few years before 1965, but as can be seen from the selected major items shown in Table 2.5, this occurred in those industries dependent on imported raw materials or on levels of activity in the construction industry.

These data have been presented here to illustrate the all too infrequently discussed different sectoral performances behind the foreign exchange crisis of 1965, and thus to point to the real nature of the rehabilitation requirements. They also reveal that the erosion of some established specialisation set in before what is usually regarded

TABLE 2.4

Area, Production and Average Yield of Major Export Crops: 1955, 1960, and 1965

	Smallholder			*Estate*		
	Area (1000 hectares)	Production (1000 metric tons)	Yield (quintals per ha.)	Area (1000 hectares)	Production (1000 metric tons)	Yield (quintals per ha.)
			Rubber			
1955	1430	507	3.54	491	266	5.42
1960	1430	404	2.82	506	216	4.26
1965	1609	504	3.13	507	220	4.32
			Dry Copra			
1955	1514	1039	6.86	23.2	16.2	6.98
1960	1610	1239	7.70	18.8	8.8	4.68
1965	1540	1235	8.02	16.6	6.6	3.98
			Coffee			
1955	148.6	47.3	3.18	48.3	16.1	3.33
1960	230.7	77.9	3.38	47.1	18.3	3.89
1965	265.8	120.7	4.54	40.4	19.8	4.90
			Tea			
1955	64.6	21.9	3.39	80.3	39.3	4.89
1960	64.4	37.3	5.79	72.9	41.9	5.75
1965	55.1	35.0	6.35	74.3	44.8	6.03
			Tobacco			
1955	100.5	35.0	3.48	11.4	7.0	6.14
1960	140.3	49.5	3.53	11.0	6.5	5.91
1965	140.5	55.5	3.95	3.7	4.8	13.21

Source: Central Bureau of Statistics, Jakarta.

TABLE 2.5

Changes in Production in Major Secondary Industry: 1961 to 1965

	1961	1962	1963	1964	1965
Paper '000 tons	8.3	10.4	11.0	11.4	11.1
Cement '000 tons	446	511	429	439	389
Glass '000 tons	12.0	14.1	11.8	7.0	9.0
Tyres '000	114	214	144	154	127

Source: H. W. Arndt, 'Survey of recent Developments', *Bulletin of Indonesian Economic Studies,* No. 4, June 1966, p.32.

as the country's period of economic decline and that it has its roots in limited land resources.

Finally this brief analysis demonstrates that the financial crisis of 1965 was not caused by an economic crisis in the mass peasant economy wherein the vast majority of Indonesians find their livelihoods. Indeed, it could be said that the positive response of smallholders to new export opportunities delayed the foreign exchange crisis. The vulnerability of the financial system lies not in any subsidisation of the mass-based economy but in the expenditure of the government on itself and in the fluctuations of the exporting foreign enclaves. That the post-1965 government has not understood this will be made clear in later chapters.

THE HISTORICAL LEGACY

The first two decades of independence saw a search for a new independent economy and therefore a re-structuring away from the colonial allocation of land and other resources. The Dutch had not developed the archipelago as one whole endogenous economy, let alone an autonomous one. The Indies, especially Java, came to be a cheap supply arm of the Netherlands economy and if there had been any 'optimisation' of resource use it was within the boundaries of Holland and its empire. The colonised parts, or even metropolitan Holland, standing alone, did not reflect the same degree of optimal resource allocation. In general it can be said that had the great colonial empires changed their boundaries by swapping colonies, resource allocation within the new empires would have been sub-optimal prior to re-organisation. Furthermore, national chauvinism, political imperatives and imperialistic military ventures made nonsense of the standard economic argument of the world's economic resources following international price ratios. The huge market imperfections caused by unequal international power make nonsense of anything but the very loosest application of comparative advantage theory as an explanation of economic development of the colonies. The truth is that on the advent of political independence the ex-colonies were saddled with economies which had never been intended to have an internal dynamic of their own or to have powers for self-generation.

In the case of Java foreign earnings capacity was locked up in sugar estates, and to a less extent coffee and tea estates, while smallholders' rubber and sugar were cultivated alongside or partly in rotation with rice. The rapid population increase presented the dilemma of choosing between bringing export crop land permanently under more labour-intensive rice cultivation, to diminish rice imports, and depending on primary export earnings to create industrial employment. The first signs that time was running out for any viable change emerged towards the end of the nineteenth century when debates took place in the Netherlands parliament over Javanese poverty. But in the following forty years the Dutch resisted both the decline of the plantations and the transfer of profits from the plantations to new industries. Lists of possible industries were drawn up several times, only to be discarded. After the Second World War and independence popular western theory promoted the idea of an export-orientated development whereby the proceeds of continuing with the colonial economy should be put into an expanding industrial sector. But prices of exports were depressed by the monopolistic price-fixing of western companies, while the advanced industrial technology offered to poor countries meant that the cost of creating one industrial job was high and rising all the time.

Under Sukarno the early rehabilitation plans and the first Five Year Plan, 1956–60, tried to develop indigenous small-scale industries located in rural and semi-rural areas. Textile enterprises and small repair workshops were ostensibly supported by cheap credit and capital imports. Attempts were made at intensifying rice cultivation through extension services and cheap fertiliser supplies. It amounted to a policy which, after decades of failure of more grandiose development plans in developing countries, is today gaining currency. But in Indonesia during the 1950s it fell between two stools: on the one hand the capricious nature of world commodity markets, and on the other hand the drawing off of rural national talent and economic surpluses into urbanised activity which simulated a state of development.

The latter had a special effect on the successful promotion of a small-scale informal sector. This sector is not characterised by the economies of scale of plantations or of industrial development. There is no parallel in western development for the burden on planning and administrative resources it demands. The Indonesian intelligentsia was, for all the anti-western posturing, only too willing to accept the westerner's dictum, "Imitate me if you wish to develop". The aura of political independence and imitative consumerism left behind by European influences created the illusion that development was much easier than it was and that mechanistic planning methods could substitute for a new set of social and economic relations. The failure of Sukarno to inspire a dedicated cadre class to carry through the plans of the 1950s, his failure to be even more anti-western in cultural terms than he was, meant that part of his legacy was a weak small-scale secondary sector in rural areas which fell before the massive capital-intensive foreign investment after 1966.

The unexploited regions of the archipelago led Sukarno to the fatal assumption that Indonesia had time on her side. The demographic arithmetic of Java could not, and still cannot, be solved by transmigration and industrialisation. Sukarno cannot be blamed for not having economists briefing him on the necessary conditions for a successful, labour-intensive, high-value-added rural strategy of development—for such people were not being produced by the western-dominated schools of economic thought. What he can be blamed for is his unsympathetic attitude towards family planning and his romantic (or machismo-based) belief in God's help. He can also be blamed for not giving more support to the demands by the peasants for implementation of the land reform legislation without which the necessary radical reallocation of resources on Java cannot take place.

In the long run these acts of irresponsibility constituted a far, far worse legacy than his military debts and financial bankruptcy. The few brief years of foreign aid needed to rectify those latter ailments testify to this assertion. The other problems he failed to ameliorate remain as daunting as ever.

Suffice it to say here that if Sukarno was unable to take development far enough the present military government, with its sycophantic attitude towards western economic theory and technology, is hardly likely to do any better. What its performance has been in the last eight years is the subject of the following chapters.

We have then a picture of an export-oriented colonial legacy being eroded more by years of inflation than by a deliberate reallocation of land resources towards promotion of a development dynamic internal to the country. The policy of productivity improvements in the small-scale informal secondary production sector was gradual and its success depended on a long period of tranquillity.

THE GAMBLE ON INSTANT PRICE STABILISATION AND POSTPONED REHABILITATION

Because of the lack of foreign exchange and external credit-worthiness Indonesia was in no position to import raw materials and spare parts to re-activate her industrial productive capacity. The first hurdle that had to be cleared before the question of options on extricating the economy from a situation of internal and external imbalance and on rehabilitation strategies could even be considered was to regain a measure of credibility in the eyes of foreign governments. But clearing this hurdle in itself determined the range of options because of the leverage available to foreign governments in imposing their ideas on Indonesia. Since the communists were being liquidated and the New Order was in the hands of western sympathisers it was credibility in the eyes of western governments that mattered. Therefore, the options available were those acceptable to the economic thinking of the World Bank, the International Monetary Fund and of governments being pressed by their oligopolistic interests to find for them an *entrée* into the Indonesian economy. However, there were ready counterparts in Indonesian society, for most of the country's leading economists had had spells at western graduate schools, notably in Berkeley, California. The experience of the past for sections of the Jakarta middle class was that close and protracted fraternisation with the many emissaries of the western business world would greatly benefit them.

There was, therefore, no real divergence of opinion between Indonesian leaders and western governments as to what road the economy should take. The procrastination of the West in granting new aid in the first six months after October 1965 can fairly be attributed to their questioning whether the new regime was firmly in the saddle or whether Sukarno could, at this late stage, make a successful comeback.

The stages of economic rectification might be put in simple terms as stabilisation of consumer markets (1966–7), rehabilitation of productive capacity (1967–9), and the Five Year Development Plan (1969–74). In reality, there was much overlapping. The stabilisation of consumer markets affected rehabilitation, mainly of rice and manufacturing production, by bringing on to the market competitive imports, while the rehabilitation of sectors, such as irrigation and estate perennials, was still taking place at the end of the Five Year Plan. The difficulties of rolling one phase on to the next were recognised by the government, which sensibly took the attitude that inflation should be wound down rather than be expected to stop immediately.

Producers' liquidity had suffered badly from inflation which in the last two to three years before 1965 amounted annually to several hundred per cent. At the same time restoration of confidence in production and profit expectations was bound to take time. The main danger was that short-term price stabilisation via foreign credits would postpone even further the fuller utilisation of existing capacity. Were precious credits to be spent on consumer imports (and therefore on maximising future debts) to hold down market prices, or on estate rehabilitation and rice inputs to expand exports and limit imports? What proportion of emergency credit imports were to include value added which might have been contributed by Indonesian work? What was to be the time horizon of progressive targets?

In the event the government chose an expensive way and one which made it unnecessarily hard for indigenous producers to regain full utilisation of existing capacity. This might be put down to the government's belief that it was most necessary to buy the loyalties of the urban population by injecting supplies of consumer goods into the markets as well as to the lack of farming and business representatives in the government. The indifference shown towards the paralysed state of domestic producers can also be explained by the military and academic composition of the new government.

The slow process of restoring utilisation of domestic production capacity had the effect of synchronising the rehabilitation of industry with the inflow of competitive foreign investment. Instead of restoring the economy first and seeing where new foreign investment could make up the deficiencies (a policy frequently officially propounded) domestic enterprise found itself competing against foreign capital to regain its own domestic markets. The example of textiles suffices to illustrate these points.

Textile manufacturers found difficulties in obtaining imported raw materials because the anti-inflationary policies of the government led to a tight credit policy while prices were still rising at 10 to 15 per cent a month. Given the ensuing liquidity crisis tenders for raw materials imports were weak compared with the bids for foreign exchange for cloth imports for which working capital could be rapidly turned over. Moreover, since the government had a strong desire to demonstrate price stability as soon as possible after the September 1966 monetary reform, it imported such huge quantities of textiles for Christmas, Lebaran and Chinese New Year that textile prices actually fell 25 per cent. At the same time it was announced that dependence would be made on the market mechanism to settle prices. Prices of public utilities were raised in late 1966 to eliminate deficits. All these measures were regarded at the time as making matters more difficult for domestic producers. In spite of budgetary pruning the money supply was rising by about one-third each quarter, most going to the government sector. New money to private enterprise rose less than 0.5 per cent (Penny and Thalib, 1967). Thus domestic producers were caught between competition from credit imports and the continued inflation of government sector spending. It has been pointed out (Boucherie, 1969) that the poor liquidity and low profitability of textile producers meant that they could not purchase imports of both raw materials and spare parts. The latter were foregone and existing machinery was cannibalised.

The progress towards monetary stabilisation was said to be partly at the price of stagnation and even of some decline in business activity (Arndt, 1967). One year after the coup-attempt there was no significant expansion of textile capacity utilisation. Writing in early 1967, Penny and Thalib (1967) concluded that it did not appear likely that the economic situation would improve markedly until *deflationary* pressures were relaxed. At the same time the government admitted to something resembling a recession as a result of its stabilisation programme. Industry was not only stagnating in the first quarter of 1967 but still deteriorating.

Huge imports of finished textiles left textile manufacturers demoralised. In 1967 $15·9 million of credits were spent on all textile materials purchased from the U.S. and Japan, $12·7 million of which was spent on finished textiles. Throughout 1967, 230 million metres were produced (out of a capacity of 700 million metres) against 220 million metres imported. It was clear that while preferential exchange rates were awarded all textile materials the market prices for other inputs in the domestic production process were making domestic production, and therefore imported raw materials, quite uncompetitive.

Only eighteen months after the coup-attempt did the government announce measures to stimulate production. In March and April 1967, the authorities, declaring that conditions warranted a change of emphasis from 'checking inflation' to 'stimulating production', relaxed restraint. Bank credit was eased; official interest rates were lowered (from 6 to 9 per cent to 4 to 7 per cent a month).

But domestic enterprise was about to face a greater threat. Concurrently with the first meeting of what was to become the Inter-Governmental Group on Indonesia, the law laying down the basic principles governing foreign investment was being drafted. It was finally passed in April 1947.

The Foreign Investment Law stated that it was intended that the economic potential of Indonesia should be developed by Indonesians but that development was to be accelerated by foreign investment. Foreign investment should be channelled into projects which national capital could not undertake for reasons of expertise or size of capital outlay. Since foreign investment was to be part of long-term development, not of rehabilitation, it was expected to contribute to expanding job opportunities. No technological constraints were placed on investors.

One of the articles of faith of the Law was that domestic investors would respond to being shown the way by foreign investors. It should have been expected that the most profitable, least risky ventures would have been taken up by those first in the field, and that later investments would not be so profitable. The assumption that anything else could have occurred must have rested on the belief that employment and income multipliers would have been activated by foreign investment to produce new markets for domestic enterprise. With hindsight a more accurate description of foreign investment would be that it is timid, selective and has absolutely no interest in what its investment might do for the organic body of the economy.

There was, however, one group of Indonesians which was to benefit from foreign investment, namely the Chinese. But this group was not what was meant by the government as the intended responding domestic enterprise. That it was ever imagined that the Chinese would not take most of the domestic benefits of foreign investment attests to the whole dreamlike attitude the government had to external assistance in developing the economy.

Another field of conflict over the strategy of development embarked on in 1967 was the regional distribution of benefits of aid and investment. Until employment and income multipliers were activated Java offered little prospect to foreign investors apart from displacing less technologically advanced indigenous capacity and replacing some imports. On the other hand, estate, forestry and mineral development could make a local impact on the less densely populated outer islands. Inter-island jealousies, therefore, could be aroused by the open-door policy to foreign investment.

THE FIRST FIVE YEAR PLAN, 1969 TO 1974 (Repelita I)

The presumptions about the future development strategy cannot be completely described without a brief reference to the later Five Year Plan commencing in 1969.

The Plan was not intended to introduce fundamental changes in the economy as it was seen only as the front-runner of a series of similar plans. As the date of its commencement drew near it became increasingly apparent that the share of rehabilitation in it would have to be larger than at first anticipated. Lack of statistics precluded any detailed mapping out of the plan but sectoral targets were laid down such that their achievement would seem to maintain a 5 per cent annual overall growth rate.

Since there was no time to make micro-feasibility studies on individual projects, annual plans were allocated the responsibility of allowing flexibility in the Plan as feasibility conclusions surfaced. Then project details would be incorporated in state budgets.

The pivotal field of development was to be the rice sector which would aim for a completed 'green revolution' and national rice self-sufficiency by 1974. To achieve this there would be interdependent activity in agriculture, industry and infra-structure. Were this not to be achieved then hopes for rural employment would be slight and enlarged fertiliser factories and infra-structural investment would not be able to pay their way.

Table 2.6 displays the output increases expected over the whole plan period. The relatively low percentage increases for agriculture must be seen in the light of the already advanced state of its specialism, whereas fertilisers and paper were to face a hugely expanded domestic demand.

The only modest expectation of the table is the 50 per cent increase in petroleum output, but at the time this might have appeared ambitious.

TABLE 2.6

Expected Production Increases: Five Year Plan, 1969-74

		1969-70	1973-4	Percentage increase
AGRICULTURE				
rice	million tons	10.52	15.42	46.5
palm oil (export)	1000 tons	172	275	59.8
sugar	1000 tons	677	907	33.9
logs (export)	1000 cu. metres	2900	7900	172.4
MINING				
petroleum	million barrels	293	440	50.1
tin	metric tons	16.16	19.4	19.9
bauxite	1000 tons	1000	1200	20.0
INDUSTRY				
textiles	million metres	450	900	100
Fertilizer: nitrogen	1000 tons	46.5	403.5	767
phosphate	1000 tons	18(1971)	168	833
cement	1000 tons	600	1650	175
paper	1000 tons	16	166.5	940.6
ELECTRIC POWER	1000 KW	659	1084	64.4

Source: Repelita I, quoted in J. Panglaykim and K. D. Thomas, *Economic Planning Experience in Indonesia,* Occasional Paper 5, Institute of Business Studies, Nanyang University, Singapore, 1971, p. 35.

Of the total allocation of government expenditure on the plan of Rupiah 1,420 billion, irrigation alone was to take Rupiah 236 billion (Panglaykim and Thomas, 1971). This is almost as much as the total for industry, Rupiah 251 billion, which would attract both domestic and foreign investment.

The appallingly low figure of Rupiah 50 billion for village development is in marked contrast to, and helps to define the style of, the rice intensification programme. Another expenditure-paring affecting the quality of development is the derisory sum of Rupiah 172 billion for all social expenditure. This figure is 30 per cent below that projected for government expenditure on commerce and tourism.

Sources of finance for the plan are shown in Table 2.7. The projected routine budget surplus and project aid was to rise by about three times over the five year period, while counterpart funds were to expand only 33 per cent. Assumptions that the routine budget would gather so much more in taxes (especially income tax) and would successfully combat inflationary aspects of government expenditure were highly ambitious. The shift from counterpart funds (from the different kinds of programme aid) to project aid reflects the expected shift from stabilisation and rehabilitation to long-run development. The reversal is quite sharp and is a measure of the confidence of the government in its own scheme for economic growth. It was to present problems in the councils of the Inter-Governmental Group on Indonesia as the donor countries had a more sober view than the Indonesian government of success possibilities.

TABLE 2.7

Sources of Finance (Rupiah billion – 1968 prices), Five Year Plan 1969-70 to 1973-4

	1969-70	*1970-1*	*1971-2*	*1972-3*	*1973-4*	*Total*
DEVELOPMENT BUDGET	123	153	223	264	296	1059
budget surplus (routine)	24	33	43	55	71	226
counterpart funds*	63	75	85	85	85	393
project aid	36	45	95	124	140	440
OTHER	38	54	72	89	108	361
increase in medium-long run bank credit	13	15	19	22	26	95
direct capital investment**	25	39	53	67	82	226
TOTAL	161	207	295	353	404	1420
Counterpart funds and project aid as percentage of total:	61.5	58	61	59	56	59

US$ 1 = Rupiah 350.

* Includes normal foreign 'BE' credit and surplus agricultural commodities on PL 480.

** Domestie, foreign and state enterprises.

Source: J. Panglaykim and K. D. Thomas (1971), p. 39.

Exports were to make their own strong contribution to foreign exchange availability, rising from $672 million in 1969–70 to $924 million in 1973–4. But imports, especially of raw materials and capital goods, would climb much faster. Both the absolute and proportional deficit on the balance of trade would enlarge, requiring ever increasing amounts of foreign credit. The balance of payments projections reveal the ambition of a rapid developmental spree generously backed by foreign governments and international agencies. From an alleged bankruptcy in 1965, overseas loans under the Five Year Plan would steadily rise faster than total exports until the former actually exceeded the latter. As it happened these aid projections were very close to what eventuated although they were much greater than the Inter-Governmental Group on Indonesia itself would have chosen to predict in 1969.

Of total anticipated export earnings in 1973–4, $124 million was to come from petroleum, leaving $800 million to be realised by all other exports. These commodities had been detrimentally affected by years of physical neglect, and doubt was cast at the time upon their ability to show marked improvement until well into the seventies.

There had been little replanting of palm oil since independence and together with small increases in acreage it seemed inevitable that output must decline in the near future. Rehabilitation of rubber estates was also necessary before startling increases in output could have been expected. Estate rubber earnings had fallen more than world rubber prices. Coffee and tea appeared to have been generally maintained in the face of big price falls. Copra output reached a high plateau in the early fifties from which it had since fallen. World copra price fluctuations have been no greater than those of other crops, yet copra's earnings have been highly volatile.

Yields of these perennials are not easily raised in the short run, and unless there was to be a boost to world prices it was difficult, in 1969, to see non-petroleum exports expanding a great deal during the Five Year Plan period.

CONCLUSION

Separate viewing of the financial crisis and the crisis of production in some sectors in 1965 helps to assess the policy priorities that were needed after 1965 and to judge the value of the policies that were actually followed. The latter is left to the following chapters, but this chapter shows that inflation and the particular foreign exchange crisis severely affected the economy only after 1963 and that earlier trends in export production could not be put down to inflation. The tenacity of producers, aided by periodic devaluation of the currency, has been grossly underestimated by economic analysts. The particular problems of foreign-owned estates bore little relation to the financial crisis, while the looming crisis in the smallholding sector was to do with lack of replanting since colonial times. Therefore policies to boost production in these sectors need not have concentrated on measures to overcome disincentives caused by inflation.

In the food staple sector production was slowly edging forward in the early 1960s though largely due to irrigation and land extension in the outer islands. The increasing failure of Java to feed itself was not due to the financial drama which culminated in 1965.

Those industries that did suffer serious declines in production were mainly those dependent upon imported raw materials. It was reasonable to expect, therefore, that an easing of their situation would coincide with an easing of the foreign exchange situation when aid flows commenced. This, however, did not happen.

At the same time there were bound to be difficulties in reconciling the objectives of the different phases of price stabilisation, production rehabilitation (and consolidation) and further expansion. But it is fair to say that too much of a short-term policy nature was subsumed in the search for confidence of western creditors and their economic advisors, and too little attention was given to the inability of domestic entrepreneurs to hold their ground against tied foreign aid and foreign investment. It is also fair to add that this arose from a faulty diagnosis of the production crisis as distinct from the financial crisis.

Chapter 3

Stabilisation and its Maintenance

This chapter describes in detail the step-by-step approach towards stabilisation and rehabilitation. What was undertaken comprised an interesting, though not necessarily ideal, model of economic resuscitation. Nor, given the large amount of aid, can it be regarded in any sense as a miracle. But the mechanics of the policy, sometimes appearing as *ad hoc* measures, must be of interest to all development economicsts whatever their ideology.

THE POLITICS OF AID

That the new regime would practise the utmost possible sobriety in its monetary policy there was never any doubt. The memory of persistent inflation throughout the independence period was imprinted forever on the minds of Indonesian economists. Between 1950 and 1965 the consumer price index had risen to over 121,000. But in 1960 it had stood at only 660. The economic haemorrhage of the last few years of Sukarno's rule gave rise to what can reasonably be described as an obsession about monetary restraint. In 1966 the issue of armed forces expenditure was set aside. There was, no doubt, a tacit agreement between Indonesian economists and western creditors that no significant reduction of military costs could be expected while the armed forces pursued their mania over security. In political terms the civilian part of the government had to behave obsequiously towards its military counterparts. The consequences of that arrangement could only mean a protracted and costly recovery of price stabilisation during which domestic enterprises would receive an otherwise unnecessary degree of mauling.

The pinning of hopes for recovery on freeing markets by means of adequate foreign credits was very risky. One observer (Glassburner, 1971) wrote:

> She [Indonesia] is now placing a frighteningly heavy bet on a handful of economists to bring order out of economic chaos; and these economists have placed their heaviest bets on the revival of the market system.

For almost a year after September 1965 the Indonesian economy was left to bleed on its own. Emergency aid had arrived but not of the amount with which to commence stabilisation, let alone rehabilitation. When aid did arrive it was in generous and increasing helpings. It is worth pondering on these mysteries, because answering the two questions, 'Why was debt rescheduling and further aid delayed?' and, 'Why was so much aid finally granted?' helps to explain the motivations and future influence of foreign groups.

We have already mentioned the desire of western oligopolists to enter the Indonesian economy. No one can question the existence of this pressure group. The later tying of aid and the huge investments in Indonesia's, then untapped, natural resources are telling evidence of this. But to suggest that this was the only explanation of these two mysteries is a gross over-simplification of the total 1965 setting.

To begin with, Indonesia was still nominally pursuing a policy of confrontation to the young Malaysian Federation. While the clandestine suing for peace by army officers and overseas ambassadors, even before October 1965, was a well-known secret, President Sukarno's political life was known for its elastic quality. Until the handover of the formal instruments of power to Suharto in March 1966, there was no means of knowing whether or not there would be a return to the Old Order. And even after March 1966 there was some breath-holding. Nor had the 'New Order' made it clear what was to be done with seized foreign enterprises, a fact which rankled bitterly with the Dutch and the British.

On this occasion the customary aid generosity of the United States for right wing military regimes appears to have been surprisingly weak. It is true that American interests, especially oil interests, had suffered during the last years of Sukarno's regime but this alone does not satisfactorily explain America's tardiness in aid-giving. There were three other reasons for this. Firstly, the new government refused to support American policy in Vietnam. Indeed, the new Foreign Minister, Adam Malik, was quite candid in public about his thoughts on Vietnam. In 1969 before a closed hearing of the Senate Committee on Foreign Aid, the Director of USAID, John Hannah, referring to Indonesia's diplomatic recognition of North Vietnam, North Korea and China, said that he had found Indonesia's recognition of America's enemies in Asia disappointing (Warta Harian, 31.10.1969). Secondly the United States government, with one ear cocked to Congress, was restless over the unwillingness of other rich countries to share the aid burden. Again and again, American representatives pressed home the point that their government would only provide a fixed share of total aid. It was up to Indonesia then to help the United States to make other rich countries commit themselves to a rescue operation. Thirdly, almost half the total

Sukarno debt was to communist countries and the United States government baulked at the thought of providing aid to maintain debt repayments to them.

THE EMERGENCE OF THE INTER-GOVERNMENTAL GROUP ON INDONESIA

The chief answer to the second question, 'Why so much aid when it did materialise?', lies in the new ideas on development aid emerging at that time. Previously the International Monetary Fund had granted loans to restore external equilibrium (the balance of payments) under conditions which imposed brakes on domestic economic activity and which failed to meet long-term structural defects. Furthermore, at the time when the world's rich were eyeing the prostrate Indonesian economy the notion of 'Country Programmes' was gaining ground in United Nations circles. The idea of a County Programme is that various bodies giving project aid compare notes so that all aid fits into a recognisable national plan of the recipient country. Posthumus (1971) had provided a little of the background of aid consortium thinking in 1966. He has pointed out that aid policies were invariably short-term while the conditions on which aid was given were important only in the long-term. But he also stated that the October 1966 tight credit measures were designed both to overcome the financial and economic crises and to reorganize Indonesia's economic system. This is preposterous. It is rare that any economic measure anywhere has resolved both short- and long-term problems. There are obvious contradictions and trade-offs in the interests of different time horizons. It is difficult to imagine a situation in which this was not more true than in Indonesia in 1966. It is argued in these chapters that meeting the short-run crisis in the way chosen damaged unnecessarily the long-term interests of the endogenous (and indigenous) body of the economy.

The only explanation Posthumus offers for his assertion of both immediate and reorganisational measures being taken in October 1966, was that the aid to meet the short-term crisis was on very easy, very long-term conditions; unless he means that the rehabilitation of traditional exports through foreign exchange liberalisation measures was the reorganisational measure. However, it is interesting that he also defends Indonesia's creditors' unwillingness to discuss Indonesia's long-term prospects, at least in the shape of the Five Year Plan (1969–74), on the grounds that individual donor countries could not be expected to make open-ended commitments to details of the Plan. That may be quite correct, but at the same time it casts doubt on the capacity of 1966 aid to meet Indonesia's long-term problems, let alone reconcile short- and long-term problems. The truth is that the portentous deliberations of the international creditor community failed to camouflage the inability of the government—on its own—to reconcile short- and long-term problems of the endogenous economy.

While the aid practitioners were burying their differences and surrendering some sovereignty over their former territories, the theoreticians were making their contribution to a new aid ideology by suggesting that if a state of underdevelopment were to be overcome it had to be attacked by everything one had—or could borrow. A veritable avalanche of external aid finance would break down all resistance to growth before the state of underdevelopment had time to muster its forces against the attack made upon it. That the anticipated success of this aid policy would be conducive to foreign investment merely made it easier to bring in western aid at nominal give-away prices. The new philosophy is best summarised by Chenery *et al.* (1967):

> ... if we have in mind a given target, which might be a given growth rate or a given level of per capita income, the most effective way to get there is to grow as fast as possible ... the more effective the country is in increasing its investment, the more aid it will need.

Doctors frequently practise a similar policy in their applications of heavy doses of antibiotics. But whereas the antibiotic absorptive capacity of the human body appears to be large relative to that of the bug under attack, one is hesitant to say that the analogy can be drawn that the aid absorptive capacity of the active economy is greater than that of the consumption and corruption leakages.

But that is rushing the story. Suffice it to say that it was a measure of the response won by this new aid ideology that it was so swiftly put into action in spite of the bureaucratic and political obstacles one might normally have expected to encompass it. It was a time when some of the world's economists were learning for the first time where Indonesia was. They were hearing stories of the empty treasury, of unruly inflation, of beggaring *Konfrontasi,* of debts and expensive monuments.

The United States was the first country to break the silence in early 1966 with emergency credits of $59 million, of which $19 million was for PL 480 cotton, yarn and rice. Japan then offered $30 million of credits (at 5 per cent interest, four years' grace period and another five and a half years to pay.) Then came West Germany with $7·5 million and, after the settlement of $157 million of compensation from Indonesia (payable in 30 years after a grace period of 7 years), the Netherlands with $18 million. Singapore added $32·7 million, making a total of $174 million of emergency credits available by late October 1966. The terms were still harsh and the sum involved clearly inadequate. In May and June of 1966 the government had been able to release just \$18 million for tender for imports of raw materials and spare parts. Exports for 1966 were concurrently being estimated at only \$430 million.

In September 1966 a meeting of the major western creditors (United States, United Kingdom, the Netherlands, France, West Germany, Japan and Italy), which later became known as the Paris Club, was held in Tokyo. Present as observers were Australia and the IMF. The Soviet Union turned down an invitation to attend, not surprisingly since the mass extermination of the left was still in very recent memory. This absence did, however, affect the proceedings of the Tokyo meeting, for the West was less than enthusiastic about granting new credits while the Soviet bloc was still demanding its money back. Despite this it was solemnly agreed that Indonesia could not meet her debts, and re-scheduling of them was accepted in principle. Nevertheless no new aid was offered except emergency aid from the Netherlands which had extracted the *quid pro quo* of recognition of compensation for seizure of assets of its nationals in 1957–8. Such recognition was a significant political gesture for the western creditors to go away with and think about.

By November 1966 the Soviet Union had indicated that it also agreed to the principle of a debt moratorium. This paved the way for another meeting of the western creditors in Paris in December 1966. Further emergency bilateral credits were provided for a minimum level of imports and a moratorium (until the 1970s) of \$357 million of the approximate \$1,000 million debt to the West was agreed upon.

The first conclusive meeting of the Paris Club was in Amsterdam two months later. The first of a long series of calculations of Indonesia's aid requirements was tabled. Indonesia's earnings deficit for 1967 was estimated to be \$200 million. In spite of the fact that \$43 million of what had already been offered had not yet been taken up new offerings amounted to \$95·5 million—the United States \$65 million; West Germany \$12·5 million; and the Netherlands \$18 million. To the embarrassment of the other participants Japan insisted on the now out-dated style of aid-giving and was holding out for 5¾ per cent interest on her offer against United States pressure for acceptance of a standard 3 per cent.

From these meetings of the Paris Club emerged the Inter-Governmental Group on Indonesia, with Australia quickly joining as a full member and Canada and a host of West European countries adding themselves later to the membership list. The observer status of the IMF and the World Bank soon changed into the roles of guide, secretariat and broker. There followed an important meeting in Scheveningen in June when the practice of reviewing the current state of the Indonesian economy was established. The IGGI finally settled down to two meetings a year; one in December to review Indonesia's economic progress and future needs and one in May to settle individual donors' credits. Indonesia had been re-admitted to the United Nations in 1966, but signed on with the IMF only in February 1967 (although the IMF had actually sent a mission to Jakarta in June 1966) and with the World Bank in May 1967. Its membership of the new Asian Development Bank concluded the list of international aid agencies which were to play such an important role in the IGGI meetings. Advice to the IGGI came in the form of a 'Report on Indonesia's Recent Performance' compiled for each of IGGI's meetings by the East Asia and Pacific department of the World Bank. These reports make dreary reading on the whole, hotch-potch of aggregate statistics and summary of government economic manoeuvres as they are. They belong to the pedantic old-fashioned school of economic reporting and are strangely at odds with the skilful diplomacy of IMF and World Bank negotiators at the IGGI meetings. But insofar as they constituted the basic material for other minds to utilize it is significant that they exhibit an almost total disregard for social development and their authors appear never to have heard of the new interest in human resources—with the exception of family planning. They also ignore obvious conclusions on unemployment, linkages and leakages and the dynamic of the informal sector. The paucity of social and national enterprise content of World Bank reports to the IGGI was faithfully reflected by the negotiators until only recently with the arrival of Dutch Minister Pronk as the IGGI's chairperson. By 1968 the World Bank, by taking the (then) unprecedented step of setting up a permanent mission in Jakarta, declared its continuing involvement in the recovery and progress of the economy. With offices in the same building as the National Planning Bureau its entire operation confirmed the new aid style of working closely with a country's national planning apparatus. Its advisors were, likewise, strongly influential in designing that plan. The IMF too had its say. In 1970 its managing director, Pierre Paul Schweitzer, expressing his pleasure with the economy, commented (Pedoman, 30.10.1970):

> We gave advice, but the decision and its implementation was in the hands of the Indonesian Government.

Where the United States was instrumental in pushing the original Paris Club towards new responsibilities it was the World Bank which stage-managed the final debt-rescheduling. The earlier partial moratorium covered only the early 1970s. It soon became apparent that this was inadequate. The bulk of repayment was obviously coming too soon. The United States and the Netherlands were the first to agree to new proposals from the World Bank that repayment should be in 30 equal annual instalments such that debt repayment should never be more than 20 per cent of foreign exchange earnings. By December 1969 all the other western creditors had agreed to postpone the debt repayment for 1970.

In August 1970 the Soviet debt was renegotiated. The $750 million was to be repaid in 30 annual instalments commencing September 1970 (Nusantara, 31.8.1970). By the same month Indonesia had repaid the Soviet Union $15·8 million, the Netherlands $0·5 million (out of $29 million), and, by December, France $1·5 million (out of $90 million). Payments agreements had not been signed then with the major western creditor countries. But it was anticipated that the World Bank's recommendations of repayment in 30 instalments, 1970 to 1999, would finally be accepted by all.

By mid-1971 the Soviet Union, East Germany, Czechoslovakia, Poland and Rumania had signed debt agreements along the IGGI-prescribed lines. Italy followed in January 1972 and Bulgaria in May. That left Hungary, Yugoslavia and the United Kingdom. The finalist, the United kingdom, signed in October 1972.

THE QUANTITY OF AID

Before the problems faced by the government in channelling the new aid to the economy are described it is useful to present the order of magnitude of total aid, its composition and its rate of utilisation.

The terms of the IGGI credit became progressively easier. Some countries, such as the United States and the United Kingdom (together with the World Bank) were granting aid at zero interest in 1969 while Australia moved quickly to placing all her aid in grant form and the Netherlands two-thirds in grant form. A summary view of this progression is given below (Posthumus, 1971). If we summarize the terms as repayment period; grace period; interest rate, the selected data shown in Table 3.1 indicate this trend:

TABLE 3.1

Terms of new credits: repayment period (years); grace period (years); interest rate (per cent)

Australia	1967 to 1970/1	Grants
Canada	1968 to 1970/1	Grants
France	1968	20; 7; 3.5
	1969/70	25; 7; 3.5
	1970/1	22; 4; 3.5
West Germany	1967	25; 7; 3
	1968	25; 7; 3
	1969/70	30; 8; 2.5
	1970/1	30; 8; 2.5

Japan	1967	20; 7; 5
	1968	20; 7; 3
	1969/70	20; 7; 3
	1970/1	20; 7; 3 and grants
		30: 10; 2 and grants
Netherlands	1967	25; 7; 3 and grants
	1968	25; 7; 3 and grants
	1969/70	30; 10; 3 and grants
	1970/1	30; 8; 2.5 and grants
United Kingdom	1967	25; 7; 0
	1968	25; 7; 0
	1969/70	25; 7; 0
	1970/1	25; 7; 0
United States	1967	25; 7; 3
		40; 10; 1-2.5
	1968	40; 10; 2-2.5
	1969/70	40; 10; 2-3
	1970/1	40; 10; 2-3
IDA	1968	40; 10; 1-3
	1969/70	50; 10; 0.75
	1970/1	50; 10; 0.75
ADB	1969/70	25; 7; 3
	1970/1	30; 8; 2.5

Some countries, including the United Kingdom and West Germany, offered even softer terms in later years.

Today IGGI donors must charge no more than 3 per cent interest and allow at least 25 years to repay.

Between 1968 and October 1972 the World Bank, through itself and its affiliate, the International Development Association, made loans valued at $350 million in 23 different kinds of credit. The bulk came in very soft loans from the International Development Association for repair work, rehabilitation of roads, agriculture, electricity, telecommunications, the purchase of large scale equipment for rehabilitation, tourism and more recently in stock-raising in South Sulawesi. The World Bank has also given technical evaluation assistance to the National Planning Board and joined with the World Health Organisation to study the urban water supply situation. The United Nations has been slower than the World Bank in involving itself in Indonesia. UNDP has financed an advisory service to the government's highway authority, and in 1972 granted $35 million in technical assistance over a five-year period for drawing up an inventory of infrastructure, including a big programme on irrigation facilities. UN agencies have combined with the Ford Foundation to provide assistance on a national assessment of the education system. The Food and Agricultural Organisation has joined with Japanese interests to work in agriculture. USAID and the World Food Programme have also entered the field of aid for directly productive projects, the former with a loan of $6·3 million in 1969 to expand the Gresik cement plant and the latter providing millions of dollars for food for transmigrants in South Sumatra and for irrigation and soil improvement in Java and Bali.

The only notable funding in the social field to come from international agencies, apart from UNICEFs educational experiments, has been the interest of the World Bank, the International Planned Parenthood Association, the Ford Foundation, the Population Council and USAID in a large scale family planning programme, which has had a very mixed reception.

The rapidly escalating requests by the government for assistance soon came to be granted with alacrity. There was a tendency in the earlier years for aid requests to be somewhat greater than final offers, but later the reverse was the case. For instance, in 1971/2 the government stated its needs to be $640 million and IGGI granted only $627 million, but in the next financial year the figures were $670 million and $723 million (although this was partly due to the revaluation of some currencies). In 1973/4 the early conceding of $760 million was raised to $877 million, principally due to the rice crisis.

These differences reveal that the IGGI secretariat was mustering a form of intelligence on Indonesia and acting with a mind of its own. The difference between IGGI and government estimates was most noticeable at the time when their views on the allocation of aid between programme and project categories conflicted most sharply. Since this bears on their two views of short term development possibilities it will be discussed at greater length later. Here referential data on aid are presented in Table 3.2.

TABLE 3.2

Programme and Project Aid Totals: 1968 to 1973/4 ($ million)

	1968	*1969/70*	*1970/1*	*1971/2*	*1972/3*	*1973/4*
Programme	294.7	320.4	341.1	325	202.8	402
—of which food	100.8	125.2	151.4	140	118.3	160
Project	77.1	202.1	263.4	302.0	402.5	474.6
Total	371.8	522.5	604.5	627.0	723.6	876.6

N.B. After 1968 the accounting year was changed from the calendar year to a new financial year.

Source: Amongst others:
1972/3: *Bulletin of Indonesian Economic Studies (BIES)*, 8, (2), July 1972, p. 6.
1971/2: *BIES,* 7, (2), July 1971, p. 11.
1973/4: *BIES,* 9, (2), July 1973, p. 21.

The jump in project aid's share of the total came quickly after 1968 although it can be seen that it fell somewhat in 1973/4 mainly due to large quantities of food aid. Much of the project aid has been rehabilitating the infra-structure rather than for development promotion, and the rapid rise in project aid can be taken to indicate increasing capital absorptive capacity of the infrastructure as surveys indicated what had to be done. After 1973–4 the share of project aid rose sharply with virtually all of the record aid figure of $1·1 to $1·3 billion in 1976–7 going to project aid. In the special circumstances of the impact of Pertamina's liquidity crisis on the foreign exchange reserves, there have been assurances from creditor countries of an additional $1 billion of commercial credits in the latter year.

One of the most significant points that emerges from Table 3.3 is that of the two major donor countries, the United States tended to specialise in programme aid while Japan tended to specialise in project aid. Japan also took over from the United States as the biggest donor in 1973–4, and was offering $133 million of aid in 1976–7 compared with the United States' $99 million. The Netherlands, West Germany and Australia are the most significant aid donors. The United States, the Netherlands and Australia were the prime movers of consortium aid, with Japan brought into a significant role at the beginning because of her wealth and geographical position. But whereas the former three have continued to exhibit more than the other countries a purer form of 'consortium' outlook, Japan has manipulated her aid towards her economic penetration of Indonesia much more uninhibitedly than the European countries. Another recent event is the hugely expanded role of the World Bank and the Asian Development Bank, together now accounting for half of total aid. The former committed $550 million in aid to Indonesia for 1976–7 and the latter $120 million.

NEW ECONOMIC MANAGEMENT

The *quid pro quo* for all this aid diplomacy was a new active financial policy of the Indonesian government.

The first response to the 1965 crisis had been to form a government monopoly of importing in November 1965 accompanied by a takeover of rice mills and all textile trading. It was stated that 'in order to safeguard the revolution, the government will take measures against those privately-owned enterprises whose operations are crucial to the material well-being of the people.' The economic dislocation was encouraging the government to place under its control those parts which were still functioning in order to meet minimal goals.

In December 1965 a currency reform was undertaken by converting 1,000 old Rupiahs into one new Rupiah and announcing

TABLE 3.3

Programme and Project Aid by Donor Country and Agency ($ million)

	PROGRAMME						PROJECT					
	1968	*1969/70*	*1970/1*	*1971/2*	*1972/3*	*1973/4*	*1968*	*1969/70*	*1970/1*	*1971/2*	*1972/3*	*1973/4*
United States	169.4	191.1	187.3	155	135.0	90	5.2	26.3	46.4	45.7	68.0	60.0
Japan	70.0	65.0	79.4	85	90.0	64.2	40.0	55.0	39.3	66.0	95.0	115.8
Netherlands	19.4	19.3	17.9	19.1	23.0	26.0	6.5	27.8	7.6	15.0	21.2	25.7
West Germany	12.5	15.6	16.7	20.3	22.4	22.8	10.5	14.2	14.6	24.7	24.4	34.2
Australia	12.0	12.7	13.8	15.0	19.0*	11.8*	2.8	3.9	11.4	7.1	6.9*	15.5*
France	6.9	7.9	8.1	8.5≠	9.8	10.4	4.3	6.3	6.3	—	10.8	15.9
Canada	0.8	1.9	5.0	8.0	10.2	3.0	—	0.4	1.3	5.0	6.5	10.0
United Kingdom	4.3	4.4	8.6	11.3	7.8	10.0	0.9	1.0	1.8	12.0	18.3	19.8
Belgium	0.4	2.1	2.8	n.a.	3.9	3.8	—	0.8	1.7	—	2.2	3.7
Italy	—	0.4	0.9	n.a.	—	—	—	—	—	—	—	4.0
Denmark	—	—	—	—	—	—	—	4.0	—	—	4.2	—
Switzerland	—	—	—	—	—	—	—	—	—	—	—	6.0
IBRD/IDA	—	—	—	—	—	—	7.0	59.0	104.9	56.5	145.0	133.0
ADB	—	—	—	—	—	—	—	3.4	20.2	35.0	—	31.0

N.B. These figures cannot be guaranteed as actual final commitments. Different sources have been seen to vary a little.
≠This includes Belgium and Italy also. *Includes New Zealand.

Sources: Bappenas, Jakarta.
BIES, 7 (2), July 1971, p. 11; 9, (2), July 1973; p. 21; 8, (2), July 1972, p. 6.

that notes of Rupiah 5,000 upwards would not be legal tender after 30 days. Converting these notes to the new currency would be at the cost of a 10 per cent tax. The same tax was levied on bank deposits. It was believed at the time that 57 per cent of currency in circulation was in the form of Rupiah 5,000 and 10,000 notes. But about the same time as these measures were promulgated the government was putting into circulation the equivalent of 20 per cent of the money supply by way of bonuses to civil servants whose basic salaries were concurrently elevated by 175 per cent. The armed forces received a 500 per cent rise. Immediately then the pattern was set: that producers' liquidity was to be squeezed to allow the defence of the government sector. But few saw much hope in these options. The monetary reform of December 1965 proved illusory while the first attempts at budget balancing resulted in a more uncontrolled budget.

To make things harder for producers subsidies to public utilities and on petroleum products were terminated. This led to big rises in the petrol price, in bus and rail fares, and in postal charges.

But the crucial aid meeting, set for September 1966, required more evidence of financial rectitude, and the transfer of power in March 1966 provided the political impetus. In August and September the government raised the curtain on its stabilisation policy.

As presented at the Tokyo meeting the measures included a return to market forces; achievement of a balanced budget; pursuance of a rigid but well-directed credit policy; and establishment of a realistic foreign exchange rate.

The item which concerns us immediately is the third. Most prices of public utilities had already been raised to reduce subsidies to the public sector. Credit became very tight indeed and in November interest rates were raised to 6 per cent per month for the food and industry sectors, 7½ per cent for the transportation and export production sectors and 9 per cent for commerce in basic commodities.

However, all the measures for paring down a huge budget deficit could constitute little more than window-dressing. For reasons outlined in the previous chapter the simultaneous amelioration of external and internal imbalances could only be achieved through the injection of foreign aid and how this extra purchasing power was to be channelled would determine the relative priorities of the stabilisation strategy. The resolution of the external imbalance meant that in the long term exports had to rise faster than imports, but an activation of domestic production to do this was bound to aggravate the internal imbalance and sustain or worsen inflation. Foreign aid meant that for every level of inflation a greater level of domestic production was being tolerated than with no aid at all. Or in other words, for a tolerated rate of price rises, production could rise at a faster rate with aid than without. What volume and quality of aid were necessary for each possible phased combination of internal and external imbalance amelioration would have been extremely difficult to estimate, even approximately. However, no serious attempt at these evaluations was made because the goal of price stabilisation was a rigid article of faith of all the influential economists of the time, regardless of the level of production at which it would be found or the cost in terms of mortgaged future export earnings.

In normal circumstances an inflow of funds is inflationary as domestic credit is generated against it. In the Indonesian case the inflow occurred against a fiercely tight credit policy, so that the foreign currency now available for purchase was mopping up part of the existing money supply. But the incentives for manufacturers to purchase the foreign exchange were not strong enough, as became apparent in the next few years. The new foreign exchange regulations did, however, affect primary export incentives significantly with the result that this sector proceeded towards rehabilitation well ahead of the non-exporting sector.

LIBERALISATION OF THE FOREIGN EXCHANGE MARKET

The government set out to liberalise the foreign exchange market by ending multiple exchange rates and by reducing cumbersome regulations. But it had to face the problem that 'parcels' of foreign exchange were becoming available under unequal conditions and were therefore received with unequal popularity. Until the total sum of foreign exchange available became much greater there was no hope of effectively homogenizing the entire foreign exchange market. Therefore, the government was still saddled with multiple rate equivalents. The sources of foreign exchange were of two main groups.

Firstly, a percentage of exchange earnings could be retained by exporters for sale on a virtual free market. This free market rate was about Rupiah 43 = \$1.00 in early 1966 (against the official rate of Rupiah 10), rising to Rupiah 150 by October 1967. Currency sold on the free market was called General BE (General *Bukti Ekspor,* or export bonus), arising from BE Quotas (that is percentages). The quotas were different according to whether the exports were strong or weak. This discrimination was an attempt to maximise foreign currency appropriated by the government without discouraging exporters from expanding the volume of their trade. In February 1966 there were three such categories of exports with quotas of 10, 15 and 50 per cent, respectively, but in July 1967 after a re-ordering of exports and amalgamation of categories only two were used, and the quotas retainable by exporters were much higher, 75 and 90 per cent respectively. Thus within eighteen months liberalisation of the domestic supply side of the foreign exchange market was very largely accomplished. There can be no doubt that this was one of the more successful aspects of the stabilisation strategy.

Items on a long 'BE list' could be bought with this source of foreign exchange by both public and government agencies. In addition there was a corner of the foreign exchange market taken by exporters' earnings in excess of a government-stipulated 'check price' for Category A exports. This device is examined further in the next chapter, but here it is mentioned as a source of foreign exchange available for imports outside the BE list of essentials. The greater the difference between the actual market price of exports and the government's check price the greater the supply of this Complementary Foreign Exchange (DPA). Needless to say it had a higher exchange rate than the General BE but the difference was surprisingly small.

The second main source, was, of course, the foreign credits coming through programme aid and subject to individual idiosyncrasies of the donor country. Apart from being tied to the donor's exports there were other imperfections arising through selling practices and pressures. Japanese credits were the most popular and United States credits the least so. They were made available intermittently, commitments not synchronising with disbursements, and all disbursements not synchronising with each other. For reasons of diplomacy and of simplifying the market as much as possible they were subject to one common exchange rate. Although embarrassment might have occurred with Japanese credits disappearing swiftly and United States credits remaining unsold, the main headache was to settle on an overall rate which would clear the market of these credits by some desired date. Furthermore, with the ultimate goal of merging General BE with this latter Credit BE, the closer the Credit BE rate could be set to the floating General rate the better. Another problem was that, in what was still a nervous market, an irregular overall flow of foreign currency could provoke periodic speculation particularly if exporters' or importers' credit terms were being altered. Therefore, although exchange rates were in theory being determined by a free floating General BE rate the Central Bank evolved a practice of open market operations buying and selling foreign exchange to steady the floating rate. This required a delicate monitoring service which, apart from a few bad miscalculations, must be judged successful within its narrow goal of exchange rate stabilisation.

The July 1967 liberalisation of exporters' quotas was made possible by the expanding PL 480 aid and project aid available for the government's own importing programme, but it signified a readiness to disperse further export-producing incentives on the earliest possible occasion. At the same time the recessive policy on non-export producing enterprise was eased by import duties being raised on some finished products and those on some raw materials being reduced. Sales tax on selected import-competing manufactures was also reduced or eliminated. However, the decrease in required prepayments made on consumer goods imports from 100 per cent to 50 per cent as against the decrease to 25 per cent of the value of other imports may not have been properly offset by the impact of lower short-term interest rates for all Credit BE imports.

The goals of the Central Bank's periodic intervention in the foreign exchange market were (1) to keep all exchange rates as close together as possible and, as urged by the IMF, to finally unify them, and (2) to monitor the relationship between internal price rises and exchange rates. The latter was intended to cushion exchange rates from the effects of domestic inflation as well as to prevent foreign exchange speculation (such as hoarding BEs) from provoking speculation of goods internally. It can fairly be said that cushioning exchange rates from domestic upsets was regarded as the more sacred since the government appeared to hold to the belief that stabilisation in the foreign exchange market was the prime mover of stabilisation in other sectors. It was, of course, the easiest to control too.

The easing of credit in July 1967 was not without its problems and the banking crisis which followed revealed just how carefully the liberalisation policy has to tread while opening the dam gates.

When the munificent sum of $200 million of Credit BE became available there was a rush for it and large sums of credit were released. Within three weeks $60 million of Credit BE was sold. In August the private banks were asked to cover their clearing debts within seven days and many could not do so and were thus suspended. They had over-extended themselves and their liquidity ratios were dangerously low. When the banks restricted cash withdrawals, panic spread, even though private bank credit comprised only 20 per cent of total bank credit.

The government moved fast and decisively. Credit BE sales were halted on 25 August and the banks were investigated. Although the panic was over in a few weeks new banking legislation followed quickly. It amounted to a reorganisation of state banks along the lines of increasing their specialisations and obliging private banks to abide by certain regulations to obtain their licences to function. Foreign banks were permitted to establish themselves for reasons of bringing in more capital and improving banking expertise.

But a quite unforeseen crisis was about to break. The rice harvest in 1967 was poor owing to drought, and the domestic price level was dragged up by the price of rice. This, together with the slowness of arrival of programme aid, encouraged speculation in BEs which, once bought, were retained awaiting an increase in their value. In January 1968 the government began selling more BEs to bring down their price, while a reduction in the period of validity of BEs (once bought) from three months to three weeks forced a disgorging of hoarded BEs onto the market. Tough as this policy was it was not enough to end speculation in foreign exchange in the face of domestic inflation, and in April 1968 importers were forbidden to resell their BEs and instead were obliged to open letters of credit for imports within ten working days. But it was only in May that exporters themselves were told they could no longer retain their BE earnings indefinitely. At the same time their practice of selling direct to importers was ended. In future they would have to sell their BE earnings to foreign exchange banks which in turn were obliged to offer them for sale immediately. Although these events were assisted by the simultaneous announcement of more Japanese aid they signified the government's new decisiveness in jumping on speculators rather than resorting to the tired old policy of credit repression.

These measures also meant that the Central Bank was no longer operating in the dark. It had the information on available foreign exchange at the ready, and by bringing foreign exchange into the formal banking system had greatly increased its powers of regulating the flow. Such instruments of policy need never have conflicted with the basic provision of export incentives and one can only conclude that their introduction was long overdue.

Not so a concurrent step: this was the end of the difference between General BE and Credit BE exchange rates. Their equalisation in price, though not in conditions, would create the long sought after uniform rate. But to undertake this in a crisis was a gamble and one which was to lead opinion to believe that it was also a premature act for basic structural reasons. In July 1968 there was an announcement to the effect that even General BE had to be spent on imports from IGGI countries. There was a strong desire to merge the two BE markets but one was 'tied'. So rather than continue with the differentiated market, make the second tied too! There followed, very naturally, a rush on the totally free DPA (excess of checkprice earnings) foreign currency. The announcement was countermanded a few weeks later. During the last three months of 1968 the Central Bank did a great deal of buying of BE and selling it in the DPA market to reduce the latter's price. One might ask 'Why bother if

DPAs are to be spent on non-essentials?' But the government's central goal was the maintenance of confidence in the Rupiah and it could not afford the psychological disadvantages of allowing backsliding in any one of the foreign exchange markets since it had publicised so clearly that it was pinning its shirt on foreign exchange liberalisation.

When prices of strong exports, particularly rubber, began falling in 1969 the supply of DPA foreign exchange fell correspondingly. The fall was no small matter. For each cent drop per pound weight in the market price (and therefore the overprice) of rubber the supply of DPA declined by about $1·2 million per month. The Central Bank once again found itself in the market, on the insistence of the authorities that the DPA rate should not move away or out of sight of the other exchange rates.

While all this firmness was coming off the commanding heights, the authorities were becoming slowly aware of some massive embezzlement of BEs. Letters of credit were being manipulated with either incorrect descriptions of imports or no imports at all. The problem seemed to be confined to ghost shipments from Hong Kong and Singapore, and trade with these two places was halted with alacrity. Officials simply had to be involved in the conspiracy somewhere, although they might not have been responsible for the recording of two addresses which turned out to be a playing field and a Chinese temple, respectively. Thirty-five million dollars was known to be involved, with suspicions that the final amount was £100 million (Sinar Harapan, 30 Sept. 1968). Documents concerning the shipments were found to have been burned by the foreign exchange banks (Angkatan Bersendjata, 12 Sept. 1968).

Furthermore, by 1970 internal price stabilisation appeared to have been achieved and attention was moving to the balance of payments. Both imports and exports were burgeoning under forces which were not wholly expected. The enormous increase in the foreign trade turnover since 1966 meant that the problem of allocative preferences for scarce foreign exchange had virtually been passed. It now became more important to see expanding imports and exports subject to criteria of competitive efficiency and this was to be promoted by uniformity throughout the foreign exchange market.

There was, therefore, a case for both an effective devaluation and a lumping together of the sources of foreign exchange—even if it meant shutting one's eyes and jumping into the unknown.

In April 1970 the checkprice/overprice system, and therefore DPA exchange, was abolished. In future exporters had to surrender their entire f.o.b. value of exports to foreign exchange banks. The General BE became the DU (*Devisa Umum*—General Foreign Exchange).

Essential imports were to compete with non-essentials for DU, and protection would depend more heavily on the tariff structure. The evaluation of tariffs thus became a priority. Credit BE (now *Devisa Kredit*—DK) was sold at a slightly lower rate, justified on the still movement of some tied aid.

The Central Bank would continue to support the 'floating' exchange rate but at a rate which was effectively devalued after the merging of DPA and General BE; and the fact that there would only be one rate to work on was believed to strengthen the controlling ability of the government.

In December 1970 DU and DK were merged. Some writers have commented that the continued slowness of sales of programme aid caused the unification of Credit and General BE to be premature. That the Central Bank had to remain active in the market after that is true, but it is still open to debate that management problems within the foreign exchange market would have continued to be more difficult with the necessity of estimating and supporting price differentials. The criticism arose because of the structural imbalance in the foreign sector. What was not foreseen was the continued rapid expansion of imports. The liberalisation of import items permissible under this one source of foreign exchange would, alone, have encouraged the volume of imports. But the concurrent reduction in interest rates had put a spurt on imports of industrial materials and wage goods.

In addition in May 1970 importers had been allowed to use merchant letters of credit of up to 180 days from overseas suppliers at interest rates less than half of those in Indonesia. Imports via this means quickly rose to 29 per cent of total imports in the second half of 1970. Anxiety was aroused because the uneven repayment of these letters of credit could exert abrupt pressures on foreign exchange reserves, especially since prices of rubber, copra, pepper and palm oil were falling.

The result of this build up of pressure meant that whereas the government had to step in with support for the Rupiah, amounting to $13 million in the last six months of 1970, it had to sell $95 million in the first six months of 1971. The fall in foreign exchange reserves caused some alarm and it encouraged the belief that the unified exchange rate had been premature. There was nothing the authorities could do about export prices and there was extreme reluctance to put the clock back on industrial and commercial rehabilitation through raising interest rates. Instead a regulation was introduced obliging merchant letters of credit to be opened through the foreign exchange banks so that their volume could be monitored; and an effective prepayment of 25 per cent was also demanded. But because of the still favourable conditions of these import credits merchant letters of credit continued to grow.

In August 1971 the government took the opportunity provided by the devaluation of the United States dollar to make a formal devaluation of the Rupiah amounting to 9·5 per cent against the dollar itself, claiming that there had been a serious fall in reserves. Nevertheless the move was criticised as unnecessary on the grounds that the loss in reserves had been the result of a structural problem which was bound to continue after devaluation.

Nor could the need for devaluation be said to have arisen due to internal inflation. The Jakarta cost of living index rose only 9 per cent in 1970 and actually fell 1 per cent in 1971. What is difficult to explain is why the government did not allow a genuine floating of the foreign exchange rate without official intervention. It had always been against a policy allowing internal balance to be achieved at the expense of external balance and the formal devaluation showed that this consideration continued. The only explanation is that the authorities were fearful of the consequences of releasing the market from real control even for a few weeks in order to find its natural level. The satisfaction of its fetish about a unified exchange rate and its desire to put as much distance between its policies and those of Sukarno led it into a situation where its basic insecurity was revealed, even after several years of generous shoring up of the economy by external aid.

The government must have come round to acknowledging the validity of the argument on structural imbalance, in part at least, for in August 1971 a form of multiple exchange rates was introduced, passing right across the main thrust of the liberalisation policies of the previous four years. It was, above all, an extraordinary curtain call after having finally rung down the curtain on the saga of the evolving unified foreign exchange market.

We leave the record of the relationship between aid and the foreign exchange market here, since the issues of rising domestic economic activity and imports, of merchant letters of credit, of the 1972 rice crisis and the 1973/74 oil price increases were to assume greater importance. The management of the combined foreign exchange market was, on the whole, skilful within its highly conservative framework. There were flashes of brilliance and decisiveness, and gambles were inevitable considering the rigidly phased progress the authorities set themselves. What was not excusable was the strict adherence to textbook orthodoxies of market liberalisation at the expense of a long delayed solution to the national liquidity crisis. Providing incentives to exporters in the early days after 1965 was one thing; to hasten towards a unified exchange rate and to permit competition between essential and non-essential imports before the rehabilitation of domestic activity was another. Merchant letters of credit, used mainly for vehicles, chemical products, textiles and machinery, at far lower interest rates than prevailed domestically, were unfair competition to exhausted industry. In addition a Foreign Investment Law, passed as early as February 1967, allowed foreign capital, again raised at lower overseas costs, to cut a swathe into nationally-owned production capacity.

FOREIGN AID AND THE BALANCE OF PAYMENTS

Although imports and exports were rising together their net balance was highly volatile. The deficit in the total balance of trade declined temporarily during 1967 and 1968 when exports were being encouraged. But the partial release of the brakes in 1969 set in motion the rapid expansion of imports (see Table 3.4) which kept in step with exports until the oil price increases after 1973. But the enlarging of the deficit on the balance of trade in 1972–3 was largely due to investment income sent abroad.

The authorities had anticipated a continuation of the deficit, in spite of a substantial rise in exports, because imports and debt-servicing were expected to rise by equal amounts. Thus deficits on the balance of payments were planned for. However it is doubtful whether such a large share of the rise in the deficit between 1967 and 1972/3 taken by investment income had been expected.

According to the Five Year Plan, by 1974 exports would reach $800 million a year and the deficit would be $1,081 million, covered by aid of $910 million. That Indonesian economists had planned for such dependency on aid is an indication that they at any rate did not read concern or failure in the trend in aid commitments. It would appear that the IGGI had also finally come round to the view that 'the more effective the country was in increasing its investment, the more aid it would need' (Chenery *et al.,* 1967). As it turned out, the unexpected rise in exports (non-oil exports were $1·9 billion and net oil exports were $3·1 billion in 1974/5) and the very generous debt rescheduling led to a smaller deficit in spite of imports reaching $5·7 billion (McCawley, 1976).

It can be seen from Table 3.5 that the share of imports financed by aid increased significantly up to 1970, when the merchant letters of credit began to make a strong showing. The data on the latter illustrate well their ability to cause short-term upsets should their repayments occur unevenly. But by 1972–3 general commercial imports had emerged as by far the biggest source of import financing.

The Pertamina troubles of 1975 introduced a startingly different picture of the overall balance of payments. As a result of falling (non-

TABLE 3.4
Balance of Trade in Goods and Services: 1966 to 1972/3 ($ million)

	1966	*1967*	*1968*	*1969*	*1969/70*	*1970/1*	*1971/2*	*1972/3*
A. GOODS								
Exports (fob)	+417	+770	+872	+995	+1044	+1204	+1374	+1939
(of which oil)			(+303)	(+358)	(+380)			
Imports (fob)	−604	−805	−831	−993	−1097	−1102	−1287	−1832
(of which oil)			(−80)	(−82)	(−91			
Balance	−187	−35	+41	+2	−53	+102	+87	+107
B. SERVICES								
Freight and insurance related to imports	−63	−86	−92	−107	−139	−140	−153	−205
Other transportation	−7	−9	−3	−3	−4	−5	−10	−20
Travel	−18	−4	−14	−10	−3	−16	−26	−22
Investment Income	−47	−63	−78	−107	−116	−135	−199	−360
Government	−35	−23	−23	−18	−20	−20	−20	−14
Other services	−72	−62	−82	−118	−139	−139	−131	−146
Balance	−242	−247	−292	−363	−421	−455	−539	−767
TOTAL TRADE BALANCE	−429	−282	−251	−361	−474*	−353	−452	−660

Sources: *Bank Indonesia Reports, 1968* (p. 74); *1970/1* (p. 45), *1971/2* (p. 42); and *1972/3,* (p. 33). Oil: H . W. Arndt, 'Survey of Recent Developments', *Bulletin of Indonesian Economic Studies,* 7, (1), March 1971, p. 3.

* Corrected from the reference.

oil) export prices and a 20 per cent increase in the value of imports, the current account deficit of $138 million in 1974/5 changed into a deficit of $991 million in 1975/6 in spite of oil price rises. At the same time the net private capital outflow was expected to increase from $131 million in 1974/5 to $1,371 million in 1975/6 due to sluggish new foreign investment. The huge anticipated deficit on the overall balance of payments was being supported by an increase of official capital inflows (aid and commercial loans) from $660 million to $2,287 million (Rice and Lim, 1976). The sharp fall of foreign exchange reserves (from a peak of $1·6 billion in mid-1974 to $0·4 billion a year later) following the government's paying off of some of Pertamina's debts was probably not enough to elicit this massive support from Indonesia's creditors. The vulnerability of the current account in spite of higher oil prices has also caused alarm. While export prices have been affected by world recession imports have risen uncontrollably. The government intended to restrain imports in 1976/7 but the upward trend of imports in 1976 and the concurrent expansionary monetary and fiscal policies suggest that imports will reach a record in 1976/7.

It can be concluded that the unsettled nature of the balance of payments in the mid 1970s, a decade after the rescue operation began on the economy, will provide IGGI with a continued full supporting role.

FOREIGN AID AND THE BUDGETS

Until 1966 the budget was clearly the biggest single source of increases in the money supply and no amount of effort in other fields could have brought about price stabilisation without some kind of an assault on the budget deficit. In the early years of the new government three items emerged as the potential equalisers of revenue and expenditure: a successful income tax drive, the end of subsidies to state enterprises, and the use of counterpart funds from the sale of programme aid as Credit BE. The last was easily the most important; by 1967 the budget deficit was less than 6 per cent of total revenue, marked by the sale of $200 million of Credit BE amounting to about 34 per cent of total government revenue. But the aid component of total revenue declined rapidly after 1971/2 to 14 per cent in 1974/5 (see table 3.6). This was facilitated, of course, by the much larger oil taxes/royalties. However, sales taxes and import duties kept pace with the rate of expansion of the total budget.

Although direct taxes increased as a percentage of total revenue from 29 per cent in 1965 to 55 per cent in 1974/5 this was due to taxes from the oil companies more than compensating for the decline in income tax (from 4·7 per cent to 1·9 per cent) and in corporation tax

TABLE 3.5

Financing of Imports: 1966 to 1972/3 ($ million)

	1966	*1967*	*1968*	*1969*	*1969/70*	*1970/1*	*1971/2*	*1972/3*
General BE imports:	340	384	416	475	469	419	361	816
DP imports:	68	114	94	125	178	32	42	19
Credit BE imports:	128	238	240	285	337	346	393	497
(programme aid)	(96)	(145)	(103)	(101)	(106)	(125)	(139)	(174)
(non-PL480 food aid)	(—)	(6)	(30)	(32)	(40)	(39)	(40)	(67)
(PL480 aid)	(32)	(25)	(89)	(90)	(135)	(105)	(111)	(126)
(project aid)	(—)	(62)	(18)	(62)	(56)	(77)	(103)	(130)
Imports under direct Investment	—	1	1	21	25	65	121	130
Imports under merchant letters of credit	—	—	—	—	—	146	238	211
Total	536	737	751	906	1009	1008	1155	1673
Imports of oil companies	68	68	80	87	88	94	132	159
Grand Total	604	805	831	993	1097	1102	1287	1832

Source: Bank Indonesia Reports 1969/70, p. 51; *1971/2*, p. 52; and *1972/3*, p. 40.

(from 9·2 per cent to 4·6 per cent).

It is possible to conclude, then, that in the first few years after 1965 counterpart funds from foreign aid were a major support of the government budget whose huge deficit was quickly cut back, and that later expansion of the budget was supported by the oil industry. Since foreign aid was intended to help national economic development and, with foreign aid, to accelerate industrialisation it would have been realistic to suppose that income and corporate tax would have taken over from aid as a support to the budget. But this did not occur, and the increase in revenues from the oil industry, especially after the fortuitous rise in oil prices in 1973, can hardly be said to have resulted from foreign aid. Had Indonesia not been blessed with oil resources the assumption that aid counterpart funds would be needed only temporarily to support the budget until development increased personal and company incomes and with them the taxable base of the economy would have proved fallacious.

That there were improvements in tax collection after 1965 is not denied. Staffed by underpaid workers the system had experienced endemic corruption and mass tax evasion. But the improvements were partly hidden by the rapid expansion of the total budget. It is also suspected that they were not sustained in the 1970s for one report (McCawley, 1972) quoted an estimate of 'leakages' as high as 40 per cent. With the government's burden of paying off Pertamina's debts in the second half of the 1970s this weakness of budget revenue sources is likely to be felt. It also goes without saying that Table 3.6 illustrates clearly that there has been no serious attempt to apply fiscal instruments to a more egalitarian redistribution of income.

The development budget was financed from three sources: the surplus on the routine budget, programme aid counterpart funds, and project aid. The sums available are shown in Table 3.7.

By the end of 1968, as prices stabilised, some IGGI countries were suggesting programme aid might be gradually reduced. This idea was overruled when it was finally acknowledged that programme aid was needed for budget counterpart funds, if not for confidence in the foreign exchange market. But before then there was an interesting, and insofar as it revealed confusion over the role of an aid consortium, an important theoretical debate.

Posthumus (1971) wrote, in retrospect, that the stabilisation policy had taken hold in the second half of 1968. This was running behind schedule, for 1968 had originally been designated as the year of rehabilitation and development. That rehabilitation was late in coming is confirmed by the fact that only in 1969 was Indonesia ready with enough surveys and evaluations of the state of infrastructure to make use of more project aid. In 1969 project aid commitments

TABLE 3.6

Budget Revenue (Rupiah million)

	1965	*1966*	*1967*	*1968*	*1969/70*	*1970/1*	*1971/2*	*1972/3*	*1973/4*	*1974/5*	*1975/6**
DIRECT TAXES	269	1,790	16,816	51,034	91,468	121,668	180,989	302,229	504,974	867,400	1,867,500
Income	43	640	3,130	9,432	12,060	13,375	17,394	23,722	34,393	49,300	52,400
Corporation	85	611	10,808	9,497	15,640	20,683	25,405	30,598	44,223	60,200	125,600
Oil	—	—	—	25,504	48,332	68,818	112,497	198,885	344,612	653,700	1,540,000
Land subscription to regional development	3	520	2,137	—	—	—	—	15,200	19,501	24,200	31,700
Withholding	—	—	—	6,369	15,268	18,591	24,610	30,195	56,745	70,100	104,800
Other	138	19	741	232	168	201	1,083	3,629	5,000	9,900	13,000
INDIRECT TAXES	604	10,744	42,018	93,963	149,069	209,823	219,538	253,770	412,949	466,400	571,600
Sales	101	1,717	5,069	15,207	30,954	40,382	46,412	62,292	105,346	131,100	198,400
Excise	133	2,220	7,657	16,566	32,090	38,879	40,391	47,279	61,674	67,800	90,200
Import duties	52	3,689	16,901	37,300	57,671	70,697	69,417	73,223	128,172	167,300	221,400
Export, BE rate differential	—	1,966	10,602	13,923	7,447	25,032	28,101	32,739	68,623	65,200	71,700
Net petroleum prepayment	—	—	—	7,743	17,460	30,417	28,213	31,563	37,634	19,300	—31,100
Stamp, levy on credits	20	219	722	—	—	—	—	—	—	—	—
Contributions for luxury goods	16	115	220	—	—	—	—	—	—	—	—
Dwikora	57	57	16	—	—	—	—	—	—	—	—
Transfer of motor vehicles	—	—	507	—	—	—	—	—	—	—	—
Other	225	761	324	3,224	3,437	4,416	7,004	6,674	11,500	15,700	21,000
Other revenue	50	608	26,066	4,749	3,167	13,112	27,494	34,609	49,764	29,600	57,000
Programme aid	—	—	—	35,537	65,761	78,951	90,527	95,500	89,869	89,100	20,200
Project aid	—	—	—	—	25,297	41,580	40,575	62,300	114,125	124,800	218,400
Total	923	13,142	84,900	185,283	334,762	465,134	559,123	748,408	1,171,681	1,577,300	2,734,700

*Planned

Sources: *Bank Indonesia Reports, 1966/7* (p. 26); *1969/70* (p. 8); *1970/1* (p. 7); *1971/2* (p. 9), and *Indonesian Financial Statistics,* 8 (3), (pp. 84-5).

jumped to $180 million against $70 million the year before. At the outset it had been agreed by all parties that aid would commence heavily weighted towards programme (BE) aid and then shift to project aid. But the government did not anticipate an absolute decline in programme aid during the Five Year Plan. Counterpart funds were to provide Rupiah 63 billion to the government budget in 1969/70 rising to Rupiah 85 billion (at constant prices) in 1973/4. This intention conflicts with the opinion of at least one donor country representative:

> Programme aid is, in the first place, a short-term and emergency measure, whose primary purpose is to correct an unfavourable balance of payments and bring inflation under control as soon as possible. The advantage of a prolonged extension of programme aid is dubious from the point of view of an effective use of foreign aid. It is to be hoped that programme aid will be reduced year by year and completely terminated as soon as it has served its purpose. (Posthumus, 1971).

This opinion gathered momentum over Indonesia's request for more programme aid in 1970–1. It was pointed out that price stabilisation (internal equilibrium) at least had been established and that great strides had been made towards external equilibrium. Indonesia argued that the latter was not strictly true since more imports were scheduled under the Five Year Plan and any external imbalance would threaten internal balance, notably via insufficient counterpart funds in the government's development budget. The discussions in the IGGI in 1969 to 1971, more than anything else, revealed the continued irresolution of aid consortiums over the real purpose of their interventions.

Posthumus points out a more pressing reason for donors preferring to give project aid. Project aid is a better means of conveying technical knowledge and of ensuring the efficient implementation of each individual development project. True as this proposition probably is, it tells us nothing of the efficiency of allocation of aid between project and programme aid, nor indeed amongst various projects.

The December 1971 meeting of IGGI probably witnessed the peak of euphoria for the Indonesian authorities. There was no doubt that the IMF and the World Bank were extremely impressed with the degree of stabilisation by the end of 1969. In accordance with the new theory of aid (that the more effectively investment is increased the more aid is needed) past success had the effect of encouraging softer loans. The increase in commitments was seen as a clear vote of confidence.

However, IGGI countries were pressing for an acceleration in project implementation, and their proposals for all projects in 1971/2 was equal to twice the amount of project aid requested. But Indonesia again pressed for priority of more programme aid since even project aid called upon some counterpart Rupiah financing. There was a detectable difference in the bases from which IGGI countries and Indonesia were arguing; the former were urging more effort in surveys and project evaluation and preparation, and the latter was stressing the money backing to project expansion via the general supporting role of programme aid.

The change from 1968 when development was being totally financed by foreign aid to 1972/3 when the surplus on the routine budget had risen to equate the total of foreign aid was creditable. It had been expected that the 1972/3 surplus would just exceed programme aid alone. This led some to point out that the main determinant of the development budget need no longer be the IGGI's generosity, and that the time was ripe for considering the government's development budget within the framework of internal economic trends and needs. More immediately it encouraged the rapid demise of programme aid.

Within six years of a position of staggering budget deficits in 1966 domestic financing of development was greater than foreign aid sources and the main problem had shifted to devising an even rate of absorption of these funds. The issue of erratic aid expenditures should not be seen only in the light of its consequences for the foreign exchange market. Its basic cause also deserves attention. Real need for new projects there certainly was. But patterning projects so that they were supportive to the overall strategy of development and preparing the technicalities of implementation placed a constraint on the capacity to absorb project aid. Had there been a waiting queue of prepared projects, phasing their expenditure outlays into a steady flow would not have been nearly so difficult. This was a point which was reiterated by donor governments and by the World Bank, and although Indonesia's economists must have been equally aware of it their training was in manipulating markets rather than in organising and inspiring skilled bureaucratic ability.

During the early years after 1965 there were two other headaches of programme aid for the planners. Firstly, the counterpart funds of programme aid were not immediately available for stabilisation policy since Central Bank credits extended for the importation of grains, fertiliser and cotton, had to be returned by borrowers before the counterpart funds could be released. These delays, or carryovers, were considerable. Secondly, aid commodities were imported at much higher than domestic market prices, and their subsidisation was subvented from the value of programme aid. An idea of the

TABLE 3.7

Sources of Funds for the Government Annual Development Budget (Rupiah million)

	1966	*1967*	*1968*	*1969/70*	*1970/1*	*1971/2*	*1972/3*	*1973/4*
Surplus on routine budget	−16,800	−11,900	—	27,200	35,600	78,900	152,500	254,400
Programme aid	—	24,700	35,500	65,800	80,200	90,522	95,500	89,869
Project aid	—	10,300	5,500	25,300	49,100	40,575	62,300	114,125
Total	−16,800	23,100	41,000	118,300	164,900	209,997	310,300	458,394

Source: Calculated from H. W. Arndt, 'Survey of Recent Developments', *Bulletin of Indonesian Economic Studies,* 7 (1), March 1971, p. 29; *Bank Indonesian Reports;* and *Indonesian Financial Statistics,* 8 (2), February 1975.

difference between programme aid and counterpart funds generated for the year 1971–2 is given in Table 3.8. The whole of programme aid was what had to be finally repaid the donors. Half the commodity aid for rice and almost half for yarn went in subsidies. On average, in this year, about 36 per cent of commodity aid value was subsidised on the domestic market.

TABLE 3.8

Generation of Counterpart Funds: 1971-2 (Rupiah billion)

	Programme aid	*Subsidies*	*Balance*
General programme aid	49.14	—	49.14
Commodity aid:			
fertiliser	11.34	3.13	8.21
cotton	13.23	5.70	7.53
yarn	5.67	3.42	2.25
rice	41.58	20.40	21.19
wheat flour	18.90	4.11	14.79
Total	139.86*	36.76	103.11

Source: Ministry of Finance, quoted in *Bulletin of Indonesian Economic Studies*, 7, (1), p. 29.

* Corrected from the reference.

It would be fair comment to say that project development was from 1969 never a fundamental problem of shortage of finance. Until 1971 the main restraint on capital absorptive capacity, in other than infrastructural works, was lack of effective demand for capital, and the development of interest rates and bank deposits highlighted this.

CREDIT AND THE RISE OF DOMESTIC SAVINGS

Confidence in the banking system could hardly have occurred until the Central Bank's management of the money supply had been properly brought under the control of government. This was done by the Banking Law of December 1967 whose regulations enforced a sober relationship between the government budget and the Central Bank.

In economically advanced countries the percentage of the money supply in bank deposits may be as high as 66 to 75 per cent. By the mid-sixties in Indonesia only about 30 per cent of the money supply was in bank deposits and this weakened the powers of the monetary authorities. Since bank deposit interest rates bore no relationship to inflation there had been little chance of rectifying this, or of encouraging small public savings, within the banking system.

In October 1966 the tight money policy turned on very high interest charges. Credit for foodstuff production was set at 6 per cent per month, on export production at 7·5 per cent, and on distribution of domestically produced goods at 9 per cent. In April 1967 this was lowered to 3 per cent per month for production and distribution of essentials, for agricultural and export production. Trade and services credits cost 4 per cent, and all other credits carried 5 per cent. During 1969 there was an attempt to shift credit away from the commercial sector into medium-term investment, but this proved difficult to implement.

As early as October 1968 there had been a serious effort made to bring savings into the banking system with an offer of 6 per cent per month interest earnings for a 12-month deposit (with no questions asked about source of money). (Interest in the unorganised market was 9 to 12 per cent per month in 1968–9.) The scheme proved unexpectedly successful. There were fears that depositors would withdraw their money when the rate was reduced in stages to 3 per cent per month on 12 month deposits in 1969, but the upward trend continued. The six-month deposit rate went to 2½ per cent, the three-month one to 1½ per cent, and less than three months to 1 per cent. When private national banks ran into liquidity troubles in 1969 there was evidence of a switching of deposits from them to foreign and state banks. Thus basic confidence in the monetary authorities held.

The deposit scheme was launched propitiously. A year before it would have run into trouble from the aftermath of the rice crisis. But in 1968–9 prices rose much less than the money supply due to a good harvest. The amounts placed in time deposits rose from Rupiah 4·5 billion in December 1968 to Rupiah 126·1 billion in March 1975, with around 67 per cent being held in 12 month deposits in the latter year.

As liquid assets moved into the formal money market so the government was able to increase its range of monetary instruments. In 1972 42 per cent of the money supply was in bank deposits. Of private funds that had been brought into the banking system by 1972, 56 per cent were in demand deposits, 33 per cent in time deposits, and 10 per cent in savings.

Being able to retain savers' confidence at new low dividends allowed attention to be given to lowering borrowing rates. The issue was becoming more pressing because of the growing fear that domestic investors were losing ground in the face of foreign investment inflow.

In June 1969 the investment credit rate was only 12 per cent per annum but it is doubtful whether this was competitive with overseas rates. However, another problem was appearing to the authorities.

When goods were in short supply money went into their purchasing, trading and hoarding. Now that the supply of goods was much greater (through the munificence of foreign aid) money was going into bank deposits, instead of production. Indeed, the supply of goods had increased so much towards the end of 1970 that there were reports that shopkeepers were selling at a discount (Kompas, 15.10.1970). Several banks were no longer accepting deposits because they suffered excess liquidity while businesses were not fulfilling their requirements to obtain bank credits. This in spite of a narrowing of interest rates between credit for domestic production and credit for purchasing Credit BE. In May 1970 interest on loans for importing under Credit BE rose from 1 per cent to 2½ per cent per month while interest on loans for production, for export, and for trade in essentials fell from 2¼ per cent to 2 per cent per month. Four years after the new economic order was introduced producers were only just placed on a par with importers of competitive imports in the credit market, but they were still paying much higher interest charges than overseas producers.

These trends in interest rates indicate that expanding domestic production was regarded merely as a residual policy for stabilisation. What is most shocking is that price stabilisation, budget surpluses, and a highly successful savings programme had been pushed so far along their paths before the domestic production sector was allowed to significantly reflate. It is extremely difficult to escape the conclusion that there was a basic antipathy on the part of the westernised gurus of the Planning Board towards production and commercially-minded national entrepreneurs. It is a form of cultural dualism which has escaped the development literature although it has been touched upon by the influential Jakarta *Business News*.

The main amelioration came towards the end of 1970 with a big expansion in medium-term bank credit. Against a (monthly) 2 per cent 12-months deposit rate, medium-term loans were going out at 1 per cent per month in early 1971. Short-term commercial loans were subsidising others by paying 2½ per cent. Even so, industrial credits were slow to catch up on domestic commercial credits. In 1971 total credits rose 26 per cent against 17 per cent in industrial credits. But the following year both expanded by 47 per cent (Bank Negara Indonesia, *Annual Reports 1971* and *1972*). Amongst the industrial investment credits the private textile sector took an increasing share, followed by chemicals.

Finally, against a background of growing world inflation, the high deposit rate was presenting the authorities with a new problem, incredible to those who were still concerned about the monetary nightmares of Sukarno's last years.To say the banks were awash with savings deposits would be an exaggeration. But the tide of capital inflow to bank deposits was causing consternation. Indonesia was becoming something of a safe-deposit box for overseas companies with liquid reserves. As with programme aid and merchant letters of credit, the authorities were suspicious of the volatility of these funds. If the high deposit rates were to be lowered would foreign depositors withdraw their funds?

By 1972 something had to be done. Export volumes and prices were causing a big expansion in the money supply. In January more stringent reserve requirements were imposed on the banks. Inflation in 1972 amounted to 25 per cent but the government held its fire because the money supply and bank credit rose by much more: by approximately 65 per cent and 47 per cent, respectively. This could only mean that there was a larger volume of transaction of goods and services which was partly mopping up the increase in money and credit. The same was true for 1973, although overall increases were less.

Then, in what might be seen as a contradiction of economic theory, deposit rates were lowered as an anti-inflationary measure. The purpose, of course, was to prevent an inflow of funds to the banks, especially from overseas. In the face of escalating world inflation Indonesia was in danger of becoming a (relatively) hard currency country. After a run of very high export prices, and with greatly enlarged oil earnings, decisive action had to be taken on the inflow of capital looking for a relatively secure home. Although the measure was actually taken when prices of traditional exports began to fall, this loss of earnings was to be more than made up by new oil earnings.

An alternative scheme, a discriminating tax against foreign depositors, was mooted at one stage, but it was argued that discriminating further amongst borrowers might have placed too much of a burden on the hard-pressed and weak bank administrative personnel. Already they had to cope with a set of complex interest rates for credits for concessional sales, credits for short-term trading, credits for favoured ethnic groups and credits for medium-term borrowing. Moreover, the government feared that a discriminating tax might mar the picture of Indonesia welcoming foreign capital. Instead with the decline in interest rates, all deposit earnings were exempt from tax, with the foreigners benefitting more because of their larger deposits.

But inflation continued and was refuelled by the oil crisis of late 1973. The Philippines ceased exporting cement to Indonesia and the cement price jumped from Rupiah 800 per bag in mid-1973 to Rupiah 3,000 in January 1974. The fertiliser price rose 100 per cent. Between March 1973 and March 1974 the Jakarta cost of living index increased 47 per cent. Time deposits were falling in real terms, but the government had committed itself to further economic expansion. The budget rose 89 per cent in 1974–5 to $3,800 million and the banks were expected to grant credits amounting to over $2,500 million.

In April 1974 there was a sharp rise in interest rates although deposit rates were still much higher than credit rates. (At the same time foreign depositors were obliged to leave 30 per cent of their deposits without interest earnings.) What contribution this made to a slower rate of inflation and what was contributed by heavy importing of consumer-goods is impossible to say. But by November 1974 inflation over the previous 12 months had been only 31 per cent. The levelling of time deposits in 1973 was ended and by August 1974 time deposits were 36 per cent higher than in the previous March. Once again savers had shown their responsiveness to interest rates. This was more than could be said of potential investors. The confidence of savers must, in the long term, represent the other side of the coin to confidence of investors, but this had not been realised in Indonesia by the mid-1970s. Although the April 1974 measures allowed for short-term credit to cost 18 per cent and medium-term credit 15 per cent against twelve month deposit rates of 18 per cent and twenty-four month deposit rates of 30 per cent this degree of subsidisation of credit was not enough to overcome the reticence of potential investors. Another factor causing a poor response of borrowers was the ceiling imposed on the amount of a loan. The excess liquidity continued throughout 1974 while there was a significant decline in domestic investment. At the end of December there was a reduction in interest rates and the government might have begun to get its monetary policy right had not the Pertamina troubles mopped up so much public sector liquidity. In early 1975 Bank Indonesia paid out the equivalent of $110 million (or around Rupiahs 60 billion) to domestic contractor debtors of the state oil company and in May it suspended publication of data on the money supply. In spite of this the support given by foreign creditors and the high domestic deposit rates returned the money market to a state of liquidity within a few months.

It is difficult to understand why the government has allowed this imbalance between private saving and investment to continue for so long, or why there was such a large difference between the twelve- and twenty-four month deposit rates. The country seemed to be turning into a nation of savers with individual creativity at a premium. In 1974 as much as 75 per cent of all fixed-term deposits were in twenty-four month deposits (Simandjuntak, 1975). Part of the explanation, no doubt, was the government's nervousness over so much money surfacing in the official money market without treasury bills and an official discount market available as policy instruments. Moreover, the merchant banks were moving painfully slowly towards establishing an Indonesian stock exchange which might have encouraged a marrying of savings and new company issues (although foreign bankers in Indonesia believe that few Indonesian companies wish to go public). But one thing is certain. The government has not yet developed a money market which encourages domestic investment to match the country's saving capacity.

EVALUATION OF THE FINANCIAL MANAGEMENT

It is not easy to state at what point price stabilisation arrived. Arndt pronounced in the July 1969 issue of the *Bulletin of Indonesian Economic Studies* that it had then been achieved: prices and exchange rates had been level for six months. But in January 1971 Professor Sumitro assured the country that it would be leaving behind the stabilisation and rehabilitation phases during that year. Towards the end of 1971 the World Bank was saying something similar. But the desire of such persons to apportion time to consecutive stages of planning later gave way to discussion of more interesting sectoral issues.

The early years after 1965 were marked by small national account totals compared with more recent years, so that although foreign aid began at about one-fifth of the aid flow finally reached in 1976 it was a major support of the government budget and the balance of payments. The emergence of a large surplus on the routine account of the budget, soon to exceed the value of programme and project aid together, was inevitable, as was the decline of programme aid. The underlying policy had been to promote exports, both traditional and new ones. To that end the foreign exchange bonuses to exporters was quite correct, although in the light of the data on export crops in Chapter 2 it can be questioned whether lack of foreign exchange incentives had been the main obstacle to an expansion of output in this sector. The allocation of scarce resources to the export sector and to urban consumer goods imports was at the cost of delaying development of heavily populated rural Java and of building up domestic industry. Since these two areas have always been seen as the keys to national economic salvation it can be concluded that while the post-1965 financial management tidied up the national accounts it made a negligible contribution to the main task of economic progress.

The progress of the balance of payments was facilitated by huge increases in oil and timber exports which exploited a national heritage and had nothing to do with financial wizardry. The fast increasing import bill would easily have swallowed up the other sources of export earnings. In 1975 even that fortuitous turn of events was threatened by the stunning cash flow problems of the state oil company, whose debts due for repayment over the following few years amounted to around $10 billion. This great money spinner, which was to spearhead massive industrialisation, caused the most serious loss of Indonesia's credibility in the international money market since 1965. Thus after a decade of extraordinarily generous foreign aid and a host of economic expertise, aid effectively doubled in 1975/6 with over $1,000 million in grants or very soft terms plus another $1,000 million in cash loans made available.

Nor can it be said that an overheating of the economy, resulting from great economic activity, contributed to the crisis. On the contrary, monetary management has created a vast amount of expensively held savings with nowhere to go. Once again the conflict between the chosen financial policy and the needs of potential entrepreneurs arose. It has been demonstrated in this chapter that the authorities frequently showed their nervousness over the foundations of stability. They were able to prove in 1976 that in spite of corruption and blunders they have no need to fear collapse in the foreign exchange market because the country's foreign creditors are prepared to bale it out at any cost. What they have less control over is the domestic rate of investment because, after ten years, they are still nowhere near a *modus vivendi* with the country's many potential entrepreneurs. It may seem a little strange that after so many years of faithful underwriting from other countries it is still necessary to pay savers so much more than borrowers are charged. But what is truly confounding is that after years of excess liquidity in the banking system potential investors still find interest charges too high to make borrowing worthwhile. The post-1965 financial management in Indonesia can only be described as sober and unimaginative. The hunches that were played were played over a very narrow field (such as export bonuses), never over the broad canvas of the whole economy.

Chapter 4

Rehabilitation and Expansion of the Endogenous Economy

This chapter includes the chief sectors of the economy which contributed to national production and employment prior to 1965. They include staple food crops, export products and a small range of manufactures. The tin industry is discussed at the end of this chapter by way of being an introduction to the mineral developments of the late sixties and early seventies, described in Chapter 5.

Various industries' outputs had been eroded by inflation and neglect in different degrees according to the fortunes of their markets and the local infrastructure. But all of them, even the long-established tin industry, can be said to have contributed to a close network of economic exchanges comprising one organic economic body, or as we have chosen to call it here, the endogenous economy. It is endogenous because an expansion in one sector would transmit growth impulses by *internal* channels to other sectors; that is to say, through the historical development of population centres and communications income and employment multipliers operate quickly and significantly in this part of the economy. Growth of the exogenous part can only be transmitted to the endogenous part through *external* channels; that is, through central government re-distribution of surplus and available foreign exchange. In this way the exogenous economy provides a stimulus to the endogenous economy only in the sense that foreign aid especially directed to the endogenous body does. Corruption, remittances, non-essential imports and other forms of leakages have to be deducted from these funds before any estimate of impact can be commenced. For these reasons rapid expansion of the oil or timber industry may have little or no effect whatever on the endogenous economy.

It is the contention of this book that the post-1965 economic developments of Indonesia have not generally expanded the endogenous economy, and that the new total economy can usefully be divided into two parts: a sluggish endogenous economy with serviceable multipliers and good linkages, and a new rapidly expanding exogenous economy with weak and very localized multipliers and linkages. One Indonesian (Dapice, 1972) put it like this:

> The pattern of export growth shows a tendency for income to fall for smallholders and increase for large corporations, of either national or foreign origin.

The question arises: 'Does all this matter if the timber and oil industries were to spawn their own separate endogenous economies elsewhere in the archipelago?' Yes, it does matter. Apart from the frightful inherent political dangers, a cursory look at the economic and demographic maps of Indonesia published in the early sixties shows that the new exogenous economy is generally outside Java and outside the centres of population and need for employment in the outer islands. The oil and timber industries have as much immediate bearing on the mass-based Indonesian economy as has the Hawaiian tourist industry—possibly even less since once at Hawaii tourists may go on to Bali and Java.

This chapter is devoted to the rehabilitation and expansion of what is termed the endogenous economy, with the exception of the manufacturing sector. The reason for this exception is that although expansion of the manufacturing sector ought normally to be regarded as a source of activating income and employment multipliers its recent highly capital-intensive nature as well as its displacement of so much pre-existing manufacturing capacity raises doubt as to whether it has expanded the mass-based economy.

The rehabilitation of the infrastructure is not recorded here for two reasons. First, the pertinent data are concerned with expenditure on its rehabilitation and it is difficult to assess from them the economic efficacy of such rehabilitation for producing units. Second, insofar as infrastructural improvement aids production rehabilitation it is the latter that we are ultimately concerned with.

A note on irrigation rehabilitation is justified since its quantification is meaningful and because it closely affected the import-substituting rice industry in Java which was marked for early improvement. One report (Panglaykim, Penny and Thalib, 1968) quoted an estimate that 75 per cent of all irrigation works in Java needed to be repaired and that the capacity of the existing systems to deliver water had declined by 30 to 40 per cent since 1942. The target in the Five Year Plan was 850,000 hectares and IDA aid in 1968 helped to provide a series of feasibility studies to identify priorities. From these it was decided to go for 600,000 hectares scattered throughout Java plus 180,000 hectares from the West Java Jatiluhur scheme. Rehabilitation costs were estimated at $130 per hectare, or a total of $101·4 million. By March 1971 loans had been secured to rehabilitate 600,000 hectares.

REHABILITATION OF TRADITIONAL EXPORTS

International credits flowed into directly productive fields as well. The World Bank lent $17 million for the rehabilitation of state-owned rubber and oil palm estates in Sumatra covering 200,000 acres (Harian Kami, 29.5.1970), $19 million for West Java tea and rubber estates (Sinar Harapan, 4.12.1970), while the ADB lent $17·5 million for recovery of sugar estates in East Java (Abadi, 7.10.1973). The IGGI was also offering funds for estate development. Together with $54·3 millions re-invested by returning foreign estate companies all these funds added up to a major rescue of estate export crops.

Since any reading of the first Five Year Plan would suggest that the government was drawing up its shopping lists firmly in the belief that the IGGI would stand in as underwriter there might appear to be little reason for bothering with an analysis of export predictions, especially since the Plan admitted to anticipated imports rising wildly out of proportion to exports. Nevertheless, there was always the vague assumption that during this spree real rehabilitation, and then expansion, of the traditional export-oriented economy would be taking place such that the livelihoods of the people would be beneficially affected. It is with the aim of questioning this assumption that we examine first the leeway that had to be made up before any statistical increase could be termed expansion.

Table 4.1 shows the performance of the main export commodities between 1955 and 1964. Apart from tea these commodities comprise nearly all of Group A exports, long regarded as those with strong foreign markets, and bringing in about four times as much foreign exchange as the minor items of Group B.

Except during the Korean War boom, Group A exports have never exceeded a total of $730 million. To reach the Five Year Plan target of $800 million by 1973-4 would require a fortuitous combination of high prices and fast rehabilitation. Little comfort was to be had from the fact that two of the hardest sectors to rehabilitate, rubber and tin, together accounted for about 70 per cent of earnings. In 1964 these main exports amounted to a mere $383 million, having returned well over $600 million in 1955. The greatest proportionate declines had, in fact, occurred with the two most significant exports, tin and rubber—especially estate rubber. But to appreciate the role, if any, of price changes in this decline we turn to Table 4.2. Exports and world prices are indexed alongside each other on base year 1957, as normal a year as could be found.

It can be seen that the erosion of rubber exports, after account is taken of price changes, began after 1957, and continued steadily in the case of estates—presumably encouraged by the exodus of Dutch personnel. Smallholders' output probably benefited from this, and

TABLE 4.1

Foreign Exchange Earnings of Main Export Commodities, 1955-1964 ($ million)

	Rubber			Tin Ore	Copra	Coffee	Tea	Tobacco	Palm Oil
	Estate	*Small-holder*	*Total*						
1955	171.9	259.7	431.6	59.5	35.4	16.0	31.2	30.8	24.2
1956	154.5	206.2	360.7	62.0	39.2	30.0	29.8	29.4	27.1
1957	145.9	203.6	349.5	55.0	40.5	29.4	29.8	33.6	26.0
1958	108.8	153.2	262.0	35.4	18.3	18.5	24.8	30.2	23.7
1959	143.4	275.9	419.3	36.2	27.6	19.0	20.3	24.4	19.2
1960	133.9	243.2	377.1	50.6	29.1	13.7	27.7	33.3	20.0
1961	122.4	184.6	307.0	33.3	34.7	13.8	25.7	24.6	21.4
1962	101.6	196.9	298.5	34.9	14.7	12.5	20.6	16.2	17.9
1963	94.1	150.8	244.9	18.9	13.6	19.9	17.8	18.9	20.0
1964	98.6	137.2	235.8	31.6	23.5	26.6	17.0	21.8	26.9

Source: J. Panglaykim and K. D. Thomas, *Indonesian Exports, Performance and Prospects 1950-70,* Rotterdam University Press, 1967, p. 13.

TABLE 4.2

Indexes of Foreign Exchange Earnings and (Dollar) Prices of Main Export Commodities on Base 1957, 1955-1964

	Rubber			*Tin*		*Copra*		*Coffee*		*Tea*		*Tobacco*		*Palm Oil*	
	Estate exports	Small holder exports	Price	Ex-ports	Price	Ex-ports	Price	Ex-ports	Price	Ex-ports	Price	Ex-ports	Price	Ex-ports	Price
1955	118	128	125	123	95	107	101	87	100	54	117	105	95	92	91
1956	106	101	110	103	105	112	99	97	102	102	90	100	99	88	100
1957	100	100	100	100	100	100	100	100	100	100	100	100	100	100	100
1958	75	75	91	75	99	64	125	45	85	63	83	120	105	90	90
1959	98	136	117	120	106	65	155	68	65	65	88	68	110	73	96
1960	92	119	124	108	105	92	122	72	64	47	91	93	108	99	90
1961	84	91	95	88	117	60	100	86	63	47	88	86	114	73	91
1962	70	97	92	85	119	63	96	36	60	43	81	69	115	48	87
1963	64	74	85	70	121	34	109	34	60	68	83	60	107	56	91
1964	68	67	81	67	164	57	115	58	83	90	81	57	106	65	98

Source: Calculated on the basis of data given by J. Panglaykim and K. D. Thomas, *Indonesian Exports, Performance and Prospects 1950-1970*. Rotterdam University Press, 1967, Tables 1 and 4.

indeed until 1962 the decline in its value kept at least in step with the decline in world price. But after 1962 along with all the other main exports (except tea) value fell faster than price or failed to rise as fast as price.

Tin exports suffered an erratic trend, scarcely related to price changes and the virtual halving of the value of tin exports between 1955 and 1964 (while the price rose about 70 per cent) suggests serious internal organizational and financing problems. The decline was very sharp after 1960.

The value of copra exports was almost halved between 1955 and 1964 while prices rose 14 per cent. The fact that the value declined sharply by about 35 per cent in the late fifties just when the price rose up to 30 per cent is indicative of serious early troubles. Coffee and palm oil seem to have had similar experiences. Tobacco exports hung on a few more years before being overcome in 1962.

There would appear to have been two periods when the bases of exports were eroded—the late fifties when the Dutch were expelled, and after 1962 when inflation worsened. Estate exports suffered through both periods, but smallholders' exports managed to avoid the effects of the first. Nevertheless, over the pre-1965 decade physical turnover of this prime foreign market-oriented endogenous sector was approximately halved. A great deal of rehabilitation had to occur before expansion could pretend to keep up with population and labour force growth.

As it happened, although they lagged behind targets in the first years of the Plan, the values of different exports rapidly accelerated later on to greatly exceed those targets.

Table 4.3 shows the actual progress of these export earnings by calendar year. In 1973 Category A exports leaped ahead of target while Category B had already moved rapidly in excess by 1970. In the latter case this was solely due to timber exports accelerating out of all proportion to the government's plans for the industry. As an export industry it was of negligible significance until 1968, but by 1974 it was accounting for over 70 per cent of Category B exports and about one third of total exports (excluding oil). So rapid was the growth of the timber industry that even by the first year of the Plan realized output was $45 million compared with a target of $22 million, and by 1974 realized output was $725 million compared with a target of $110 million. Even so the later acceleration of other Category B exports is revealed by their excess of the target of $297 million by 1974. The falling off of exports in 1975, especially the major exports of rubber and timber show how vulnerable is the balance of external trade to trends in world commodity markets. Non-oil exports fell a further 15 per cent in 1975/6 from $1,896 million to $1,615 million. The greatest

TABLE 4.3

Value of Main Traditional Exports, 1965 to 1975 ($ millions)

	1965	*1966*	*1967*	*1968*	*1969*	*1970*	*1971*	*1972*	*1973*	*1974*	*1975*
Category A (traditional strong markets)											
rubber	200	235	189	176	221	261	222	196	395	479	358
copra	18	24	15	41	19	29	15	4	6	—	3
coffee	31	39	45	45	51	66	55	73	77	98	100
tobacco	34	27	21	23	14	12	20	30	45	n.a.	n.a.
palm oil	15	22	29	22	22	37	46	42	73	157	152
palm kernels	2	2	4	6	4	5	6	4	5	10	3
pepper	9	14	18	15	10	3	25	21	28	24	23
tin	37	22	32	50	53	62	64	65	86	175	140
Selected Category B (traditional weak markets)											
timber	2	4	6	13	26	101	169	231	583	725	500
tea	14	18	10	17	10	17	29	31	30	19	—
copra cakes	6	7	4	2	2	6	11	13	18	26	25
hard fibres	—	1	1	—	—	—	—	—	—	—	—
rattan	2	1	1	1	1	1	1	1	2	n.a.	n.a.

Source: *Indonesian Financial Statistics,* vol. 6, no. 1, and vol. 7, no. 11; and Rice, R.C. and Lim, David (1976), 'Survey of Recent Developments', *Bulletin of Indonesian Economic Studies,* vol. 12, no. 2.

fall was in rubber (18 per cent), timber (21 per cent) and palm oil (28 per cent). The only major expanding export which enjoyed a price rise was coffee (up 15 per cent in price).

For our purposes of examining what happened to the endogenous body of the economy a subtraction of the timber industry is justified. Little of the value of its exports was made available to income and employment multiplier forces. Most of it went to foreign investors and to the Jakarta middle class. But we must go even further than this modification to gain an assessment of the Plan's realisation and of the rehabilitation of livelihoods in the export sector of the mass endogenous economy. It was only in 1973 that Category A exports were exceeding Plan targets and had it not been for the enclave timber industry the same would have been true of Category B exports. The explanation is simple. World commodity prices of several of Indonesia's important exports rose very greatly: between 1965 and 1973 the price of rubber rose 46 per cent, tin 30 per cent, copra (a painfully sluggish volume recovery) 113 per cent, coffee 49 per cent, and palm oil 38 per cent. Agreeable as these world price changes were they could not be relied upon for long. Moreover, the generation of new livelihoods must be evaluated largely by volume improvements.

Table 4.4 provides indexes of volume changes of main exports. The remarkable growth of traditional export values is not reflected in these changes. Apart from tobacco, palm oil and pepper, recovery could not be said to have taken place if these indexes are compared with those derived from data in Table 4.2. The volume of tobacco and palm oil exports declined very sharply after 1961. Tobacco would have exceeded its 1957 volume of exports only after 1972, and palm oil after 1971. Rubber output has probably returned to its 1961-2 level, which was still far below its achievements of the mid-1950s.

The mixed progress of Category B exports since 1965 (excluding timber) affords little relief to the picture.

One final point that should be mentioned is the impact of the early production incentives to exporters in the form of foreign exchange quotas. It will be remembered that this was amongst the first measures of the post-1965 government to resuscitate the economy. Apart from tobacco and tea most of the main exports appear to have responded. It is possible that this initial recovery phase allowed excessively ambitious extrapolations of traditional exports in the Plan, but that fortuitously these targets, offered in value terms, were saved by the world price increases of the early seventies.

We have seen then that the Indonesian miracle did not extend to the traditional export sector. Already world prices of some of these goods have fallen again. Since 1965 the population has increased by something close on 30 per cent. As far as the 'people's economy' is

TABLE 4.4

Volume of Exports, Indexed on Base 1965, 1965 to 1975

	1965	*1966*	*1967*	*1968*	*1969*	*1970*	*1971*	*1972*	*1973*	*1974*	*1975*
Category A (traditional strong markets)											
rubber	100	96	92	108	120	111	111	111	123	117	110
copra	100	96	92	174	126	149	62	28	34	—	—
coffee	100	90	148	79	118	96	69	89	93	106	113
tobacco	100	97	78	68	42	81	136	183	230	189	n.a.
palm oil	100	141	105	121	141	126	166	184	205	217	297
palm kernels	100	96	118	111	130	129	148	146	121	74	55
pepper	100	168	304	200	136	22	197	201	201	131	128
Category B (traditional weak markets)											
timber					100	216	289	385	524	461	360
tea	100	86	68	93	83	95	103	104	101	114	93
copra cakes					100	109	140	164	137	121	142
Hard fibres	100	163	363	238	213	44	69	—	—	—	—

Source: Based on data from *Indonesian Financial Statistics*, vol. 6, no. 11; vol. 7, no. 11; vol. 7, no. 1; vol. 8, no. 1; vol. 8 no. 2; and *Bank Indonesia Report 1966-7;* and S. Grenville (1971) 'Survey of Recent Developments', *Bulletin of Indonesian Economic Studies*, vol. 10, no. 1; and. R. C. Rice and David Lim (1976), 'Survey of Recent Developments', *Bulletin of Indonesian Studies*, vol. 12, no. 2.

N.B. Although the series differed somewhat between the types of sources, it was possible to calculate all indices from consecutive annual data within one series.

concerned there has probably been a contraction in this sector in job opportunity terms.

Why has recovery and expansion been so difficult in this sector? Apart from the disruptive element of uncertainty caused by inflation, traditional exports faced having to run the gauntlet of a weakened and demoralized marketing network with the resources of credit, sorting, grading and transportation inadequate for coping with a suddenly enlarged output. Moreover competing countries, notably Malaysia in the case of rubber, had moved into foreign markets lost by Indonesia. Restoring confidence in Indonesian exports within those markets would take time. All this required investments in the appropriate trading sector over a long period, but it was part of the anti-inflationary drive that speculation in the trading sector was not to be fuelled by bank credit. How was the administration to discriminate?

When in 1966 the State Trading Corporations were told that they had to break even, because they were no longer to receive privileged credit treatment, it was clear that there was to be no subsidisation of the rehabilitation of traditional exports by parastatal bodies. The rapid and generous reform of foreign exchange quotas for exporters of selected products was partly due to the recognition that credit even for this sector was going to be meagre. Thus as early as February 1966 BE Quotas of 10, 15 and 50 per cent provided *effective* exchange rates of Rupiah 13·3, 14·95 and 26·5 to the U.S.$ for categories I, II and III of exports respectively. The lowest effective exchange rate was for goods regarded as strong traditional exports (rubber, copra, pepper, tea, and tobacco—and after May 1966, coffee too). Category II included those regarded as weaker (capok, essential oil, and so on). Category III included handicrafts. In 1965-6 the three categories had supplied 90, 8 and 2 per cent of foreign exchange, respectively. In the following years the quotas were enlarged.

An additional incentive to exporters was the use of the check-price system, whereby the government determined a price for an export commodity in the light of the world market price, and earnings in excess of this could, since 1964, be retained by exporters for their own use. It was a small amount, only about 2 per cent, but sudden rises in the world price could temporarily inflate it. The further the check-price was below the market price the greater the discouragement to smuggling since exporters could acquire more foreign exchange and use it for any imports or foreign transactions through legal channels.

In 1965 and 1966 the difference between the two prices for rubber appears to have been significant. Glassburner (1971a) quotes one report that it varied between 25 and 30 per cent. An IMF report quoted it in early 1967 as 8 per cent. Because this foreign exchange

(DPA) could be used in any way its effective exchange rate on the market was higher than other sources of foreign exchange. Between February and May 1966 it rose from 4½ to 9½ times the rate at which exporters had to exchange part of their foreign earnings with the government, and in October 1966 it stood at 20 per cent above the General BE rate. This might partly explain the rise in output of rubber in 1965 and 1966. But the fall in the world price of rubber in 1967 and 1968 would have reduced the excess of the check-price, while the later progressive liberalisation of imports narrowed the difference between BE and DPA exchange rates.

Credit assistance was longer in coming. Restricted state bank credit was increasingly tightened in May and October 1966. (No credit was to be given the import sector.) It was only in April 1967 that interest rates were significantly reduced with credit for exports always slightly cheaper than credit for domestic trade.

RUBBER

This is easily the most significant of the traditional exports, but its rehabilitation was set against declining world prices from 1965 to 1968—a 24 per cent fall. This was fully reversed one year later, but the ground was more than lost again by 1971. Although the volume of exports showed much response to these price fluctuations the failure to restore the rubber industry to its former eminence was due to the absence of real development resources which could not be purchased locally by profits derived from BE Quota incentives. They involved structural support which only the central government could supply. Indeed the contrast in the prerequisites of expansion of the timber and rubber industries points to the fundamental inability of this character of government to bring about endogenous economic growth. Extension service neglect went back further than the changeover of government in 1966. In 1971, in one instance, a village in South Sumatra claimed that extension agents had not been there for ten years (Collier, 1972). As late as 1971 many areas had no extension information.

The overwhelming issue in the rubber industry was the age of the trees and the need for replanting. New rubber trees are left to mature for five to seven years before they are tapped. Their yields rise until they are fifteen or so years of age. Their life continues depending on many factors but it may end at 30 years. Maintenance of the trees, frequency and heaviness of tapping, as well as the method of tapping, all affect their life-spans. If the world price is high smallholders may find it worthwhile to go on tapping diminished quantities from a 50-year-old tree, and if the old trees are in good condition, new tapping methods can produce good yields at this age. It is believed that between 1960 and 1965 there was very little replanting, so that extrapolating from the 1960 census it could be said that out of a total of 500,000 trees, 315,000 were older than 30 years (Panglaykim and Thomas, 1967). Moreover, evidence from the Agro-Economic Survey of Indonesia suggests that those farmers that did replant did not use new breeds of trees. On the other hand, smallholders' output is highly responsive to prices and the weak prices in the early sixties might have led to an underestimation of the true potential of the smallholding sector. Also, where rubber is grown with rice in shifting cultivation, self-germinating trees are not cleared away so that there could be young trees growing in an unplanned manner.

The several expectations that estates' output would fall, and that smallholders' output would hold the line or increase a little, proved to be on the pessimistic side, although by 1972 estates' output was still short of its golden years in the mid-fifties. Table 4.5 provides the relevant data. There was alleged to be some replanting on estates in the early sixties, which may explain the spurt in output and yields in 1969, for area tapped was still declining.

TABLE 4.5

Area, Production and Average Yield of Rubber: 1955, 1960, 1965-71

	Smallholders			*Estates*		
	Area ('000s hectares)	Production ('000s metric tons)	Yield (quintals per hectare)	Area ('000s hectares)	Production ('000s metric tons)	Yield (quintals per hectare)
1955	1430	507	3.54	491	266	5.42
1960	1430	404	2.82	506	216	4.26
1965	1609	504	3.13	507	220	4.32
1966	1626	528	3.25	477	209	4.38
1967	1617	500	3.09	455	199	4.36
1968	1690	531	3.14	510	208	4.07
1969	1,771	559	3.16	486	223	4.74
1970	1813	571	3.15	486	238	5.02
1971	1853	572	3.09	475	238	5.14

Source: Central Bureau of Statistics, Jakarta, November 1972; and *Bank Indonesia Report 1972/3,* p. 61.

Smallholders' output rose unexpectedly fast after 1975, but its resources were quite different from those of the estates. Yields were declining, if anything, so that the record output was due to tapping a larger area of trees. Indeed, the figures for area tapped suggest that old, new and half-forgotten trees were brought into productive use as a response to price stabilisation and export incentives. Infrastructural and marketing improvements were probably behind the big increases in area tapped after 1968. But all this suggests a form of slaughter-tapping of the smallholding sector.

The tenacity and drive of smallholders confirms their performance in earlier years when they hung on while the estates faltered badly. But if replanting on estates has been proceeding during the sixties there will be great temptation to run down the smallholding sector. There are other factors to consider in any prognostication of the smallholders' sector.

One measure taken by the government to improve returns to rubber growers is the promotion of crumb rubber factories. With price stabilisation and simplified and more realistic exchange rates there was a new interest in upgrading rubber exports to gain the best prices that are paid for guaranteed, uniform and high quality. Previous to 1965, and in fact until 1969, the internal Rupiah price differential of low and high quality rubber was not as wide as the world price differential. Thus low quality rubber production was relatively more profitable *in Indonesia,* which may have been a factor contributing to the greater tenacity of smallholders' output up to 1966.

The government began financing the establishment of crumb rubber plants in 1968-9 through the Indonesian Development Bank and the State Trading Bank. It planned to build eight to ten plants on British credits. By July 1969 there were 170 applications from private companies to build crumb rubber factories. By the end of 1969 14 such factories were established with total capacity of 63,200 tons. But by the end of 1970, actual production was only 34,000 tons. The target output of 100,000 tons in 1971 therefore appeared to be ambitious. But in 1972 there was an acceleration of activity and the plants turned out 281,000 tons of crumb rubber.

Although the introduction of crumb rubber processing was designed to elevate the quality of rubber, especially that of smallholders, it appeared to be having the opposite effect. Local supply of rubber was insufficient to maintain the large single units at capacity so that they were buying low quality and impure rubber in various forms as their raw material. The small difference in prices for low and high grade rubber was of no help to the processors.

In September 1971 the government decided to give further encouragement to these factories by banning the export of low grade rubber. It was a pretty ruthless step and can be seen as an indication of the government's determination to protect Indonesian rubber in the international market in the long run. The measure was, of course, welcomed by crumb rubber factory managers but there was, understandably, great protest from producers and remillers.

In spite of this encouragement, the factories were having a hard time. The low grade raw material was still causing trouble. Moreover, scale and location were involving high transport costs between smallholders and factories. Taxes and levies, official and *ad hoc,* were also adding to costs. One foreign-owned crumb rubber factory with a capacity of 6,000 tons a year went bankrupt (Kompas, 16.12.1972). There were other reports of suspended production or factories changing hands.

The poor profit rates of the factories sparked off a debate on the issue of economies of scale. Collier and Werdaja (1972) suggested the setting up of small-scale local plants closer to sources of production. Barlow (1972), in a reply, disputed this by pointing to the experience of West Malaysia where small crumb rubber plants were found to be uneconomic while considerable economies of scale in crumb rubber processing could be gained. However, West Malaysia had also established a good primary collection system, manned by extension officers. And so Barlow concluded that it was better to invest in marketing improvements than in small, uneconomic crumb rubber plants. He pointed out that the numerousness of middlemen in Indonesia made it difficult to increase the quality of input of the crumb rubber factories. The rejoinder to this from Collier and Werdaja (1972a) was that the smaller crumb processing plants could be channels for advice to smallholders, as well as a cause of a decline in the number of middlemen. The poor transport infrastructure and the shortage of working capital had played into the hands of the middlemen and led to lower prices being offered the producers. Localised, and therefore small, rubber factories would offer the smallholder producers more direct access to them.

We pause here to contemplate the lessons of this for the economy in general. Between the two strategies of encouraging streamlined, large units of technological investment capable of high internal profit rates on the one hand, and supporting and improving numerous lines of communication and production skills on the other, an elite attracted to all things bearing a modern, cosmopolitan flavour will naturally choose the former. In the end in the case of the rubber industry, the neglect of the marketing system rebounded on the policy of promoting, single-mindedly, the crumb rubber factories. There was, after all, no escape from rebuilding the many short axes of the traditional endogenous economy. The large crumb rubber units could only be properly utilised given the marketing network found in West Malaysia. But this was not to be, so that economies of scale had to be sacrificed because the external economies of close proximity were greater. The only circumstances in which economies of scale will overcome diseconomies of distance would be, as Barlow has pointed out, after the government has invested in marketing. But investment in marketing and transportation can produce economies of scale in other directions also. Single traders can then cope with more functions and longer distances, and fewer traders should increase expertise in buying, grading and sorting of raw rubber.

These opposing interests of scale and externalities can be repeated in many instances within the mass-based economy.

Competition from synthetic rubber has played havoc with the investment plans of rubber-growing countries. The gestation period of capital investment is longer for natural rubber and cyclical changes in rubber prices can easily be mistaken as new secular trends. The FAO predicted that demand for synthetic rubber would rise faster than for natural rubber. However, since October 1973 high chemical prices have raised synthetic production costs greatly so that the relative profitability of natural rubber must have risen. But for how long will chemical prices remain high in real terms relative to natural primary commodities?

Demand from centrally planned economies for natural rubber has always been more difficult to predict since the profit motive does not play the role it plays in capitalist production. In 1965 the USSR took over half Indonesia's production of rubber. In 1971 it bought only 21 per cent. Political antagonisms between the two countries are receding but other political factors may emerge. The emergence of China into world trading of commodities is also a huge imponderable. Stock movements can also affect prices. In 1970 and 1971 huge stockpile releases contributed to tumbling prices. Between September 1969 and October 1970 there was a 35 per cent fall. The loss in foreign exchange earnings to Indonesia was reputed to be about $100 million.

COFFEE, TEA, TOBACCO, PALM OIL AND COPRA

Once again smallholders showed greater tenacity than estates in maintaining output during the vicissitudes of post-independence Indonesia. This is illustrated in Table 4.6. In some cases estate owners were unable to get back their land after the war and estate administration lapsed. This explains why estates performed relatively poorly even before the takeover of Dutch estates in 1957-8. Other estate owners were uncertain of their future during the fifties and so declined to invest.

Area under palm oil had remained virtually stationary since 1955 while yields had fallen. If palm oil were to recover there had to be replanting, of which there had been very little since 1950.

The remarkable expansion of smallholders' coffee before 1965, in spite of inflation and transport difficulties, allowed the proportion of production exported to rise alongside an increase in domestic consumption. Unlike the case of coffee, smallholders' tea production was never greater than estate production even though estate production in the sixties was only 55 per cent of its pre-war level. Smallholders' tobacco managed to gain ground but this might have been due to their production mainly for the domestic market.

In the case of copra, estates are insignificant and smallholders have failed to raise their output very much. Area has risen by about one-third since independence but yields have fallen. After 1961 copra production fell steeply. The issue of extension services hangs heavily over the copra sector.

TABLE 4.6

Smallholder and Estate Area, Production and Yield of Selected Main Export Crops, 1955, 1960 and 1965-71

	Smallholder			*Estate*		
	Area ('000s hectares)	Production ('000s metric tons)	Yield (quintals per hectare)	Area ('000s hectares)	Production ('000s metric tons)	Yield (quintals per hectare)
			COFFEE			
1955	148.6	47.3	3.18	48.3	16.1	3.33
1960	230.7	77.9	3.38	47.1	18.3	3.89
1965	265.8	120.7	4.54	40.4	19.8	4.90
1966	279.2	129.2	4.63	39.9	13.0	3.26
1967	289.2	140.3	4.85	38.8	19.5	5.03
1968	299.4	143.7	4.80	38.8	13.9	3.58
1969	337.3	160.8	4.77	39.2	14.7	3.75
1970	351.1	170.1	4.84	38.5	16.2	4.21
1971	353.3	177.6	5.03	39.2	19.4	4.95
			TEA			
1955	64.6	21.9	3.39	80.3	39.3	4.89
1960	64.4	37.3	5.79	72.9	41.9	5.75
1965	55.1	35.0	6.35	74.3	44.8	6.03
1966	55.1	34.6	6.28	79.2	42.4	5.35
1967	53.9	38.2	7.09	71.6	37.8	5.28
1968	50.1	33.1	6.61	69.4	43.0	6.20
1969	48.0	31.2	6.50	62.8	40.7	6.48
1970	51.7	20.6	3.98	62.4	44.0	7.05
1971	52.6	24.2	4.60	65.5	48.2	7.36
			TOBACCO*			
1955	100.5	35.0	3.48	11.4	7.0	6.14
1960	140.3	49.5	3.53	11.0	6.5	5.91
1965	140.5	55.5	3.95	3.7	4.8	13.21
1966	120.4	48.8	4.05	5.7	3.9	6.91
1967	107.7	42.4	3.94	5.9	3.9	6.66
1968	123.8	48.0	3.88	9.9	6.2	6.26
1969	175.9	66.5	3.78	10.4	5.4	5.19
1970	119.0	54.7	4.60	9.4	4.8	5.11
1971	116.0	57.0	4.91	11.1	5.6	5.05

	Smallholder			*Estate*		
	Area ('000s hectares)	Production ('000s metric tons)	Yield (quintals per hectare)	Area ('000s hectares)	Production ('000s metric tons)	Yield (quintals per hectare)
			PALM OIL			
1955				101.4	165.8	16.35
1960				104.3	141.2	13.54
1965				103.8	156.6	15.09
1966				108.5	165.7	15.27
1967				105.8	167.7	15.85
1968				119.7	181.4	15.16
1969				121.1	188.7	15.58
1970				124.2	216.5	17.43
1971				139.2	248.4	17.84
			DRY COPRA			
1955	1514	1039	6.86	23.2	16.2	6.98
1960	1610	1239	7.70	18.8	8.8	4.68
1965	1540	1235	8.02	16.6	6.6	3.98
1966	1479	1130	7.64	16.6	7.9	4.76
1967	1472	1094	7.44	19.4	7.4	3.81
1968	1590	1131	7.11	19.9	7.5	3.77
1969	1665	1165	7.00	20.2	8.0	3.96
1970	1789	1198	6.70	20.2	8.8	4.36
1971	1834	1148	6.26	n.a.	n.a.	—

*People's tobacco for smallholders; all varieties for estates.
Source: Central Bureau of Statistics, Jakarta

At the time of rehabilitation Indonesia was labouring under a coffee export quota of 81,400 tons, imposed by the International Coffee Agreement. With domestic consumption of 40,000 tons, that placed a foreign demand limit of 121,000 tons—or exactly smallholders' production alone. There was therefore a need to find markets in non-quota countries. But as production rose and the quota stayed at 81,000 tons the country still faced a large surplus in 1971. An increase in domestic consumption was urged. The International Coffee Organisation was also approached for $11 million to put coffee land in South Sumatra and Bali under cloves and cashews. In 1972 the ICA quota was actually lowered to 68,100 tons, even though total exports had been running at 70-80,000 in previous years. Annual production was running at 100-150,000 tons and the difference could not be made up by domestic consumption. Markets in non-quota countries were small and because of their status their prices were lower—by about 15 per cent. The solution seemed to lie in urging coffee producers to switch crops.

Rehabilitation of tea seems to have been confined to estates where production rose in spite of a decline in area. Area of smallholders fell a little, but their yields much more. In contrast to this tobacco smallholders enjoyed improved yields after 1965 while estate yields continued to fall. In 1970 disease affected the crop.

Replanting on the formerly Dutch-owned palm oil estates had been started in 1961. With a gestation period of six years, yield improvements should have begun to emerge in statistics from 1967 onwards. With no clear increase in area harvested, yields were already struggling back to their fifties level between 1964 and 1967. From then on there was a sharp rise in area, and yields cleared all post-independence records in 1970. By 1972 production was 269,000 tons, or about 150 per cent greater than in 1965. This was the only clear success story of crop exports.

Copra exports continued to decline between 1965 and 1967. World prices were falling slightly and with old trees there seemed no likelihood of a sudden increase. But in 1967 the volume of exports almost doubled. The small rise in price, coming only in 1967, could not have been the stimulant. Since most copra exports came from the outer islands (especially Sulawesi) it is more likely that exporters' quotas and some semblance of trading order had reduced smuggled exports and that these were now being incorporated in official statistics. (To some extent this might have been true of rubber export statistics as well.) But after 1970 weakening world prices and old age of trees led to continued serious falls in exports. Even under the impact of the enormous rise in price (274 per cent) in 1973 the volume of copra exports merely limped from 28 to 34 per cent of its 1965 volume. During this period copra trees suffered an attack of *Saxava* and in spite of efforts it had not been overcome by the time of the big rise in world commodity prices. Replanting had commenced but with a gestation period of seven years no benefits to average yields have yet been recorded.

By 1970 only coffee and palm oil had risen above 1960 output levels. The former was then to suffer demand constraints demanding a cutback in production. The latter was all estate cultivation. There was no evidence of new plantings coming into use by 1972, with the sole exceptions of palm oil and of smallholders' coffee.

SUGAR

Today Indonesia imports sugar. But in 1928 sugar accounted for 75 per cent of Java's exports. On 200,000 hectares nearly three million tons were produced, half of which was exported. Only Cuba was a greater producer. In 1971 on 134,000 hectares just over one million tons were produced. Production and average yield are less than one half of pre-war levels. In 1938 average yields were 16·2 tons per hectare. By 1963 they had fallen to 8 tons per hectare. Over the years an increasing share has been produced by smallholders. Today Java produces less than three quarters of domestic consumption.

About 60 per cent of sugar cane acreage used to be in East Java and about 10 per cent in West Java. Sugar land was rented by the sugar mills from peasants (under various degrees of coercion) who would otherwise grow rice. Rents were assessed on the basis of government-fixed sugar prices and farmers could also work as labourers on their own land. The crop takes 12 to 13 months to grow, and in Java the land is supposed to be returned to the rice farmer after 16 months (that is, after one sugar crop.) A system of sharecropping was introduced in 1963 whereby the farmer received one quarter of gross output plus rent, or 60 per cent of gross output and no rent. But farmers constantly complained that with given sugar prices rice farming was more profitable.

The general efficiency of administration of the pricing and renting system, processing and marketing were affected by the quality of personnel in the General Management Board of the mills which implemented these matters. The mills had to sell sugar to the Board which made all kinds of cost deductions (some of dubious legality) for marketing before deriving the mills' share of sales returns. In 1968 the Management Board was supplanted by several Government Estate Enterprises, each comprising a group of mills. In the following year the marketing of sugar was passed over to four syndicates of traders, which purchased sugar from each mill separately at prices fixed by the Departments of Agriculture and Trade. It is believed these prices were more generous to the mills.

The falling yields, especially on smallholders' land, are clear indication of the rehabilitation or extension work that has to be done on irrigation, fertiliser use and cultivation practices. But competition from rice and the lack of longer-term rehabilitating capital have meant that the move towards freedom from bureaucratic controls did not lead to a quick recovery.

By the late sixties the sugar mills were facing serious problems of obsolete and run-down equipment. They were extremely old and the estimated cost (in 1966) of rehabilitating the 54 mills in Java was $59 million. The decision to rehabilitate the industry largely depended upon the world price of sugar which could range between $40 and $160 a ton. The haunting issue of deciding whether land is better allocated to rice or to sugar is greatly complicated by the unpredictability of movements in the rice:sugar price ratio. But some rehabilitation did take place, first extending estate area and raising its yields, and a year later extending the area of smallholders whose produce went to the mills. But it was only in 1969 that the 1960 level of these sources of sugar was surpassed, and in 1971 that the 1955 level was exceeded. That part of smallholders' sugar output which is processed by smallholders themselves did not share in this recovery. This is probably sufficient indication that rice and other food crops were more profitable.

New larger scale sugar mills will have to face problems of input collection. Sugar cane must be crushed quickly before it deteriorates and larger scale of processing plant has raised the additional difficulty of arranging a large area of sugar cane close to the mill. Here we see again, as in the case of the crumb rubber plants, that poor communications and transport lead to a trade-off between economies of scale in processing and quality. In spite of this, in June 1974, with national domestic consumption of one million tons of refined sugar compared with production of about one million tons of unrefined sugar, and against a background of sharply rising world prices, the President urged a new drive to raise sugar output by means of large new factories outside Java.

ADVANCING THE PRINCIPAL FOOD CROPS SECTOR

We have separated export crops from domestically consumed food crops because they have been treated and affected differently by government policies.

In Chapter 2 the analysis of harvested areas of different food crops showed that root crops came into prominence and cereals and pulses declined with the inflationary spurt (and general run-down of the economy) from 1962 to 1965.

While export recovery would be dominated by external markets, by export earnings incentives and by improved infrastructure, the rehabilitation of the food crop sector must also be seen in the light of population increases over most of the decade of the 1960s. Some part of the reallocation of land under foodcrops of different nutritional value will thus be due to heavier population. We would normally expect to see this influence more clearly in Java as room to manoeuvre back to specialisation is less, but here a new factor must be taken into account. The mass guidance programmes (Bimas) for rice farmers, started in Sukarno's time, gained ground in area and intensity, and throughout most of the 1960s they were heavily concentrated in Java.

An increase in paddy output arrested the upward movement in maize plus cassava output between 1960 and 1966 (see Table 4.7). As paddy output continued to expand, output of the poorer foods (maize, cassava and sweet potatoes) continued to decline until 1972. In as much as these latter foods are eaten more by the poor the inevitable change in relative food prices must have caused a redistribution of the food budget of the poorer households. How they were finally affected would depend on what happened to their real income as a result of these shifts in production. Rice land and rice-substitute land are only partly substitutable for each other. The competition between the crops lies also in labour effort and market incentives. Arndt (July 1974) has claimed that the poor performance of rice substitutes is not due to excessive preoccupations with rice and neglect of other crops. But he goes on to say: 'The main reason has been that the increase in rice production has come largely from the use of irrigation and fertiliser to produce a second crop of rice on land previously used for other crops.' Not only does he recognise the land substitution factor but he implies neglect also. It could also be suggested that where land has been upgraded by the maturation or repair of irrigation schemes in the last decade rice cultivation has taken over from other lines of food production. Arndt (1974) writes that there was a 4·4 per cent a year rise in rice output between 1968 and 1973. The implication is that this was due to the new technology which is a factor of the future also. The faster rate of growth in the last few years is indicative of the continued pressure of the intensification programmes. The impact of the change in production relations, which they ushered in, on income distribution in rural areas is dealt with later on.

The raising of paddy output is due largely to the improvement in yields. But there has been widespread reserve felt about the official statistics of rice production. In 1968 the method of statistical collection altered and a comparison of the old and new series indicates a varying proportional difference. In 1968, for instance, the old series recorded a production of 10·2 million tons (of milled rice) and the new series 11·7 million tons, or an upward revision of 14·7 per cent (Grenville, 1974). But in 1972 the old series recorded 12·3 million tons and the new one 13·3 million tons, or an upward revision of only 8 per cent. Furthermore, the fact that only between 25 and 30 per cent of production is marketed leads any production shortfall to have a magnified effect on market supply (Grenville 1973). In as much as the accuracy of production data depends on the visibility of that production, increases in output which are largely directed to the market might exaggerate rates of growth. The fact that the rice sector has claimed so much of the limelight since 1965 could also have contributed to inflation of the statistics because it was in the interests of so many people to show that efforts at raising production were succeeding.

Soybeans and peanuts began an increase only in 1970. This would have been due to the revival of trade within Java and between the islands. Their continued expansion was also due to the intensification programmes being extended to food crops other than rice.

TABLE 4.7

Production and Yield of Principal Food Crops: 1955, 1960, 1965-74

	Production ('000s metric tons)						*Yield (quintals per hectare)*					
	Paddy	Maize	Cassava	Sweet Pota-toes	Pea-nuts	Soy-beans	Paddy	Maize	Cassava	Sweet Pota-toes	Pea-nuts	Soy-beans
1955	14,432	1,971	9,317	1,898	207	346	21.97	9.65	86.50	68.03	6.95	6.72
1960	16,860	2,460	11,377	2,670	256	443	23.14	9.32	80.29	67.94	6.79	6.80
1965	17,072	2,365	12,643	2,651	243	410	23.30	9.43	72.08	63.73	6.92	7.02
1966	17,960	3,717	11,232	2,476	263	417	23.25	9.84	74.19	61.59	6.78	6.89
1967	17,398	2,369	10,747	2,144	241	416	23.15	9.30	70.52	59.56	6.87	7.06
1968	19,550	3,166	11,356	2,364	287	420	24.37	9.83	75.56	58.51	7.28	6.20
1969	20,464	2,293	10,917	2,260	267	389	25.54	9.42	74.42	61.25	7.18	7.02
1970	23,401	2,825	10,478	2,175	281	498	28.77	9.61	74.95	60.75	7.40	7.17
1971	24,557	2,632	10,685	2,154	280	516	29.87	10.06	72.66	62.07	7.47	7.14
1972	23,734											
	(millled rice)											
1972	13,183	2,254	10,395	2,066	282	518						
1973	14,607	3,690	11,186	2,387	292	541						
1974	15,452	3,239	13,775	2,916	315	550						

Source: Central Bureau of Statistics, Jakarta, November 1972; and *Bank Indonesia Report 1972/3;* and Anon, (1975) 'Survey of Recent Developments', *Bulletin of Indonesian Economic Studies,* vol. 11, no. 3.

The speed of rehabilitation of major food crops was doubtless aided by the fact that sources of production and consumer markets were close to each other and did not require the improvements in infrastructure that, say, rubber exports required. Even so the Five Year Plan targets for food output by 1973-4 appeared very ambitious in 1971. Milled rice output of 15·42 million tons required a paddy output of between 25·7 and 28·0 million tons. Maize production would have had to experience a sudden uplift to reach the target of 4·23 million tons, while 1·4 million tons of pulses by 1973-4 would have been difficult to predict from the slow continued trend of soybeans and peanuts.

But the big boost to calorie supply that rice productivity improvements brought about was a major cause of change in the rural economy. For this reason and because it is the prime staple in the diet of Indonesians we look at the rice sector separately.

RICE

Population pressure on land in Java had served to make rice cultivation a highly labour-intensive activity, such that many of the practices introduced in the Philippines during its recent green revolution had long been standard in Java. In addition, the colonial authorities had laid down an extensive canal irrigation system, largely dependent upon the monsoons but offering some areas irrigation water in the dry period also. Fertiliser was introduced on export crops long before the war, but in as much as rice and sugar were alternately cropped in parts of Java rice farmers did not fail to notice the effect on rice yields of residual quantities of fertiliser in the soil, and became interested in the direct application of nitrogen on paddy fields. Finally, seed breeding was well advanced in the 1930s with some of the best results still in prominent use in the early 1960s and even holding their ground against the riskier IR varieties imported some years later.

With all these ingredients in cultivation practices Java experienced a green revolution even before the second World War. Its rice yields were reputed to be higher than those of Thailand, Burma, the Philippines, Cambodia and Laos, though lower than those of deltaic Vietnam (significantly another densely populated area). After post-war rehabilitation had been achieved, increases in rice output were going to be difficult especially where land extension was not possible. In 1954 rice output passed its 1940 level but by 1962 it was only 17 per cent above that pre-war level, an increase quite outmatched by population increases. The rising imports of rice in the mid-1960s encouraged a strong determination to promote import substitution of rice as the principal goal of the Five Year Plan, 1969 to 1974.

Thus since the mid-1970s Indonesia is said to have experienced something of a new green revolution using the latest imported technology. The origins of the new system for delivering techno-commercial inputs lay in the failure of the Three Year Plan, 1959 to 1962, which was to have resulted in self-sufficiency. Hundreds of paddy centres were established to provide extension information, but since farmers were expected to make their way to them without prior awakening to the technological possibilities it is not surprising that they were unsuccessful. Furthermore, the centres were responsible for procuring rice from farmers at sub-market prices and farmers' resistance grew. In the event, the hoped-for surplus of 390,000 tons in 1962 turned out to be a record deficit of one million tons.

In 1963 the Bogor Agricultural College sent twelve students to villages to undertake intensive extension work with farmers under strict rules of social conduct. The first results were encouraging and the project was expanded in 1964-5 and called *Demas (Demonstrasi Massal*—Mass Demonstration). The student extensionists operated as farmers' advocates by harassing and threatening officials regarded as responsible for delays in deliveries of agro-inputs. But the change of political ethos in 1965 gave greater opportunities to manipulators and speculators and put at risk the lives of those who challenged them. Also, from 1966 onwards, the extension programme was diluted with bureaucratic extensionists being brought in to cover very much larger numbers of farmers. These became the *Bimas* programmes *(Bimbingan Massal*—Mass Guidance) and there were frequent complaints of coercion and of resistance of them.

In mid-1967 some alterations were made to these programmes. They were divided into *Inmas (Intensifikasi Massal)* and *Bimas (Bimbingan Massal)*, the former embracing farmers who were self-financing and voluntary participants. They were an attempt to extend extension services and input supplies without placing a greater burden on public credit resources. In 1968 both *Inmas* and *Bimas* were further sub-divided into *Bimas Biasa* (ordinary seeds) and *Baru* (new seeds), the latter denoting the use of the new high-yielding seeds from the Philippines. The government's ambition to force the pace led it to promote a mechanistic approach to rice intensification which was totally in character with the general economic and political style. As far as the rice industry was concerned it reached its peak with the introduction in the 1968-9 wet season of multi-national corporations replete with fixed packages of inputs regardless of size of farm enterprise, or of factor and environmental endowments. The most famous of these was the Swiss-based CIBA company which had successfully experimented with its own pesticide on 30,000 hectares in South Sulawesi in 1966. Yields in the best endowed areas did rise substantially during this *Bimas Gotong-Royong* programme but the fixed and forced procurements of paddy on a per hectare basis as repayment for the unsolicited input package was hard on those who, for one reason or another, failed to make good use of them. In September 1969 this procurement was determined as one sixth of a pre-determined local average yield. Those farmers failing to reach that yield suffered. Some of the inputs were not wanted by the farmers, or at least not in the quantity given. Sometimes part of the package was stolen before it reached the farmer although he had to repay the whole. In particular the cash complement, the COL, which was highly favoured by the farmers, was found to be missing.

When complaints reached a crescendo in 1970, threatening civil order, the whole programme with the international corporations was suddenly terminated. In its place was ushered in a more flexible scheme allowing for personal contact and assessment, known as Improved *Bimas* (*Bimas yang Disempurnaken*). It was still ambitious as far as scale was concerned and local officials brought to bear different degrees of coercion. But it was to allow the farmer individual contact with bank and extensionist, although this was inevitably at the cost of fielding more administrative personnel. Mobile banks and fertilizer kiosks were fielded. But there was continued confusion over how much freedom farmers had to choose quantities and types of agro inputs, A village unit, the BUUD (*Budan Usaha Unit Desa*), was designed to act as an umbrella to the separate parts of the scheme. It was hoped that at a later date when local administrative resources were strong enough, the BUUD would turn into a KUD (*Koperasi Unit Desa*), and that these would form the basis of a new village development unit. But it has been the role of the BUUD as procurer of paddy from farmers at fixed prices that has caused almost continual strife. In May 1973 when new procurement prices were introduced to restore rice stocks depleted by the 1972 drought many reports of coercion and force filtered through, and in July the BUUD—based fixed procurement scheme had to be temporarily abandoned. But reports of corruption and coercion by BUUD officials have not terminated. There appears to be wide scope for mismanagement of finances by BUUD officials who inevitably are senior members of the village hierarchy which can exert a mixture of patronage and authoritarian power. The main complaint appears to be that these officials buy the paddy privately from farmers at one price and sell it to the BUUD at the higher, official price (Arndt, 1975). At other times they may ask farmers for the cash equivalent instead of the paddy. When the official price is well below the market price, both coercion and resistance are likely to grow.

We see, then, on the one hand the rice industry being offered a great deal of attention and new technological inputs, and on the other hand being squeezed by the time-honoured means of turning the terms of trade against food producers in favour of urban consumers. A much debated issue of this argument has been the choice of the rice-to-fertiliser price.

The government's horror of subsidies, except to the government sector, led to a suspension of fertiliser subsidies between 1965 and 1967 even though low-priced rice procurements were being extracted from farmers and, relatively, very high price food aid was being subsidised by almost 50 per cent. There was the popular belief amongst some economists that 'farmers' (landlords, owner-operators, tenants, debt-labouring tenants?) had done well out of inflation in the past and could be squeezed a little more. But in January 1968 a Farmer's Formula was devised equating the prices of one kilogram of milled rice (at the mill-door) and one kilogram of urea. The one-to-one ratio was thought to bear some relation to prevailing Asian price ratios, and it was of course administratively convenient. Following so quickly on a drought year some observers thought there should have been a wait-and-see policy to estimate more accurately the appropriate ratio. The fertiliser import cost was Rp. 27·06 per kilogram in 1971. If Rp. 8·76 for distribution costs were added the real cost was Rp. 35.82 compared with the actual price of Rp. 26·60 offered for farmers. This amounts to a 33 per cent subsidy. But farmers were competing against subsidised rice imports. US. PL480 rice was costing the government Rp. 73·80 per kilogram ($190 per ton) and long-term Japanese credit rice Rp. 59·8 ($155 per ton), while the maintained domestic (ex-mill) price was only Rp. 37·5.

Relative rates of subsidisation of rice and fertiliser varied during the rice crisis of 1972/3 and with continued world and domestic inflation, but in 1975/6 the fall in the world price of fertiliser meant that it was questionable whether Indonesian farmers were still enjoying subsidies on fertilisers. At the same time the world rice price of $400 a ton translated into a domestic price of Rp. 180 per kilogram but the domestic price had been fixed at Rp. 80. Consumers were therefore enjoying a subsidy of Rp. 100 per kilogram.

However, questions of whether the rural sector is or is not suffering from imposed terms of trade with urban areas are superficial because the better-off farmers, who have undoubtedly benefited from the new rice technology, can impose their own terms of trade on the indebted small farmers and the landless labourers who must all offer their labour. Even the effort of the BUUD failed to touch those rice farmers heavily in debt or to stem the current to increasing concentration of control over land via debt-labour and debt-produce. The meaning of tenancy was changing as those controlling land took a new interest in its productivity and became the applicants for credit. There had been hopes that the green revolution would raise output without making land and agrarian reforms necessary. What was foreseen by only a few critics at the outset was that the green revolution would cause agrarian regression in the absence of government intervention.

The hectarage being covered by *Bimas* and *Inmas* programmes has been increasing steadily. In 1976/7 it is planned to cover 5·5 million hectares of rice (out of a total harvested area of 8·6 million tons) and 1·6 million hectares of other crops (including vegetables). The immediate rice target is to be met by the intensification of existing hectarage. In output terms these programmes have enjoyed a fair measure of success. In spite of the savage attack of the *wereng* pest in recent years and the partial return to lower yielding, but more resistant, traditional seeds, the 1976 wet crop is expected to exceed the record 1975 crop of 15·3 million tons of paddy which fell short of the target for that year by 300,000 tons. Yet imports of rice are still found necessary. During 1974-5 imports amounted to 1·8 million tons and another 600,000 to 700,000 tons are expected to be imported during 1976-7.

With severe drought occurring every 4 to 5 years self-sufficiency might be better termed self-sufficiency after adequate stocks have been established. Because the rice price rises much more than the wheat price in world drought years (because a smaller proportion of world production is traded) the burden of a drought on foreign exchange reserves can be very heavy. In 1973 Indonesia spent $600 million on rice imports, a sum which would have wiped out total foreign exchange earnings in 1966; and this occurred the year before the green revolution was supposed to bring self-sufficiency.

The effort to raise yields managed to lift *per capita* rice output above the 1962 level, although this was due to the expansion of production on irrigated land. However, none of the other main food staples achieved this performance by 1972, and *per capita* output of sweet potatoes, in particular, has fallen sharply (see Table 4.8). *Per capita* output of only one, maize, managed to rise above the 1961 level in the last two years.

Comparisons of the years 1964 and 1974 have shown that *per capita* consumption of rice plus the rice equivalents of rice substitutes rose from 178 to 201 kilograms, an increase of 23 kilograms (Anon, Bulletin of Indonesian Economic Studies, 1975, vol. 11, no. 3). But *per capita* rice production increased by 41 kilograms and *per capita* rice imports fell by one kilogram. Thus the *per capita* rice equivalent of other staples fell by 17 kilograms.

The impact of rice improvements on mass welfare must be subject

TABLE 4.8

Per Capita Production of Food Crops (kilograms): 1961-74

	1961	*1962*	*1963*	*1964*	*1965*	*1966*	*1967*	*1968*	*1969*	*1970*	*1971*	*1972*	*1973*	*1974*
Paddy	163.2	171.7	149.7	154.0**	159.5	163.8	154.9	169.8	173.3	193.2	206.0	108.4*	117.2*	121.1*
irrigated	143.1	149.1	130.6	132.9	139.9	141.5	136.3	149.4	155.7	175.7	188.2	n.a.	n.a.	n.a.
non-irrigated	20.1	22.6	19.1	21.1	19.6	22.3	18.6	20.4	17.6	17.5	17.8	n.a.	n.a.	n.a.
Maize	23.4	32.5	23.1	36.0	22.1	33.9	21.0	27.5	19.4	23.3	22.1	18.5	29.6	25.4
Cassava	114.8	114.2	114.4	117.3	118.1	102.4	95.6	98.6	92.5	86.5	84.3	85.5	89.8	108.0
Sweet Potatoes	25.0	36.9	30.0	37.8	24.7	22.5	19.1	20.5	19.1	18.0	18.1	17.0	19.2	22.9
Peanuts	2.5	2.6	2.3	2.5	2.3	2.4	2.1	2.5	2.3	2.3	2.3	2.3	2.3	2.5
Soybeans	4.4	4.0	3.4	3.7	3.8	3.8	3.7	3.8	3.3	4.1	4.0	4.3	4.3	4.3

Sources: 1961-71: *Monthly Statistical Bulletin,* Jakarta, November 1972, p. 108.
1972-4: Anon. (1975), 'Survey of Recent Developments', *Bulletin of Indonesian Economic Studies,* vol. 11, no. 3. (The *per capita* data were calculated on the basis of total production data).

* *Per capita* milled rice production. *Per capita* paddy would be about double this amount.

** Corrected from the reference.

to further questioning because of the sharper rural class differentiation that appears to have occurred in the wake of the new production methods. But first, as with so many of the other comparisons of changes between the mid-1960s and a decade later, any conclusions about long-term improvements are undermined by the particularly bad economic conditions of 1964.

National Social and Economic Surveys (SUSENAS), which obtained data on household expenditure in value and volume, were undertaken in 1963/4, 1964/5, 1967 and 1969/70, and the results have been taken as the basis for certain distribution estimates. The Gini coefficients for *per capita* consumption expenditure in rural Java-Madura were 0·362 for 1963/4, 0·371 for 1964/5 and 0·330 for 1969/70. The worst situation in 1964/5 can be largely attributed to the regressive influence of inflation on income distribution. But instead of merely relying on the interpretation of single coefficients, percentile expenditure distributions were also examined. The results are shown in Table 4.9. The effect of inflation is clearly seen. The first and third periods show a more egalitarian distribution of *per capita* expenditure. Since 1969/70 marked a period of substantial price stabilisation but was too soon to reflect structural changes apart from those induced by the widespread rice intensification programmes, the only conclusion which can be drawn is that the stabilisation programme redressed much of inflation's regressive effects on income distribution. It is unfortunate that data for 1960/1 were not available to show a comparison with a relatively prosperous earlier period.

TABLE 4.9

Percentile Distributions of Per Capita Expenditure in Ascending Order of Expenditure Magnitude: Rural Java—Madura

	P_{10}	P_{20}	P_{30}	P_{50}	P_{80}	P_{90}
1963/4	45.8	61.8	75.7	100	167.3	213.1
1964/5	38.8	60.0	72.5	100	165.0	222.5
1969/70	44.7	59.2	75.8	100	153.2	195.3

Notes: These data are ratios. For example, the figure for P_{90} is the ratio of the income of the top 11th percentile (individual's income) to the medium income.

Thus $P_i = \dfrac{100 \times Yi}{Y_{50}}$

1963/4 refers to the period December 1963 to January 1964,
1964/5 to the period October 1964 to February 1965; and
1969/70 to the period October 1969 to April 1970.

Source: The percentile expenditures were measured from a cumulative frequency curve using the original SUSENAS Surveys' data of frequencies and class intervals.

The percentile distribution of *per capita* weekly consumption of rice (see Table 4.10) demonstrates clearly the impact of the rapid acceleration of inflation in 1964/5. The decline of rice consumption of the first and second decile groups was dramatic, although due to interpolation difficulties with only five class intervals for 1963/4, that year's consumption figures might be too high.

TABLE 4.10
Percentile Distributions of Per Capita Weekly Consumption of Rice in Physical Quantities

	P_{10}	P_{20}	P_{30}	P_{40}	P_{50}	P_{60}	P_{70}	P_{80}	P_{90}
1963/4	(0.81)	0.98	1.16	1.36	1.54	1.78	2.12	2.42	(2.82)
1964/5	(0.28)	0.56	0.84	1.08	1.32	1.60	1.86	2.22	(2.62)
1969/70	(0.55)	0.80	1.00	1.22	1.47	1.71	1.96	2.27	(2.54)

Notes:

1. Survey data were given in the form of average consumption of rice for each *per capita* expenditure class. The frequencies used pertained to each expenditure class. Cumulative frequencies were drawn on these class averages. Whatever the disadvantages of this method they should not affect the relative positioning of the three curves and therefore the relative readings from them, except perhaps for the first and last decile readings, which are placed in parentheses.

2. For 1969/70 the frequencies from which percentages were calculated were of numbers of persons in each *per capita* expenditure class. For 1963/4 and 1964/5 the frequencies from which percentages were calculated were of numbers of *households* in each *per capita* expenditure class. If household size remains constant over all expenditure classes there would be no difference. In fact, poorer households tend to be very slightly smaller than better-off households, but it is not believed that this difference affected the results.

3. In the 1963/4 survey the quantity of rice consumed was expressed in litres (volume). One litre is usually about 0.95 kilogram, but a litre can be even heavier than one kilogram if the grains are short.

Other evidence of the effect of mid-1960s inflation on income distribution was found by Deuster (1971) who compared real income changes of different categories of rural residents between 1959 and 1968. He showed that the low-income categories were more deeply affected by inflation. Small farmers were worse off while medium and large farmers were better off in the later year. The farm labouring category underwent a process of stratification with median and (upper) third quartile labourers doing a little better in 1968, but the poorer farm labourers being much worse off than in 1959.

Any reliable conclusions, therefore, that the recent strategy of development (as distinct from mere price stabilisation) has benefited the rural poor and created more livelihoods must involve comparisons with consumption and welfare levels enjoyed prior to the mid-1960s.

The other major consideration of the livelihood impact of technological changes in food production is the social differentiation resulting from that process. The final effects cannot be evaluated since there are consecutive generations of implications as emerging attitudes to commerce and profit sharpen conflicts of interest, and as capital is accumulated on a considerable scale for the first time in the villages.

The technology associated with the high yielding rice varieties and large quantities of fertiliser is, in theory, scale neutral. And yet again and again in the literature on Java's rice sector one reads that the new technology failed to make farms of less than 0·5 hectare viable without family members also undertaking off-farm labour. Sajogyo (1974), for example, writes that

> . . . . in 2 out of 3 villages, that is in Pluneng and Nganjat, for most of farmers on 0·5 hectares of rice-land, even with double-cropping, it is off-farm income that enabled them to pass the 'poverty line'.

Part of the reason why small farmers are unable to use the new technology to pull themselves above the poverty line is that indebtedness places restrictions on the mobility of family labour and obliges farmers to offer their labour below the going wage. A farmer indebted to another can be at the latter's call day and night. He can be up all night preventing landless labourers from harvesting the crop unsolicited and he can be offering his family's labour to a creditor when it is most needed on his own farm. Labour in these circumstances is invariably under-priced. In this situation 'the smallest farmers, mostly under 0·25 hectares, buy agricultural capital not only with the value of their labour at depressed wages, 25-35 per cent lower . . . . but also with their labour mobility.' They repay their debts by working on the farms of those who lend them money and rice. Thus indebtedness prevents the smallest farmers from applying the new technology and thereby increasing their income. Another reason why small and medium farmers are unable to benefit equitably from the new technology is their inability to raise working capital as cheaply as large farms.

Equally important, and probably more important from the point of view of an internal dynamic to rural development, are the chances of raising employment with the yields. Unfortunately employment creation expected from the green revolution's high technology elsewhere was already a fact in Java in colonial times. Vink (1941) made a pre-war estimate of labour use (excluding harvesting) in East Java of between 105 and 240 man-days per hectare, averaging 151 man-days. Harvesting provided another 98 man-days. This provided an average of 249 man-days per hectare, which is not much less than the figures of 286 man-days for local varieties, 297 man-days for national improved varieties, but considerably lower than the 356 man-days for IR varieties in the wet season 1969-70 quoted by Collier and Sajogyo (June 1972) for the particular area of the northern lowland coastal plain and for the river basins of Java. This last figure is far from general as samples of employment results from the Agro-Economic Survey show (Palmer, 1974). Moreover, the new harvesting and processing practices, both part of the technological revolution, are threatening serious inroads in employment in the overall rice sector.

The traditional means of harvesting was for the farmer to allow a large number of men, women and children to start cropping a field without supervision, and the farmer would then hand over a proportion of the harvested crop to them. This was traditionally one-ninth but it could be one-seventh. A new system, *tebasan,* entails the selling of the crop by a farmer to a trader while it is still standing and the use of a recruited gang of harvesters on a cash basis. The result has been that far fewer people have been involved than under the traditional method and although each harvester receives more in return, the total return to harvesters is less. A sample survey of 120 farmers in 1972 showed that the numbers of harvesters could decline from 150 to 184 to only 30 while returns to the average harvester could rise from Rp. 39 to 55 to Rp. 95 (Collier and Sajogyo, 1972). This process of differentiation in the labour market suggests that there are numbers of landless or near-landless people (especially wormen) who have lost an important part of their family income.

A second labour displacement concerns women's traditional hand-pounding. Hundreds of thousands of these seasonal jobs are alleged to have been lost to the new small village rice mills which are being promoted by the government as part of the village unit administration of rice production. The decline in hand-pounding and the concomitant use in widespread mechanical hulling and milling has been swift. Timmer (1973) reports that in 1971 80 per cent of Java's rice crop was still hand-pounded, but that in 1973 somewhere between 10 and 50 per cent was hand-pounded. He concludes that there is little need for hand-pounding or non-mechanised rice milling now in Java. Whereas with a crop the size of the 1971 crop, 399,000 full-time workers would have been required if only hand-pounding were utilized, if large-scale bulk facilities alone were in operation jobs would be available for a mere 33,000 workers.

Unlike traditional export crops, rice should have a steadily growing market. Also unlike these export crops rice has received an enormous amount of government attention and funds. And yet because livelihoods were not of central consideration and agrarian change was baulked at, the very output successes may contribute to a loss of development dynamic in the informal sector. Some of the external economies of expanded rice production may prove negative. Especially for Java this is serious for it is imperative that the largest single prevailing industry should be able to take at least some of the increase in the labour force, since those industries which do not take up much land per person employed are so costly in terms of capital.

INDUSTRIAL REHABILITATION

Producers' liquidity, eroded by years of inflation, was further weakened by the credit restraint practised by the new government. In addition, the early emergency credits for consumer goods introduced competition to domestic producers with the result that domestic industrial activity was lower in the year and a half after October 1965 than in the last year under Sukarno. It was not merely a slow recovery. There had to be new nadirs reached before the upswing commenced. The imperative of reducing inflationary pressures obliged the government to increase the flow of final consumption goods as quickly as possible and this policy placed a premium on both production credit expansion and the delay in passing raw materials through the processing stage. It is difficult to blame the rise in interest rates directly because they were still less than the rate of inflation and market interest rates. But a restriction in the volume of bank credit would, through illegal payments to bank officials, force up effective bank 'interest rates' until they approached free market rates. Perhaps even more importantly, inflation breeds uncertainty and so expected profit rates need to exceed expected inflation rates by a risk margin reflecting that uncertainty. But domestic production could not offer such profit rates when competitive imports were increasing. Profits from speculation and trade were a much safer bet, since they had the advantage of bringing into effect self-fulfilling prophecies about retail prices.

That the aggravated liquidity crisis was real can be subject to no doubt as production data revealed. But the government was determined to see the policy of restraint through this time as it had set its face against all other options. Although the overall increase in money in circulation in 1966 was 663 per cent, the final quarter's increase was only 32 per cent.

Earlier, in April 1966, in anticipation of further foreign credits, the government announced that foreign exchange would be made available by tender for imports of industrial raw materials and spare parts. But so severe was the liquidity crisis that manufacturers could not raise an effective demand for them. As a result cotton and yarn were piling up in the godowns; and the following year there were reports that stocks of these raw materials were depreciating while manufacturers could not muster sufficient liquidity to process them.

Japan had offered the first credits for textile raw materials in November 1965, the bulk being in the form of weaving yarn. The following year there were large imports of readymade cloth at Rupiah 45 to the dollar compared with a market rate of Rupiah 120-130. Although cotton and yarn were imported at this rate or less, the effective rate of tariff protection for the textile industry was negligible in view of the domestic cost of other inputs more fairly represented by the market rate of foreign exchange. The textile industry was less utilised in 1966 than in 1965. Table 4.11 shows the decline of textile raw materials and the increasing competition from cloth imports during a period when creditor countries insisted on tying credits to their own exports. The government's intended control over import priorities was, therefore, largely ineffective. In other industries also the situation was believed to have deteriorated.

TABLE 4.11

Volume of Imports of Textile Materials: 1965-1968 ('000 tons)

	1964	*1965*	*1966*	*1967*	*1968*
Weaving yarns	29.2	42.7	19.7	10.2	19.8
Cotton, dyed and coloured textiles and shirting	7.8	18.5	22.1	34.0	17.3

Sources: 1964: *Statistical Pocketbook of Indonesia, 1964-7*, p.214: 1965-68: *Monthly Statistical Bulletin*, 1970, Central Bureau of Statistics, Jakarta.

At last, in April 1967, the government took measures for a shift in emphasis from checking inflation to stimulating production. Credit terms were eased and domestic import-competing industries were granted additional tariff protection. This was probably the main cause of a reported rise in capacity utilisation of the textile industry from 20 per cent to 50 per cent in the first nine months of the year (Arndt, 1967a).

During the first half of 1968 tariff protection was raised but little relief occurred on the credit front. There were continuing complaints that credit costs were too high. Compared with the rate of inflation these were not justified but there was still great difficulty in obtaining credit and there was probably a *de facto* price mechanism rationing them out. The longer term the credit the more restricted its supply. And manufacturers needed credit on longer terms than did traders. Thus in 1968 it could still be said that profits from trading exceeded manufacturing profits.

> It is nonetheless true that the great fortunes in Indonesia have been largely made in trade, and not in industry or agriculture. The continued instability of the economy has encouraged Indonesian capitalists to concentrate on profit maximisation in the very short term, that is to engage in speculative activities, and the few capitalists who are quixotic enough to invest in industry or agriculture are often laughed at by their fellows. (Panglaykim, Penny and Thalib, 1968).

Recovery came slowly to textile manufacturing and then not as fast as the government expected even after acknowledging the recession. In 1968 planned production was 460 million metres but actual production was only 315 million metres, or just 37·6 per cent of total supply (Bank Indonesian Report, 1968).

It was only in 1968-9 that the textile industry could start to rehabilitate itself (and that was almost two years after the Foreign Investment Law was passed).

Although production statistics showed increasing activity in 1969 there was still commercial anxiety behind the scenes. One Jakarta newspaper (*Nusantara,* 6.11.1969) commented that almost all businessmen, even though they were continuing to operate, were virtually 100 per cent dependent upon bank credits which were still difficult to obtain. At the same time businessmen were being constantly threatened by tax officials. Many, rather than face production risks, decided to lodge their money in fixed deposits and thereby acquire a more guaranteed income.

There is something of a contradiction here. If there was an epidemic of businessmen placing liquid assets in fixed bank deposits then the dependence on bank credit could not have been as widespread and intense as just described. Minister of Commerce, Dr. Sumitro, took up this theme when he accused Indonesian businessmen of always saying they had no capital and of thereby trying to get funds:

> I know a lot about the ins and outs of the finances of businessmen engaged in commerce . . . . I know the way in which they turn over their money abroad, the amount of their capital abroad, and the ways in which they keep their money in Indonesia . . . . Don't you try to deceive me, because the effort at deception will probably be useless. (Sinar Harapan, 8.4.1969)

There is a mass of confused threads in this issue. Firstly, the government failed to appreciate that whenever there is uncertainty in the economic field businessmen will choose a venture which turns over their capital fast. Only a fool will lock up liquid assets in a slow production process, especially when tax officials come peering at the all-too-obvious form of fixed and working assets. The difference between the attractions of trading and producing is therefore not fully represented by differences in anticipated profits. This the government has never appreciated. Secondly, the attention danced on foreigners while national businessmen were getting this kind of treatment must have made many Indonesian businessmen wonder whether they were ever going to be allowed to revive themselves, or whether the military and the western educated economists would settle for an alliance between themselves and foreign capital. Thirdly, there are varying degrees of professionalism amongst Indonesians in placing their money abroad. To accuse the manufacturing sector in general of doing this is foolish, and coming from an economist like Sumitro, an unexpected over-simplification.

What cannot be lightly dismissed by planners is the competition between bank deposits and manufacturing activity for the liquid funds that did exist. The very rapid expansion of deposits and savings funds suggest that it was something more than the fast acceptance of a novel institution by numerous small savers, and that many people placed their liquid assets in deposits with a huge sigh of relief. This idea has occurred in several places in the literature on Indonesia, and one newspaper (*Pedoman,* 24.3.1969) described the rush of fixed deposits as giving banks a flood of liquidity while drying up liquidity in industrial and commercial enterprises. There certainly were periods when the banks were left with a surplus of savings and deposits. If the implication here is that *ex ante* effective demand for savings was less than *ex ante* effective supply, then this is merely further evidence that the government fumbled the rehabilitation of the manufacturing sector.

Four years of new government had failed to inject confidence in this sector of the economy. In August 1969 President Suharto complained that stabilisation was not being utilised sufficiently and that remedial action would be found in terms of technical and administrative adjustments in the use of budgetary allocations for projects. It would seem that the government was never able to find the right words when addressing the national manufacturing sector.

The progress of some of the principal mass-produced industrial products is shown in Table 4.12.

Progress in weaving output was accelerated by new foreign investment which, at the same time, was alleged to have driven many national firms out of business. Fertiliser expansion was to jump in 1974 with the extension of the Pusri factory in South Sumatra. The cement industry had a prosperous progress with so much new construction going on, although much was still imported. Paper likewise received a boost with so much modernisation abounding, not to mention all the paper-pushing in Jakarta. More traditional items in Indonesian households did not share quite so much in the expansion.

TABLE 4.12
Production of Selected Industrial Items: 1967 to 1972/3

	1967	*1968*	*1969*	*1969/70*	*1970/1*	*1971/2*	*1972/3*
Cloth (million metres)	n.a.	316	415	450	598	732	852
Yarn (1000 bales)	n.a.	130	160	177	217	239	287
Fertilizer (1000 tons)	93	96	84	84	103	106	n.a.
Cement (1000 tons)	322	411	534	542	577	516	n.a.
Paper (1000 tons)	7.7	11.2	15.8	17	22	30	38
Coconut oil (1000 tons)	35	208	250	250	257	261	265
Cooking oil (1000 tons)	17	23	28	28	27	27	29

Source: 1967: *Bank Indonesia Report,* 1968, pp. 187, 190.
1968 and 1969: Ministry of Finance, *Nota Keuangan,* January 1971, quoted in Anonymous (1971), 'Survey of Recent Developments', *Bulletin of Indonesian Economic Studies,* vol. 7, no. 1, 1969/70 to 1971/2: P. McCawley (1973), 'Survey of Recent Developments', *Bulletin of Indonesian Economic Studies,* vol. 8, no. 3.
1972/3: *Bank Indonesia report* 1972/3, p. 73.

Compared with the target for the last year of the Five Year Plan, 1973-4, textiles did well. In the event, they exceeded by a comfortable margin the target of 900 million metres. The furore in the industry was due to the fact that this was only achieved by the invading foreign capital whereas the existing textile industry never fully rehabilitated itself. The target for urea fertiliser of 403,000 tons was not reached, but soon would be. The goal of 1.65 million tons of cement (a 175 per cent increase) failed utterly.

It was a mixed performance by industry, but on the whole the manufacturing sector failed to achieve the targets of the Plan. Success was to be found in other sectors far removed from employment and consumption goals. The new consumer durable industries are dealt with in the next chapter for they represent, with their capital intensity and upper middle class market, a new dimension to the economy. They cannot be seen as part of the rehabilitation of the mass economy with which we are concerned in this chapter.

MINING REHABILITATION

This chapter ends in a sector whose more recent history is continued in the following chapter. But the rehabilitation of the tin industry has a place here for, being long-established, it has attracted populations and supporting economic activity and must be regarded as part of the endogenous economy.

The tin industry suffered badly from neglect, inflation and competition in the world market. The expulsion of the Dutch in 1957-8 meant that the usual supply of spare parts was cut off. In 1963 output was only about 60 per cent of its 1954 level. Enormous capital sums were required to rehabilitate it but uncertainty of contract, as well as of Indonesia's place in the future world market, induced reluctance on the part of foreigners to supply this capital.

Over the years 1966 to 1968 a figure of $59 million was recommended for rehabilitation. But gross annual earnings in the early sixties had only been of the order of $40 million. After a slow pickup period, the rehabilitation of the industry was soon seen to press against Indonesia's export quota set by the International Tin Council, and surpluses started accumulating. From production levels of 14,900 tons in 1965 and 12,800 tons in 1966, output rose to 22,000 tons by 1974 with a projection of 25,480 tons by 1979 (*Monthly Economic Letter,* October 1974). About 96 per cent was exported. Therefore any constraint on exports would be fully felt on output.

In 1972 world tin stocks were high and in the following year the United States released large quantities. But in October 1973 the export quota was lifted partly as a result of the inoperation of large-scale smelting in Bolivia. With the current tin price very high Indonesia is looking to a shake-up of the industry.

Table 4.13 summarises changes in major mining industries over a decade which included the change in government in the middle. The slow recovery of tin output is in contrast to the continued decline in coal output. Nickel and bauxite production has expanded under the impact of foreign investment and really belongs to the next chapter.

TABLE 4.13
Mining Production: 1961-74 ('000s tons)

	Tin	*Nickel*	*Bauxite*	*Coal*
1961	18.5	13.7	447.6	560.4
1962	18.1	10.8	460.3	471.1
1963	13.8	45.5	487.3	598.3
1964	16.6	49.2	647.8	445.8
1965	14.9	101.1	688.3	590.5
1966	12.8	117.4	701.2	319.8
1967	13.8	170.6	920.2	208.4
1968	16.9	261.8	879.3	175.6
1969	17.4	256.2	926.6	190.9
1970	19.1	600.9	1,229	176.5
1971	19.8	900.0	1,238	197.9
1972	21.4	935	1,276	179.2
1973	22.5	867	1,229	148.8
1974	25.7	879	1,290	156.0

Sources: Monthly Economic Letter, First National City Bank, Jakarta, June 1974. *Summary of Mining Development in Indonesia during 1974,* quoted in Bank Dagang Negara, Annual Report 1974.

But just within the mining sector we can see that what already existed did not enjoy the progress of minerals newly exploited. This example is a microcosm of the whole economy.

Although the immediate goal of price stabilisation was achieved, those who were designated as having to tighten their belts suffered more intensely than anticipated. Recovery was more laborious than expected and the rehabilitation and expansion written into the Five Year Plan was not achieved in those parts regarded as representing the mass endogenous economy. The outstanding successes were to be found elsewhere, in sectors where 'growth' and 'development' part company.

For all the emphasis on foreign capital accelerating industrialisation, between 1969 and 1972 the share of manufacturing in gross domestic product remained constant at 9·2 per cent. More disturbing, in spite of the great opening up of the timber industry, the share of agriculture, forestry and fishing declined from 49.3 per cent to 40.9 per cent. This indicates the alarming decline in the share of pre-existing labour-intensive agriculture.

CONCLUSION

When reviewing the progress of the endogenous, mass-based sector, comparisons of production performance need to be made with the best years of Sukarno's rule. Moreover, since changes in the capacity of productive enterprise to offer livelihoods directly is, with constant technology, indicated by changes in the volume of production rather than changes in earnings, indexes of production and export volumes over a long period of time provided valuable information.

When these calculations were made it was noted that by the early 1970s the capacity of all the important traditional export crops to generate livelihoods had not matched the best years of the pre-1965 period. With greater population and labour force this is enough cause for serious disquiet. In particular smallholders, producing export crops, who had shown such tenacity during years of inflation, and who had ably filled the vacuum left by the decline of estate production since early independence, failed to continue their advances upon the estate sector, in spite of increases of area under smallholder production. The main reason appeared to be the continued lower yields of smallholders and, except in the cases of coffee and tobacco, their inability to halt the average (and therefore marginal) decline in yields, in contrast to the experience of yields of most estate crops.

The neglect of smallholders' yields extends back beyond the 1960s. It is doubtful whether measures to raise profits in this sector are a priority, for in the long-run smallholders' greater output requires resources such as improved strains of crop seedlings, replanting programmes, extension workers and better transportation and trading facilities—resources that must come from the central government.

Apart from in the rice intensification programmes (which have had questionable effects on provision of decent livelihoods of the poorest rural residents) these badly needed resources were given low priority in planning rehabilitation and expansion.

Together with the enforced and prolonged liquidity crisis in domestic manufacturing, this signifies that the strategy of development since 1965 has not been to start from the poorest sections of the community, from the bottom up, but instead followed the old form of relying on the spread of prosperity from sectors which happened to be the easiest to develop.

Chapter 5

New Investment and Exogenous Growth

We have reviewed the pluses and minuses of the rehabilitation of the established mass-based economy. It could hardly be said that this amounted to what has often been referred to as the Indonesian economic miracle. For that we must examine the capital investment in new sectors and in the, formerly, very small, industrial sector. Given the vulnerability of the traditional primary export sector to neglect, now that, with proper financial management of the oil industry, its foreign earnings are no longer so badly needed for external balance and the hardness of the currency, it is in post-1965 capital investment that hope for future mass livelihoods must be sought.

But few can doubt that the nature of the ownership of capital influences the choice of industry and mode of production. The motivation to invest, the access to new technology, and geographical mobility of management and capital across the archipelago, and the historical association with districts and with allied industries are very different for domestic and foreign capital. Also the size of the company, the 'externalities' that one activity can offer its subsidiaries, its purposes in discounting rates of return and its access to differentiated capital markets, all highlight the different investment choices that can reasonably be expected of domestic and foreign capital, respectively. The differences point to the question, 'What is it about foreign capital that makes it relevant to the development of the host country?' Certainly the inflow of capital tidies up the balance of external payments, but once in the country that capital can commandeer real physical resources which are likely to have a *real* opportunity cost.

In the plans prior to 1965 foreign investment was not seen as the catalyst to domestic enterprise. When a Foreign Investment Bill was passed in November 1958 it came at about the worst possible time for its effective success with Dutch management personnel being expelled.

Domestic pressures to implement anti-neo-imperialism concentrated on the oil industry and by late 1964 rumours of complete nationalisation were being avidly studied by the public on a day-to-day basis. Meanwhile their takeover was proceeding by degrees.

All this changed radically in 1965–6. Foreign investment was desired in order to develop the economy as fast as possible. This emphasis on speed was compatible with the new aid philosophy, which stated that the greater and the faster, the more effective.

The vocal opposition to foreign investment had been wiped out or temporarily silenced. As late as 1969 a workers' delegation went to Europe (*Nusantara,* 30 July 1969) to tell rich countries that Indonesian workers guaranteed the security of foreign capital. Indonesian workers were said to be patriotic and were bound to the national interest.

But the most revealing quotation on acceptance of foreign investment and one carrying a hint of the later disenchantment was from the Chairman of the Indonesian Board of Investments, Moh. Sadeli, in 1971

> After all we are four years older and the situation has changed here and there. When we started out attracting foreign investment in 1967 everything and everyone was welcome. We did not dare to refuse; we did not even dare to ask for bonafidity of credentials. We needed a list of names and dollar figures of intended investments, to give credence to our drive. The first mining company virtually wrote its own ticket. Since we had no conception about a mining contract we accepted the draft written by the company as basis for negotiation and only common sense and the desire to bag the first contract were our guidelines. We still do not regret this.

THE FOREIGN AND DOMESTIC INVESTMENT LAWS

The Foreign Investment Bill was introduced in Parliament in November 1966, one month before the crucial Paris meeting of creditors. It finally became Law No. 1. of 1967. In the spirit of the above quotation there was no delay over the finer points of investment regulations and it was anticipated that there would be amendments. The Law did, however, lay down the guiding principles.

The Law stated that it was intended that the economic potential of Indonesia should be developed by Indonesians but that development was to be accelerated by foreign investment which should be channelled into projects which national capital could not undertake for reasons of lack of expertise and capital.

The Law provided for a variety of combinations of domestic and foreign enterprise: joint ventures, contractual arrangements, management contracts, etc. It also stipulated that foreign enterprises operating predominantly in Indonesia must be registered there and operate under the domestic investment law. Foreign investment was given a 30-year guarantee of non-nationalisation and then compensation for nationalisation. An official document describes the nationalisation issue thus: 'It is not intended to express a policy of expulsion or forced acquisition at the end of 30 years. It is simply the maximum duration of the first set of assurances and inducements given to new foreign investors by the government.' The government could review the terms of a company in the last two years of the contract and could establish criteria by which to assess the value of an extended contract.

According to the Law, tax holidays could be awarded for between two and six years depending on the priority of the investment awarded by the government and contingent upon the enterprise being a joint venture if capital were less than $2·5 million. This prerequisite did not prove useful and the law on tax holidays was quickly made more flexible with no capital sum mentioned. Company tax was to be 20 per cent of net profits on the first Rupiah 5 million, then 45 per cent. Exemptions were given for import duties on machinery, equipment, raw materials, spare parts, etc; on sales taxes on certain initial imports such as machinery; and on stamp duty. Losses could be carried forward for up to six years, and there was an investment allowance of 5 per cent a year up to four years on additional investment made from profits before taxes. Foreign managerial and technical personnel could be used where qualified Indonesians were not yet available. Profits could be remitted but transfers in the form of capital repatriation not.

In April 1967 the first major contract under the Law was signed with (U.S.A.) Freeport Sulphur Inc. to explore and exploit copper reserves in Irian Jaya. The sum to be invested was $75 million. There was to be a tax holiday of three years starting after four and a half years for exploration and construction. After that the government would get 35 per cent of the net profit, or 5 per cent of sales, whichever was the larger.

In quite another field the government assured foreign owners that their estates would be returned to them but that a joint venture basis was preferred. When foreign companies held out for compensation for past seizure, the government argued that any compensation ought to be spent on rehabilitating the estates. In 1970 many of the foreign companies seized were handed back with leases for another 30 years. By 1973 a total of 55 companies had been returned with assets totalling $88 million (Angkatan Bersendjata, 21 June 1973).

There were two main kinds of contract: the working contract and the production-sharing contract. The working contract meant that management would be in foreign hands but that costs were shared.

The production-sharing contract was less attractive to foreign companies because all risks were to be carried by foreign capital with a return of only 40 per cent of gains. These contracts were really capital advance arrangements whereby the credit was frequently worked off by export sales to the donor country. The advantages to Indonesia include a guaranteed market and a great deal of capital equipment left hostage in the country.

As time passed restrictive clauses began appearing in new contracts. They concerned using Indonesian personnel and resources as much as possible, processing raw materials in the country and selling shares to Indonesians.

The slow implementation of industrial investments (only 30 projects out of 112 approved had been built by mid-1970) brought about a threat to cancel 10 per cent of foreign investment agreements in industry if investment was not implemented within a certain time period. But 1970 was a year of flux with both government and foreign investors demanding concessions. There was believed to be a decline in interest on the part of the latter while the bonanza in the extractive industries had encouraged a new militancy in the government.

Foreign investors had many complaints. Firstly, they were annoyed with the practices of the bureaucracy and with the large number of offices that had to be passed through. A major difficulty was the legal/procedural process when, after having run the gauntlet of many offices, an applicant was still uncertain whether the request had been granted. Foreign investors have persistently asked for a single body to be responsible for all these matters with the various ministries subordinated to this agency. Some moves towards this were made in 1974.

Secondly, there were complaints that company tax (60 per cent) was about the highest in the world. In rich countries it was about 35 to 38 per cent, and in Hong Kong it was less than 30 per cent. Tax conditions were revised. By the end of 1973 tax averaged 50 per cent of taxable income at Rupiah 4·8 million, but averaged only 25 per cent when taxable income was Rupiah 2 million. Priority projects now have larger investment allowances. Also, since 1970, tax holidays have been granted only in priority fields, and there have been complaints that these were not very real given the various local levies that were imposed.

Thirdly, there is confusion over whether the whole of the capital investment must take the form of authorised equity capital. The investor's preference is for a small initial share capital with later additions through loans from abroad. The Indonesian reply has been to make judgments case by case. The more recent moves to pass over majority shareholding to Indonesians after a certain number of years is likely to reinforce the foreigner's preference for low equity.

Fourthly, the acquisition of land presents both procedural and legal problems. Foreign companies can enjoy only the use, not the ownership, of land; although use rights can be mortgaged but are looked upon with suspicion. The right of *exploitation* is valid for 25 to 35 years, and the right of *use* may be for a fixed period or for as long as the land is used for a specific purpose. Once the foreigner has found a 'seller' of land, the seller releases his right of ownership after receiving the purchase price from the investor. The land then becomes 'state land'. The foreign investor *then* submits an application to the appropriate Minister or Director-General to use the land, and these Rights are then registered at the local land Registration Office which issues certificates. However, it has occurred that after the purchase price has been paid another individual turns up with a better legal title to the land, such titles not being very clear in Indonesia. The introduction of formal industrial estates supervised by the authorities should resolve this problem as all contenders to title of demarcated land should come forward early on.

Fifthly, foreign investors operating in the regions had to face many surprises of local taxes and levies after they believed all had been settled. There was no basis to them in the Foreign Investment Law and the central government regarded them as illegal. But insofar as the foreign investor depended on local cooperation he had to pay them. The setting up, in 1974, of regional branches of the Investment Coordination Board should have the effect of diminishing this form of unpredictable harrassment since formal region checking boards will pre-empt unofficial bribes by officialising them along the lines of practice in Jakarta.

While concessions designed to make things easier for foreign investors have been introduced since the first edition of the Investment Law, other curbs have been placed on foreigners directing them to certain industries and paving the way for future partnership with the Indonesian middle class. Since these measures have been in response to criticisms of the pattern of development they are discussed at greater length in Chapter 7.

The fear is often expressed by western businessmen that they start at a disadvantage where state enterprises enjoy privileges. With the emphasis in Indonesia on state enterprises paying their way and being regarded as private firms in a competitive economy, and where the prevailing economic wisdom is against protection of high-cost industry, it can be expected that monopolistic practices are frowned upon. But except in the case of obtaining licences, far from state enterprises holding back competition it may well be foreign private industry that is introducing monopoly practices. One graduate thesis from Monash University (Lie, 1974) described a number of cases where foreign investors were able to persuade the government to offer them tariff protection and protection against other internal producers. One example was given by Australian Balm Paints (Dulux), an ICI subsidiary, which did basic research in Indonesia for its parent company and succeeded in obtaining an undertaking from the government that competing imports would be prohibited, once the local plant could supply more than 50 per cent of the market. Another company, P.T. Kiwi Indonesia, gave as its most important reason for investing in Indonesia exploiting a market protected by tariff barriers and other import restrictions.

A great deal of demystification needs to be done on the assumption that foreign enterprise encourages competition. A factor which facilitates monopoly by foreign investment is the size of the market relative to the minimum acceptable size of the factory. If a foreign investor can argue successfully that he needs a very large factory to break even he can cover the whole market for a small item (such as shoe polish) on the 'others' list of consumer goods imports. With a compradore class more than willing to listen appreciatively, such arguments should be easily won.

It has been difficult to find any literature on the Domestic Investment Law which was passed in 1968, the year after the enactment of the Foreign Investment Law. The absence of discussion of this Law in the articles on the Indonesian economy in western journals is in itself curious, especially in view of the many bitter criticisms by national entrepreneurs that they were not granted the same import duty exemptions that foreign investors enjoyed.

Part of this neglect was due to the contents of the Domestic Investment Law largely being a confirmation of past regulations; but part also to the overweening presumption that foreign investment would be the catalyst to general growth and development and that domestic investment would, at most, respond to the incentives created by foreign investment. When domestic investment started rising after a lag of several years, this seemed to confirm such a simple view. But as we shall see, there were precious few incentives created by foreign investment outside of West Java and Kalimantan, if by incentives is meant derived demand and other economic externalities such as infrastructure and communications. The slower response of national investors was due not to the fact that their Law was passed one year after the Foreign Investment Law but that they had not nearly the same access to capital as their foreign counterparts. Differentiated supplies of capital were bound to determine the relative pace of investments.

The Domestic Investment Law of 1968 became relevant to joint ventures as it governed the Indonesian participant. Later regulations concerning the *pribumi* issue were also to affect foreign investment.

TRENDS OF FOREIGN INVESTMENT BY COUNTRY

One of the most serious criticisms of foreign investment that has emerged is the potential danger of having large parts of important sectors dominated by capital from one or two foreign countries. Only an innocent would dismiss this charge lightly, for the pattern of early foreign investment in Indonesia after 1965 reveals vividly how different countries have dominated different sources of raw materials in Indonesia. Japan has come in strongly for timber and oil; North America for oil and minerals. Because foreign investment in extractive industries invariably determines destination of those exports, foreign investment monopoly in a sector is tantamount to monopsony in Indonesian exports; that is, the foreign investor becomes the sole buyer of Indonesian exports in that sector. When, at a later date, Indonesia wishes to process its exports to gain value-added earnings, it has to negotiate with foreign investors both as owners of capacity in Indonesia and as marketing agents of the product. And so the trouble begins. There is little doubt that this has occurred in the timber industry. It is happening in oil refining and it is bound to happen in minerals once Indonesia builds up her hydroelectric power.

Sectoral distribution of foreign investments is shown in Table 5.1. The share of Japanese investment in the textile industry carries a different kind of market problem. It is often said that by investing in South East Asian manufacturing Japan is exporting her (relatively) labour-intensive industries—as well as exporting surplus capital—in anticipation of rising wage demands in Japan. Textile equipment and spare parts would, of course, come from the more capital-intensive Japanese investment goods industry. But Japan also has a surplus of textile production which she exports. Given that the huge textile corporations producing in Japan and Indonesia are one and the same, there could occur competition between their branches in certain circumstances. These circumstances arose in 1973 when the world recession led to cheap textiles—from Singapore and Hong Kong as well as from Japan—being dumped in Indonesia affecting, not the unmechanised factories, but the new mechanised factories in Java. The close competition occurred most amongst closest qualities of textiles.

The question must arise, 'If there is a contraction in world-wide markets of the big corporations will their factories in developing countries, such as Indonesia, suffer first and most, even in local markets?'

TABLE 5.1

Approved Foreign Investment Projects by Sector and Country of Origin, 1967—August 1974 ($ million)
(figures in brackets indicate number of projects)

Country of Origin	Agriculture and Forestry		Mining		Industry: Textile		Industry: Chemicals		Industry: Electrical goods and Electronics		Industry: Others		Hotel construction Real Estate		Services		Total	
NORTH AMERICA																		
U.S.A.	42.5	(12)	602.9	(9)	21.7	(3)	17.8	(18)	18.6	(8)	89.0	(29)	47.3	(18)	13.3	(11)	851.1	(108)
Canada	—		76.5	(1)	—		0.3	(1)	—		2.4	(2)	—		—		79.2	(4)
Panama	3.0	(2)	—		—		—		2.0	(1)	1.0	(1)	7.0	(1)	1.5	(2)	22.5	(7)
Bahamas	—		—		9.0	(1)	—		—		2.0	(1)	—		0.4	(1)	11.4	(3)
Subtotal	45.5	(14)	679.4	(10)	30.7	(4)	18.1	(19)	20.6	(9)	94.4	(33)	54.3	(19)	15.2	(14)	964.2	(122)
EUROPE																		
West Germany	—		—		—		11.5	(9)	8.0	(3)	142.6	(16)	—		—		162.1	(28)
United Kingdom	18.5	(18)	—		4.9	(1)	8.1	(4)	0.3	(1)	3.6	(7)	14.6	(5)	8.5	(4)	58.5	(40)
Netherlands	1.5	(3)	7.0	(1)	75.8	(3)	9.4	(8)	11.8	(3)	18.2	(17)	28.0	(5)	3.6	(5)	155.1	(45)
Others	37.0	(23)	—		33.0	(1)	12.4	(10)	1.4	(2)	44.9	(12)	14.5	(6)	4.0	(2)	147.2	(56)
Subtotal	57.0	(44)	7.0	(1)	113.7	(5)	41.4	(31)	21.3	(9)	209.3	(52)	57.1	(16)	16.1	(11)	522.9	(169)
ASIA																		
Japan	93.5	(33)	76.0	(2)	516.5	(29)	31.0	(12)	9.5	(9)	234.5	(67)	62.1	(16)	16.3	(6)	1,038.9	(174)
Hong Kong	35.1	(14)	—		129.0	(19)	9.9	(9)	2.2	(2)	78.3	(42)	174.7	(21)	14.1	(9)	442.9	(111)
Singapore	13.6	(8)	—		1.5	(1)	6.7	(5)	3.1	(3)	52.1	(19)	48.7	(9)	—		126.1	(45)
Others	379.3	(41)	2.1	(3)	52.3	(10)	17.6	(8)	1.4	(2)	33.2	(18)	9.9	(7)	5.5	(3)	501.3	(92)
Subtotal	521.5	(96)	78.1	(5)	69.3	(59)	65.2	(34)	16.2	(16)	398.1	(146)	295.4	(53)	35.9	(18)	2,109.2	(422)
Australia	—		96.0	(3)	—		3.7	(5)	0.6	(1)	67.8	(23)	3.5	(5)	1.5	(3)	173.1	(40)
AFRICA	—		0.5	(1)	—		—		—		—		—		—		0.5	(1)
TOTAL	624.0	(154)	861.5	(20)	843.2	(68)	128.4	(89)	58.7	(35)	777.6	(254)	408.3	(88)	68.7	(46)	3,771.9	(754)

Source: Investment Coordinating Board, quoted in Monthly Economic Letter, First National City Bank, Jakarta, October 1974.

The momentum of investment by different countries is of interest in the light of what has just been mentioned. This is illustrated in Table 5.2. It can be seen that Japan is sustaining its interest, actually moving into manufacturing. Some of the other Asian investments, especially from Hong Kong, must be seen as part Japanese investment, too. North America, having taken the obvious mineral investments, is slackening. European countries, mainly West Germany and the Netherlands, are also maintaining interest although at a much slower rate than Japan.

Japanese investment is well on the way to exceeding the combined North American and European investment. In fact, if the Japanese component of Hong Kong, Singaporean, South Korean and Philippine investments could be properly identified it is possible that Japanese investment has already exceeded this.

We cannot explain the differences in the data from the two sources in Table 5.2, but they in no way affect the overall view.

INVESTMENT BY SECTOR AND BY PROVINCE

The early foreign investments were in minerals and timber (see Table 5.3). Agriculture and fisheries attracted relatively little funds, and had the money put into rehabilitation of foreign estates been subvented it would be more clearly seen that new capacity in agriculture has been neglected by foreign investment. Today foreign investment is not allowed in agriculture except in rice estates.

Later foreign investments went in the main to manufacturing and tourist facilities, but these were to be concentrated in West Java and Bali. Within these areas new investments could rapidly become extensions to the local endogenous economy, although the size of the income multiplier of investment in tourism is much debated.

Domestic investment approvals (see Table 5.4) in forestry increased sharply in 1973 and 1974 to equal \$398 million (Rupiah 165·4 billion) compared with foreign investment of \$500·5 million. But there was little following of domestic investment into the minerals sector.

Total domestic investment approvals surpassed total foreign investment approvals by December 1973 but then lost ground to foreign investment in 1974, notably in manufacturing. This would have been partly, at least, caused by tightened credit restrictions in the country.

We see an interesting contrast of foreign and domestic investment approvals in the different sectors. Indonesian entrepreneurs responded to a demonstration effect from foreign investment when capital became available and where skills allowed. This meant domestic investment moved into forestry and manufacturing but not

TABLE 5.2

Foreign Investment Approvals by Country of Capital Origin at Different Dates

	November 1970		December 1971		August 1974		1970	1971	1972	1973	September 1974
	No.	$ million	No.	$ million	No.	$ million	$million	$million	$ million	$ million	$ million
North America	*61*	*606.9*	*82*	*650.3*	*122*	*964.2*	*562.5*	*591.1*	*625.4*	*651.7*	*656.9*
U.S.A.	55	517.6	72	549.7	108	851.1*	403.0	422.5	449.7	474.1	479.3
Canada	3	77.3	4	78.7	4	79.2	150.2	150.2	151.4	151.4	151.4
Panama	3	12.0	4	12.5	7	22.5	9.3	9.7	15.6	17.5	17.5
Bahamas	—	—	2	9.4	3	11.4	—	8.7	8.7	8.7	8.7
Europe	*82*	*108.1*	*117*	*145.5*	*169*	*522.9*	*188.3*	*198.1*	*207.9*	*243.7*	*427.5*
West Germany	17	19.3	20	22.0	28	162.1	16.5	19.1	20.0	23.2	134.6
United Kingdom	15	12.7	28	29.9	40	58.5	6.3	7.9	9.1	18.3	33.3
Netherlands	16	31.1	26	37.9	45	155.1	125.2	127.6	135.3	155.7	155.7
Belgium	11	8.3	15	10.6)			8.4	8.4	8.4	8.4	8.4
Switzerland	10	12.9	11	16.2)			8.2	8.2	8.2	9.5	33.5
France	5	13.4	8	15.9)			12.6	15.0	15.0	15.4	48.8
Denmark	4	5.0	4	5.0)	56	147.2	5.1	5.1	5.1	5.1	5.1
Norway	3	4.2	3	5.8)			5.4	5.4	5.4	5.4	5.4
Sweden	1	1.2	1	1.2)			0.6	0.6	0.6	0.6	0.6
Italy	—	—	1	1.0)			—	0.8	0.8	2.1	2.1
Asia	*161*	*567.9*	*226*	*815.5*	*422*	*2,109.2*	*613.5*	*805.8*	*971.3*	*1,302.7*	*1,825.1*
Japan	52	156.2	79	277.4	174	1,038.9**	170.0	277.9	344.7	544.2	900.6
Hong Kong	42	45.7	58	105.5	111	442.9	73.6	124.2	169.2	246.8	366.3
Singapore	25	39.1	31	62.7	45	126.1	29.7	45.6	67.3	72.5	95.0

* 71 per cent in mining
** mainly in manufacturing

(continued on page 109)

TABLE 5.2 (cont.)

Foreign Investment Approvals by Country of Capital Origin at Different Dates

	November 1970		December 1971		August 1974		1970	1971	1972	1973	September 1974
	No.	$ million	No.	$ million	No.	$ million	$million	$million	$ million	$ million	$ million
Asia (cont.):											
Philippines	13	261.5	15	264.0)			261.0	263.9	271.1	279.8	279.8
South Korea	4	53.3	4	53.4)			51.4	51.4	53.8	74.7	91.4
Thailand	6	6.1	9	9.3)	92	501.3	5.1	6.5	6.5	6.8	6.8
Malaysia	18	5.4	29	42.6)			22.7	32.3	39.3	40.1	40.1
India	1	0.6	1	0.6)			—	4.0	4.0	22.4	27.4
Taiwan	—	—	—	—	—	—	—	—	15.4	15.4	17.7
Australia	8	4.6	21	19.9	40	173.1	9.7	91.0	93.2	105.5	124.1
New Zealand	—	—	—	—	—	—	0.1	0.1	1.0	1.0	1.3
Africa	1	1.0	1	1.0	1	1.0	—	—	—	0.4	0.4
TOTAL	312	1,288.5	447	1,632.2	754	3,770.4	1,374.1	1,686.1	1,898.8	2,305.0	3,035.3

Source: Data for the first three dates came from *Monthly Economic Letters,* First National City Bank, Jakarta, up to October 1974, quoting Foreign Investment Board, Jakarta. The other data are calculated on the basis of figures in *Indonesian Financial Statistics,* vol. 7, no. 10, October 1974, pp. 158-9.

TABLE 5.3
Foreign Investment Approvals by Sector at Different Dates ($ million)

	November 1970	December 1971	December 1972	December 1973	August 1974
Forestry	381.4	397.4	446.0	495.5	500.5
Agriculture	48.2	67.9)	104.5	113.0	123.5
Fisheries	13.4	16.2)			
Mining	535.0	541.4	860.5	860.5	861.5
Manufacturing	267.4	383.5	669.8	1045.1	1807.9
(textiles)	(54.0)	(149.4)	(253.0)	(436.9)	(843.2)
(chemicals and pharmaceuticals)	(72.4)	(110.3)*	(77.3)	(101.7)	(128.4)
Tourism, hotels, Real estate	40.8	n.a.	144.4	195.9	408.3
Other	23.4	n.a.	81.5	118.3	70.2
Total	1309.6	1632.5	2306.7	2828.3	3771.9

*Inexplicable. Obtained from list from Foreign Investment Board.

Source: Foreign Investment Board, Jakarta.
Investment Coordinating Board, Jakarta.
Monthly Economic Letter, First National City Bank, Jakarta, September, 1974.

into minerals exploration and development. With huge forest reserves, timber could not be cornered by foreigners before nationals began to gain financial strength. But Indonesians are facing stiff competition from foreigners in tourism and hotels.

For an entrepreneurial class weakened by years of inflation and a tight monetary policy this was a creditable showing and the question must arise, 'Where did domestic investors obtain their capital?' Domestic investors in priority projects had to find 25 per cent of the total sum by their own resources and then could obtain the remainder on long-term credit. For other projects only 50 per cent could be borrowed from the state banks. That there was a great deal of Chinese national capital involved there can be no doubt, but the bureaucracy and military were developing into a new socio-economic class (or one originally spawned in Sukarno's time and mushrooming under the 'New Order'), which was accumulating wealth through its protracted fraternisation with the foreign aid and investment apparatus. When corruption of capital inflows reaches the level it has in Indonesia there is bound to be a saturation point in the purchasing, by a minority, of cars, cameras, televisions and other expensive toys; the 'surplus' then turns to another outlet.

The response of domestic investment appears to have been underestimated. Approvals exceeded expectations written into the Five Year Plan, and the Planning Bureau's prediction of actual

TABLE 5.4
Cumulative Domestic Investment Approvals at Different Dates

	December 1968		December 1969		December 1970		June 1972		December 1973		July 1974	
	No.	Rupiah billion	No.	Rupiah billion	No.	Rupiah billion	No.	Rupiah billion	No.	Rupiah billion	no.	Rupiah billion
Forestry	—	—	9	5.1	32	12.7	99	71.7	176	148.1	197	165.4
Agriculture and Fisheries	3	1.4	30	5.5	45	15.8	136	53.2	205	96.5	215	105.3
Mining	—	—	—	—	2	1.4	5	18.9	6	19.2	8	21.0
Industry	4	0.6	95	26.2	209	59.8	693	287.5	1338	722.5	1480	847.4
(textiles)									(310)	(311.0)	(333)	(346.1)
Infrastructure/ Construction	—	—	3	1.3	3	1.3	7	2.4	9	4.0	9	4.0
Housing	—	—	1	0.03	1	0.03	5	3.0	9	77.1	9	77.1
Tourism/Hotels	—	—	8	3.3	19	7.4	65	38.5	93	83.0	95	84.8
Other	—	—	14	7.6	14	7.6	48	29.9	80	85.7	86	92.1
Total	7	2.0	160	49	325	106.0	1058	505.1	1916	1236.1	2099	1397.1
US$ equivalent (millions)		4.8		112		255		1214		2972		3359

Sources: Investment Coordinating Board, Jakarta; and, *Monthly economic Letter*, First National City Bank, Jakarta, September 1974.

implementation of Rupiah 59 millions in 1972 would have represented only little more than 10 per cent of actual approvals. Inflation would partly account for the difference.

Table 5.5 confirms the shift of foreign investment in forestry (Kalimantan) and minerals (Irian Jaya) to manufacturing (Java). Sulawesi and Sumatra remain in the position of minor attractions to investors. Java's share of foreign investment rose from 34 per cent in December 1971 to 53 per cent in May 1974, and Kalimantan's share fell from 22 per cent to 12 per cent.

Within Java, Jakarta and West Java continue to retain the lion's share although proportionately Central Java has gained a little.

In contrast to foreign investment, domestic investment has concentrated more on Java (67 per cent) but spread funds slightly more evenly throughout the other islands (see Table 5.6). This is an improvement on the earlier concentration on forestry in the outer islands, and some might say it is in accordance with the 'oil spot theory' whereby initial investment has widening secondary effects. However, it remains to be seen whether that oil spot can spread to the more densely populated Central and East Java provinces.
There is practically no domestic investment in Irian Jaya but 10 per

TABLE 5.5

Geographical Distribution of Cumulative Foreign Investment Approvals at Different Dates ($ million)

	December 1971	*June 1972*	*May 1972*
Jakarta	337.2	367.0	784.8
West Java	178.6	209.0	720.1
Central Java	13.5	n.a.	123.2
East Java	32.1	75.0	171.0
JAVA	561.4	664.5*	1,799.1
SUMATRA	125.2	146.0	313.0
SULAWESI	92.3	92.3	187.3
KALIMANTAN	352.9	363.0	414.0
IRIAN JAYA	280.1	204.0**	447.2
OTHER	220.6	303.1	217.8
TOTAL	1,632.5	1,772.0	3,378.4

*Assuming the figure for Central Java is $13.5 million.
**Unexplained decline.
Source: Coordinating Investment Board, Jakarta.

cent was in Kalimantan by June 1974. Sulawesi continues to be relatively neglected by domestic investment too, but Sumatra has done well (assisted by domestic investment in agriculture).

In 1974 the rate of increase of foreign investment approvals was still rising in almost all sectors, but since then there has been a sharp decline in annual totals of approvals. Excluding the Asahan hydro-electric project there was only a 4 per cent addition to total approvals. With the Asahan project the increase was 30 per cent (Jenkins, 1976a). American investors in particular showed lack of interest. The total of these approvals was only $26 million outside the oil sector in 1975. The new approvals for all countries were mostly in industry followed by hotels and tourism.

The reasons for this decline include the changes in the Foreign Investment Law governing shares between foreign and Indonesian partners and the contraction of the international capital market. Because of the former there is apprehension on the part of foreign investors that even the latest regulations will not be the last and that the 30-year guarantees of freedom from nationalisation or expropriation will be revised for those investments already made, and of course for new ones. Indonesian commentators have attempted to put a brave face on the new situation by suggesting that it is due to the

TABLE 5.6

Percentage Distribution of Cumulative Domestic Investment Approvals by Geographical Area

	December 1970	*December 1971*	*December 1972*	*April 1973*	*June 1974*
Jakarta	37	32	30	30	27
West Java	15	11	16	18	25
Central Java	10	6	6	6	6
Yogyakarta	—	1	1	1	
East Java	9	7	9	8	9
JAVA	71	56	61	63	67
SUMATRA	31	22	18	17	15
KALIMANTAN	11	14	12	11	10
OTHER	4	8	9	8	8
	100	100	100	100	100

Sources: P. McCawley, 'Survey of Recent Developments', *Bulletin of Indonesian Economic Studies,* vol. 9, no. 3, November 1973, p.13.
Monthly Economic Letter, First National City Bank, Jakarta, June and April 1974.

fact that Indonesians are now capable of exploiting investment opportunities in certain fields. To some extent this is true, but domestic investment has also declined significantly since 1974, reputedly mainly due to the higher interest rates resulting from the April 1974 anti-inflation measures. The slowing up of investment approvals has been matched by a slowing up of investment implementation. One report (Pelita, 4 March 1976) quoted official encouragement to Indonesian partners to write to their foreign partners asking for proof of sincerity within two weeks or else other partners would be sought. If the period stipulated was allowed to lapse the government would declare that the foreign participant had withdrawn. However, altering the status of the approval from a foreign investment to a domestic investment might not encourage faster implementation since the foreign partner puts up most of the capital.

JOB CREATION BY NEW INVESTMENT APPROVALS

Investment approvals as at August 1974 are used here as basic data for estimating employment creation, although in fact these jobs will mature some time in the future.

Guidance on the capital cost of establishing jobs was difficult to come by and sources contradicted each other. In Western Europe the latest technology may provide a figure as high as $30,000 per job in some industries. P.T. Kiwi Indonesia's cost per job was reported to be $6,000 (i.e., 1974). This is not much different from the figure of

TABLE 5.7

Domestic Investment Approvals Data: 1970

	Total cost of investment ($ million)	Manpower	Cost per job ($)
Agriculture	5.63	3,162	1,781
Estates	35.48	3,657	9,700
Forestry	33.47	26,503	1,263
Fishery	0.54	10	54,000
Livestock	0.29	40	7,250
Mining	3.69	676	5,459
Industry	158.09	29,064	5,439
Transportation	19.79	5,384	3,67[illegible]
Real Estate	0.1	—	
Tourism	19.49	4,873	4,000
Infrastructure	3,56	156	22,821

Source: Domestic Investment Board, Jakarta.

$5,439 given by the Domestic Investment Board in Jakarta for all manufacturing. Little advantage is to be gained by further research as product processed and technology chosen must lead to deviations from an average. Table 5.7 gives capital costs of jobs by sector derived from investment and manpower data of domestic investment obtained from the Domestic Investment Board. It is unlikely that foreign investors would implement a technology less capital-intensive, and with post-1970 world inflation these estimates can be regarded as very low. What we have been concerned with here is to keep the cost as low as possible in order to indicate the maximum possible job creation directly generated by investment.

It is also necessary to bear in mind that the investment data used are those concerning approvals and not actual implementation. Taking into account the long procrastination of investors, the slow gestation period of investment and those companies that had second thoughts about committing their capital to Indonesia even after approval by the authorities, it may be that a more realistic figure of

TABLE 5.8

Number of Jobs Created by Foreign and Domestic Investment by Sector

		By ALL Investment	By Foreign Investment (August 1974)	By Domestic Investment (July 1974)
Forestry		711,085	396,279	314,806
Agriculture/ Fisheries/Livestock*		211,471	69,343	142,128
Manufacturing**		640,817	301,317	339,500
Tourism		153,038	102,075	50,963
'Other'***		53,032	14,040	38,992
Subtotal		1,769,443	883,054	886,389
Plus mining	(a)	167,060	157,813	9,247
	(b)	45,599	43,075	2,524
Total	(a)	1,936,503	1,040,867	895,636
	(b)	1,815,042	926,129	888,913

* This is a very generous amalgamation of different capital costs of jobs:. Agriculture $1,781; fisheries $54,000; livestock $7,250. We have taken the first one for use here—$1,781.

** The Domestic Investment Board's figure of $5,439 per job has been discarded in favour of P.T. Kiwi's admitted $6,000.

*** 'Other'. This proved difficult as most of this category would be from Trade and Construction. We used $5,000 cost per job for lack of information. But the amount invested was only about 2 per cent of the total.

(a) Assuming the Domestic Investment Board's $5,439 cost per job.

(b) Including exploration costs, a much higher figure is used—$20,000 cost per job.

total direct job creation would be half of the figure estimated in the following pages.

Table 5.8 shows sectoral employment creation of foreign and domestic investments, respectively, based on the data in Table 5.7. Their totals (excluding mining) are surprisingly equal with domestic investment offering more jobs in manufacturing and in 'other', and foreign investment more in forestry and tourism. Mining employment would alter the picture and give foreign investment employment creation a strong overall lead, but the actual amount in this sector must remain speculative. Moreover, given the recent

TABLE 5.9

Imputed Geographical Distribution of Employment Created by Foreign Investment in Forestry, Industry, Tourism and Housing by Approvals to August 1974

	Forestry	(Textiles)	All Industry	Tourism, Housing, Construction, etc.	Total Direct Job Creation
Jakarta	627	41,758	89,529	32,239	164,153
West Java	—	81,000	173,664	62,528	317,192
Central Java	—	3,398	7,285	2,623	13,306
East Java	300	28,807	61,762	22,238	113,107
Java	927	154,963	332,240	119,628	607,758
South Sumatra	4,595	—	—	—	4,595
North Sumatra	11,611	—	—	—	11,611
West Sumatra	6,056	—	—	—	6,056
SUMATRA	22,262	—	—	—	22,262
East Kalimantan	259,214	—	—	—	259,214
West Kalimantan	8,771	—	—	—	8,771
Central Kalimantan	16,706	—	—	—	16,706
South Kalimantan	47,613	—	—	—	47,613
KALIMANTAN	332,304	—	—	—	332,304
South & Central Sulawesi	19,337	—	—	—	19,337
North Sulawesi	12,533	—	—	—	12,533
SULAWESI	31,870	—	—	—	31,870
JAMBU & RIAU	20,047	—	—	—	20,047
TOTAL	407,410	154,963	332,240	119,628	1,014,241

Source: Calculated on the basis of data in previous tables.

Notes on Table 5.9:

1. Unfortunately the only sector for which distributional data by province of foreign investment was available was forestry. Therefore, estimates for this kind of employment were made separately.

2. Employment resulting from mining investment was totally ignored. Its distribution by province was quite different from all other sectors, the overwhelming part of it in Sulawesi and Irian Jaya. Some approximations could have been made concerning the provincial distribution of mining investment but the cost per job in it is the most dubious of all figures.
Therefore, it was thought better to set aside mining investment totally, bringing it in at the last in the form of a reminder of its existence.

3. The distribution of foreign investment in 'All Industry' and 'Tourism, Housing and Construction' is assumed to follow the distribution of foreign investment in the textile industry up to September 1973, for which individual company data were available. The limitations are obvious, but they are listed here nonetheless:
(i) foreign investments in the textile industry after September 1973 might have been distributed differently;
(ii) foreign investments in other manufacturing industries might have been distributed differently from those in textiles;
(iii) foreign investments in Tourism, Housing and Construction might have been distributed differently from those in textiles.
The mitigating circumstances here are the following: firstly, these latter foreign investments were heavily concentrated in Java and were not, in total, distributed in a wildly different manner from those in the textile industry; and secondly, it is not the purpose here to reach statistical accuracy before revealing the outline of one of the most important issues of Indonesian development strategy. A rough estimate of the order of magnitude of the impact of foreign investment on the labour market is desired here.

4. Foreign investment in agriculture is totally ignored here because of lack of information on distribution and because it is believed that much of it was used to rehabilitate estates—that is, to restore employment. It was, anyway, not a significant sum—$124 million out of $3,772 million.

strides made by domestic investment it can be only a matter of one or two years before domestic investment (since 1966) offers more jobs than foreign investment—always assuming full implementation of investment approvals.

Given the very uneven population distribution in the country, the geographical distribution of direct job creation is just as important as the overall figure. In Table 5.9 only foreign investment is used for these figures because of the unavailability of individual company data for domestic investment in forestry and textiles, which were the basic data used. However, enough data are available in all these tables for simple and rough extrapolations if they are desired.

Over a seven-year period about one million jobs were potentially created by foreign investment approvals. Sixty per cent were located in Java (with 63 per cent of the country's population). But another 33 per cent of the job potential was in Kalimantan (with only 4·6 per cent of the population).

Within Java, Jakarta and West Java emerge as highly privileged areas, and what is left for Central and East Java to pick up places these, the most-densely populated of all provinces, as badly off as any other province in the country. Domestic investment would have improved on this distributional situation only slightly.

Comparing Tables 5,5, 5.6 and 5.7 it could be said that foreign and domestic investment together has brought an approximate potential of about 1·2 million jobs to Java over a seven-year period, during which the labour force has increased by about 8 million. But outside of West Java and Kalimantan it cannot be said that labour has gained anything significant from new investment. In these other areas the greatest service the government has done is to rehabilitate the labour market to its early sixties level of activity which, however, does not take into account the expansion in their populations seeking work.

However, this is only the direct impact and does not indicate the relative final effects after income multipliers have worked themselves out. With manufacturing and hotels and tourism concentrated in Java the final job creation is likely to be proportionately greater on this island, but again this effect will be concentrated in Jakarta. Little wonder that some visitors to Indonesia believe in the country's economic miracle! However, with extremely low mass wages and with high import leakages of middle class and rentier incomes, the effective distribution of this multiplier effect cannot be seen in western terms.

Central and East Java, already with the highest population densities in the country, have gained nothing that would make a visible impact on the labour market. With the sugar industry failing and with rice cultivation becoming less labour-intensive, these provinces must be carrying the full increment of their workforces in the ranks of the unemployed or seriously underemployed. Sumatra and Sulawesi came off badly. Sumatra has an expanded oil industry and will have the Asahan Power Project in future. But it is not thought that the, mostly off-shore, oil investments would have increased indigenous employment much. With a rubber industry which has only been restored to former levels unemployment must be rising more sharply in Sumatra than elsewhere. Sulawesi has bauxite and nickel investments, but it is not known how much employment these have created.

Total direct job creation of just over two millions (from both foreign and domestic investment approvals) must be seen against an increase in the total workforce of about 12·5 million over a seven-year period. But if rates of actual implementation and the higher true costs of job creation were available, the figure for total direct job creation by August 1974 might be only around one million. This, however, is not the end of the story. Already, reference has been made to the bankruptcies of national manufacturing enterprises as a result of the invasion of foreign investment. It is not possible, therefore, to view the impact of new investment on employment in accretive terms. Subventions for labour redundancies would have to be made in pursuit of the true situation. The only known data on this subject refer to the textile industry in which a maximum potential of just over 300,000 jobs could have been created by foreign and domestic investments. (The figure in Table 5.9 is doubled to take cognisance of domestic investment.) The net effect of the transformation of the textile industry which formerly employed almost one-third of all workers in manufacturing has been described thus (International Labour Office, 1973):

> During the period 1966 to 1971, when production rose from 250 to 600 million metres, the industry as a whole lost more than half its workforce. The handloom and batik sectors lost all but 100,000 of the 510,000 workers who had been previously employed there . . . according to our estimation more than 70 per cent of the total workers employed in both sectors were unemployed.

Another ILO report (Sethuraman, 1976) provides data showing that between 1961 and 1971 employment even in Jakarta fell from 147,000 to 110,000.

There is evidence (Sundrum, 1975) that over the decade of the 1960s manufacturing employment increased substantially. The 1961 and 1971 censuses show an increase from 1,856,000 to 2,932,000 manufacturing jobs, or of 63 per cent. Surprisingly, this was totally due to an increase in rural areas: urban manufacturing employment actually fell by 3·2 per cent alongside an increase of 94 per cent in rural manufacturing employment. Since most of the new actual investment after 1967 was in urban areas this structural change, and the change in overall manufacturing employment, cannot be put down to economic changes under the new government. Moreover, since small-scale manufacturing in 1971/2 provided 64 per cent of total manufacturing employment it is reasonable to suppose that a large part of the explanation must lie with an expansion of small-scale rural manufacturing. (This percentage was obtained from the data derived from a 1971 survey of large and medium enterprises and a 1972 survey of small enterprises.)

Unfortunately there are no inter-censal data. A plausible explanation lies in the way the rural economy adjusted to inflation and the balance of payments crisis of the mid-1960s, when imports of raw materials, equipment and spare parts dried up. Workshops of all kinds flourished. Servicing and repairing increasingly became backyard enterprises. Far from assuming that there were steady accretions to rural manufacturing employment since 1961 it might be more realistic to assume that rural manufacturing employment peaked somewhere between 1964 and 1968 and has declined (at least as a percentage of total manufacturing employment) since. There is nothing in new investment patterns to suggest that rural manufacturing employment should continue its past performance, and since most of the post-1965 manufacturing investment came to fruition after 1971 rural manufacturing employment might well have declined in recent years.

TIMBER

Foreign investment in timber has been one of the phenomena of economic changes in Indonesia since 1965. After oil, it has come to be known as the major prop of the balance of payments surpassing even the rubber industry. Its progress has been prompted by the decline, or exhaustion, of the Philippine timber industry, and the exceedingly great Japanese demand for timber imports (part of which is re-exported to the United States after processing.) The depression in the industry in 1974/5 exposed this dependency upon Japan. The critical comment on recent Indonesian development, 'one country, two goods', refers to Japan, and oil and timber.

The development of the timber industry has probably come in for more criticism than any other industry, with charges ranging from denuding of soil and absence of re-afforestation, through coercion of small farmers to surrender their land to logging interests, to speculative brokerage of timber concessions. But above all, as in the oil industry, policy in this industry has been marked by the assumption that the national economy can 'take off' after a few decades of plundering this national heritage for re-investible funds.

There can have been few instances in developing countries of an output target being exceeded so much as Indonesian timber. What might have appeared ambitious at the start of the First Five Year Plan was clearly a gross underestimation. The target for 1969-70, 1·2 million cubic metres ($22·4 million) was turned into an actual output of 4·6 million cubic metres ($44·7 million). But the 1973–4 target of 5·1 million cubic metres ($110 million) turned into an actual output of 21·5 million cubic metres ($768 million) (Monthly Economic Letter, May 1974).

The total area of timberland amounts to around 120 million hectares. The great forests are in Sumatra, Kalimantan, Irian Jaya and Nusa Tenggara. The first giant foreign concession was granted in 1963 to a 30-company Japanese consortium which, together with the state company P.N. Perhutani, comprised the Kalimantan Forest Development Corporation. Initial capital was $2·2 million. The concession covered 2·4 million hectares in north-east Kalimantan.

Later Japanese timber ventures in Kalimantan included (i) Mitsui Company with P.T. (private) Pancha Karya, South Kalimantan (and Buru Island), an investment of $2·65 million for a final annual output of 96,000 cubic metres—agreed in 1965; (ii) Nanpo Ringyo Kaisha Ltd. and Mitsui with P.N. Perhutani, 19,000 hectares in South Kalimantan, an investment of $4·2 million for a final annual output of 122,000 cubic metres—agreed in 1965; (iii) Mitsubishi Shoji Kaisha with P.T. Kaju, 100,000 hectares in East Kalimantan near Balikpapan, an investment of $3·9 million to produce annual exports to Japan of 240,000 cubic metres—agreed in 1969. This last one became the subject of complaints by rice growers that they were forced to stop rice production and work for the timber contractors (Indonesia Raya, 7 July 1969).

A huge Korean investment (Korea Sudeco jointly with P.T. Indeco) of $10·9 million covered a 1965 concession of 300,000 hectares in South Kalimantan. Another Korean company, Keang Nam Enterprise, acquired 150,000 hectares in North Sumatra. In East Kalimantan the Kyongnam Enterprise surveyed 200,000 hectares and planned to exploit it with $2·5 million provided by the South Korean Government (Harian Kami, 2 Sept. 1970 and 2 Nov. 1970).

Ostensibly Philippine money poured into Indonesian logging. The Philippines had been the major producer of timber in the area but the exhaustion of her lucrative timber areas caused financiers to move on to Indonesia. The Philippine Consortium for Forest Development Inc. joined with P.T. Swarga to exploit 80,000 hectares in East Kalimantan at a cost of $2·5 million over the first five years; and joined with P.N. Perhutani over 250,000 hectares in East Kalimantan at a cost of $5 million over the first five years (El Bahar, 13 Dec. 1968). Together with P.T. Samodra Guna Dharma, which was said to be backed by an Indonesian naval unit, the same corporation acquired a further 100,000 hectares concession in East Kalimantan to cost $2·5 million over the first five years. A joint Philippine-Indonesian company named P.T. Padam National Trading Company gained 200,000 hectares of concessions in North Sumatra and Riau (Abadi, 8 April 1969). The Philippine International Production Association with P.T. Putri Hidjau Medan gained a 200,000 hectare concession in North Sumatra. And another unnamed Philippine company together with P.T. Surya Sakti gained a 30,000 hectare concession in North Sumatra. In 1972 the military was again involved with a Philippine Company (the Army Strategic Reserves—Dharma Rimba Kentjana—and Far East Managers and Investors Inc.) to start felling 100,000 hectares in East Kalimantan in October 1972 (Abadi, 17 April 1969).

Against these Asian interests other countries are poorly represented in Indonesian logging. Inkopad, covering 50,000 hectares in North Sumatra, is a joint venture with an American company. A French-Indonesian joint venture is operating on 250,000 hectares in Central Sumatra and intends to produce 300,000 cubic metres in 1970 with a capital investment of \$7·5 million (Warta Harian, 19 January 1970).

The attractions of this kind of investment included the short gestation period and quick returns. Within months of the promulgation of the Foreign Investment Law in 1967 twenty foreign companies had shown interest. Already by November 1969 \$165 million had been invested over an area of 5·8 million hectares (or 5 per cent of the resources) by foreigners in timber.

The bitterness of Indonesians towards foreign timber interests was to flare up quickly. By the end of 1968 the government had frozen applications by Philippine investors on the suspicion that Philippine investors were merely brokers for parts of their timber concessions on the world market (Harian Kami, 19 Dec. 1968). The buying and selling of forestry concessions appears to have continued, for the then Director-General of Forestry, Sudjarwo, was still complaining publicly in mid-1970 (Angkatan Bersendjata, 9 May 1970). The standard defence of all investors was inability to raise the capital. The chief lack of capital was found in domestic enterprises or partners in joint ventures. National companies, such as P.N. Perhutani, obtained concessions which were too large for them to capitalise so that they had to finance themselves through various forms of joint venture.

A major complaint against timber companies was the damage they did to the environment. In November 1969 a Forestry Seminar at Gadjah Mada University called for more vigilance because unregulated felling had caused the spread of elephant grass (El Bahar, 4 Nov. 1969).

At one state, in 1970, the granting of new concessions in Kalimantan and Riau had been stopped because of infringements of the regulations, such as existed. A major difficulty was that no overall forest boundaries had been established. A little later new concessions everywhere were temporarily halted except in North and Central Sulawesi, Southeast Sulawesi, West Irian, and East and West Nusa Tenggara (Harian Kami, 4 Nov. 1970).

But the anticipation of big profits could not slow the pace of extraction. A Danish-French timber company in Riau was reported to have cleaned out 20,000 hectares of a 70,000 hectare concession within two years while the entire concession was supposed to last twenty years (El Bahar, 6 Nov. 1970).

Moreover, the huge profits to be made out of forestry were bound to excite the avarice and authoritarianism of the powerful local hierarchies. Investment returns of 40 per cent have been recorded as normal (Goldstone, 1974). The local hierarchies' own short-term private capital accumulation was in direct conflict with the long-term ecological basis of mass livelihoods. There can be no doubt that a number of bureaucrats and officers were party to the ravages by foreign investment.

In 1969 it was reported that the provincial government in East Kalimantan, in Pasir Shire and Balikpapan, had ordered farmers not to plant rice, which was their usual activity (Mingguan Chas, October 1969). This was cutting at the very root of the local economy. Instead, the land around was to be exploited by timber enterprises. The reasons given for this move were the development of the local economy and the increase in employment. Since some timber enterprises were having difficulty recruiting adequate labour it is thought that the chief reason was to force farmers to offer their labour to these enterprises. In addition, since timber, unlike rice, was exported it brought into the provincial treasury a percentage of the total foreign exchange earned which could then, hopefully, use it for development. The system of returning export profits to the provinces had given the local government something of an alibi in ordering this stunning command.

In 1959 timber had accounted for only one per cent of exports, but the big jumps in recent years brought timber to represent about 10 per cent of total exports, and 32 per cent of non-oil exports in 1974. A temporary setback in the growth rate in 1971 was caused by a fall in Japanese demand and therefore price due to the US recession. For a while logs were choking the rivers in Kalimantan. But the longer term expansion of the industry's exports appears guaranteed by the depletion of Philippine forests and by the long-term income elasticity of world demand. Philippine timber exports are expected to fall by 5 to 10 per cent a year according to one source (Bank Indonesian Report, 1971–2).

A major complaint which came increasingly to catch official attention was that the country's resources were being taken away at their lowest, unprocessed, value whereas both local employment and foreign earnings would gain by adding value to the industry's product by undertaking progressive stages of processing. The objection that returns to investment in extraction had to be assured before investment in processing could take place was less valid in the case of timber than of oil. The nature of exploration was totally different in the two cases; the capital sunk in extraction per unit of output was much less in the case of timber and its gestation period considerably briefer. Indonesian concern with including value added in timber exports was a natural corollary to such a rapid growth in the export of a raw material.

Japan is the biggest importer of wood in the world and is overwhelmingly the chief importer of Indonesian wood. Timber accounts for over 7 per cent of Japanese imports against about 17 per cent for oil. So far the processing of Asian timber has been done mainly in the Asian industrialised countries. Obstacles to processing at source include roads (logs are floated downstream), shortage of capital and skilled manpower. Shipping monopolies (96 per cent Japanese) have also given foreign buyers a bargaining edge in demanding the raw material. It is, therefore, a measure of Indonesia's new bargaining power with raw material-hungry Japan that it has been able to win foreign investment to the wood processing industry. Today, timber concessionaires must set up processing plants within three years of commencing felling, and 60 per cent of logs must be processed within 10 years. Importing countries might retaliate with tariffs but, were Indonesia and Malaysia to stand firm together on a joint policy of exporting wood products only, Japan itself would be the loser in such action. Moreover, in August 1972 Japan found it desirable to lower tariffs on processed timber in an attempt to restrain the expansion of its own timber processing industry. In eleven years, 1963 to 1974, Indonesia's timber exports had expanded 14 times and the derived effect on the corresponding Japanese industry had proved disconcerting Applications for timber exploitation rights were far more numerous than approvals. Nevertheless, by November 1971, 84 foreign and domestic enterprises had been approved for a total investment sum of $471 million covering 11 million hectares (or 10 per cent of reserves). Table 5.10 shows the geographical distribution of foreign forestry investment as well as overseas sources of funds. Most of the investments were with Indonesian partners. (Records for approvals granted between July and December 1972 and between July and September 1973 were not available for inclusion. In addition, a giant investment of $100 million in East Kalimantan was proposed in 1971 as a joint venture between Indonesian Forest Resources Development Company (mainly Japanese) and P.T. Perhutani. It was to cover 700,000 hectares according to one report (Abadi, 9 Sept. 1971). It has not been possible to trace this project amongst available records of approvals, and it may only mature in the 1980s. It has been described as an integrated wood industry including a sawmill, a plywood factory and a pulp paper factory.)

Foreign investment approvals in 1974 were little more than one-third of the value in 1973, but this might have been partly due to increasing domestic investors' interest in the sector. However the concurrent slump in the Japanese construction industry led to a fall in

TABLE 5.10

Foreign Investment Approvals in Forestry to December 1973 ($ million)

	Total	East Kali-man-tan	West Kali-man-tan	Cen-tral Kali-man-tan	South Kali-man-	North Sum-atra	West Sum-atra	South Sum-atra Teng-gara	Mal-uku and West Nusa	Dj-ambi	Riau	South Sula-wesi	North Sula-wesi	East Java	Jak-arta
Japan	36.26	9.0				2.0					1.0	23.15		0.36	0.75
South Korea	57.5	3.0		3.5	48.5	2.5									
Philippines	285.05	16.3 235.0*			5.0		4.25		19.0		4.0		1.5		
Malaysia	40.5	12.5	5.5	13.0	3.5	6.0									
Singapore	9.5	0.5	1.0					2.5	2.0	2.5	1.0				
Hong Kong	18.0	4.0		3.5			2.0	3.0		5.5					
Panama	3.0					3.0									
U.S.A.	40.0	30.0					1.0				9.0				
France	2.5						—2.5—								
Netherlands	1.0										1.0				
Italy	4.0		4.0												
W. Germany	0.4					0.4									
		310.3	10.5	20.0	57.0	13.9	7.25	5.5	21.0	8.0	16.0	23.15	1.5	0.36	0.75
			397.8**				26.25			45.0					

*A. Soriano Y Cia (wholly owned logging/sawmilling integrated wood industry) approved 21 November 1969.

**The overwhelming share of investment in forestry has been in the least populated provinces of Indonesia.

Source: Foreign Investment Board. These data omit approvals given in the periods July to December 1972 and July to September 1973.

demand for Indonesian timber. The price fell from $65 to $28 per cubic metre and 30 of the 150 timber companies in East Kalimantan went bankrupt in 1975 (McDonald, 1976e). Timber exports fell 30 per cent in value in 1975. Although there has been a recovery in demand (by mid-1976 the price was back to $50 per cubic metre) foreign investors are anticipating a government request for larger shares in the companies' profits. As timber is second only to oil in export earnings the recent experience of the foreign oil companies must be seen as something of an example. It is unlikely that there will be a second round of foreign investors' interest to compare with the bonanza of 1968 to 1973.

Table 5.8 gave job creation by foreign and domestic investment in timber of 396,000 and 314,800 respectively. If about 85 per cent of all investment is in Kalimantan (as is foreign investment alone) then all but about 107,000 out of the total of 711,100 jobs will be in Kalimantan. Java's employment possibilities in forestry are next to zero. But perhaps it is as well that forestry exploitation is being undertaken in least populated areas, for unless some of the profits are re-invested in the soil the damage to the environment could produce later a calamitous employment situation.

A more immediate ecological threat to localised economies posed by timber exploitation was explained by Governor Subardjo of South Kalimantan in September 1973 (Berita Buana, 8 Sept. 1973):

> With the long dry season, which has caused rivers to become shallow, the timber concerns have dammed up the river water until it reached a height of 15 metres, and then just let all go together with the logs loose, not on rafts. The consequence of damming up the river is that the people who live in the environs have been short of water and when the dam was opened to carry down the logs, many of the people's houses were smashed by the logs running into them. Besides this, rice fields and latrines were also destroyed.

It must be said that this shocking case was of a domestic investment in forestry. The same report stated that if local residents attempted to continue their traditional rights of tree felling to make homes they would be accused of being thieves!

ESTATE REHABILITATION

Following the successful establishment of the IGGI and the promulgation of the Foreign Investment Law, overseas companies began by returning to their estates under one of two contract styles. They were (a) a joint venture with the Indonesian government, or (b) complete repossession but payment in full for rehabilitation. The company could otherwise opt for compensation. American companies were the first to return, followed by one Swiss and six

Belgian. Four British companies (three in rubber and one in tea) came next, but the great P & T Lands Company ran into great difficulties and finally settled in late 1971. Nearly all the estate rehabilitation contracts were settled by early 1971 with promises of capital injections totalling $54·3 million.

NON-OIL MINING

Ore mining investments were amongst the first to be attracted to Indonesia after the passing of the Foreign Investment Law. The acquisition of a concession was akin to cornering a future supply of a raw material whose world demand was bound to increase significantly in future. In attracting foreign capital to this sector the government informed known companies about possible fields and then called for tenders. The government was looking in the tenders for commitments other than to mere extractive installations. Some of the largest and best-known investments are described here.

The first company to show interest was Freeport Sulphur which obtained a contract to explore for copper in Irian Jaya. Freeport Indonesia submitted its findings in 1970. Proved deposits were 33 million tons of ore with 2·5 per cent copper content. Total investment required would be $120 million ($90 million for construction and the remainder for working capital). Production would be 60–65,000 tons of copper a year. By 1974 investment in copper in Irian Jaya had risen to $175 million, providing employment for 700 persons (at $250,000 per job) (Monthly Economic Letter, October 1974). In 1976 Freeport was offering dividends of 5 per cent (or a total of $400,000) and the government bought 8·5 per cent of the company's shares (Angkatan Bersendjata, 2 July 1976).

Another early entry was the Canadian-based International Nickel Corporation seeking its material in South and Central Sulawesi. The INC agreed to build a deep-water port and an electricity generating plant which sufficiently impressed the government. In 1969 it commenced survey work (over 6·6 million hectares) which was due to be completed in 1974. Already by 1972 very large deposits were found. Mining and smelting facilities worth $200 million were planned to be ready by 1975 (Go, 1971) and in 1974 it was confirmed that the Corporation had been awarded a $135 million contract to build a nickel matte plant (Grenville, 1974). This would finally produce more than one million tons of nickel ore a year and employ 14,000 persons. There were also some long-term plans for another $400 million of investment leading to 50,000 tons of nickel concentrate a year by 1990.

Five Japanese nickel smelting companies joined with P.T. Nikkel to form Sulawesi Nickel Development Corporation, in open-cut mining under a seven-year production-sharing contract. The entire future ouptut of 120,000 tons a year would be exported to Japan during the seven-year period, 40 per cent of which would pay off the capital advanced with 5 per cent interest.

But nickel output had been expanding rapidly prior to 1965 as a result of a Japanese production-sharing project. In 1961 13,700 tons had been produced and in 1965 78,800 tons; virtually all exported to Japan. In 1973 nickel ore production had reached 867,300 tons (Monthly Economic Letter, October 1974); or about 12 times the 1965 production level.

Bauxite production has increased very rapidly as a result of a great deal of foreign interest. The Aluminium Company of America and the government signed a contract in 1969 to form a subsidiary, Alcoa Minerals of Indonesia (Alcomin), to undertake general exploration

TABLE 5.11

Foreign Investment Approvals in Non-Oil Mining to December 1973 ($ million)

	Tin	Nickel	Bauxite	Copper	General	Diamond	Granite	Total
USA			76.5	135.46*	75.78			287.74
Canada		76.5						76.5
Netherlands	7.0							7.0
USA/Canada/Netherlands		76.5						76.5
USA/UK					0.3			0.3
Brunei						1.0		1.0
Australia	3.0				0.1			3.1
Japan		76.5						76.5
Malaysia							2.0	2.0
USA/Japan/Aust—ralia					2.0			2.0
USA/West Germany/Australia					4.0			4.0
Total	10.0	229.5	76.5	135.46	82.18	1.0	2.0	536.64

*Including West Germany and Japan.

Source: Foreign Investment Board, Jakarta.

N.B. These data omit approvals in the periods July to December 1972, July to December 1973.

for bauxite in East Sumatra, South-west and South-east Kalimantan, Sulawesi, the Moluccas, Irian Jaya, Central Java and Sumba. This was to take 5 to 6 years. Construction of bauxite mines, an alumina works and an aluminium refinery would follow with an initial capacity of 200,000 tons of alumina and 30,000 tons of aluminium a year. This part appears to have been visualised well into the future since Alcomin was put down for using electricity from the Asahan project. Total investment was to be no less than $100 million and the contract would last 30 years in the first instance.

Since 1967 327 licences for mining have been issued, of which 248 were granted to Indonesian nationals. But in 1973 only 13 national licence-holders were actively engaged in mining exploitation while 199 were in exploration. Many of the Indonesians were waiting to raise the necessary capital through entering into joint ventures with others, presumably foreign companies.

Table 5.11 lists the foreign mining investments that have been traced up to December 1973.

Compared with the total of $537 million for foreign investment, domestic investment approvals were very small—only $45 million. This is in contrast to the showing made by domestic investors in forestry.

As a result of investments mining production has been rehabilitated and some lines expanded. Tin production rose from 12·8 thousand tons in 1966 to 22·5 thousand tons in 1973 or about 22 per cent more than in 1961. Coal production, on the other hand, continued its decline so that in 1973 it was less than half the level of 1966 and about 27 per cent of 1961 production. But bauxite production increased from 701 to 1,229 thousand tons, and nickel ore from 117 to 867 thousand tons. Copper concentrate made its debut with 225,000 tons in 1973.

The decline in coal production is planned to be dramatically reversed. The enormous deposits of low-sulphur coal (believed to be the largest in the world) in South Sumatra are to be exploited by Royal Dutch Shell and the Indonesian government under a 30-year contract, with a production target of 30 million metric tons by the mid-1960s (Coggin, 1975). Royal Dutch Shell is to put up $1·2 billion of capital. If this plan succeeds then, at present prices, coal exports should exceed timber exports and be second only to oil exports.

SECONDARY INDUSTRY

In the general manufacturing field the first foreign investment inquiries were made by companies like Philips, Unilever, Goodyear and Uniroyal who were familiar with the indonesian scene. They were quickly followed by new companies interested in the textile industry (mainly from Japan) and the pharmaceutical industry (led by such European worthies as Ciba, Arco, Hoechst, Bayer and Dumex—bringing in small countries such as Denmark and Switzerland).

The rate of implementation of investment approvals in manufacturing was slow: by the end of 1970 $56 million of $280 million approved had been realised. Realisation of domestic investment in manufacturing was only slightly better than this ($34 million out of $150 million).

While forestry and mining saw original developments in many areas, the manufacturing sector that existed in 1965 was directly threatened by foreign investment because the tight money policy of the late sixties held back its rehabilitation for several years after the 1967 Foreign Investment Law came into effect. The textile industry was the chief example since it was an obvious developmental industry even in a low income country. After 1965 Japanese investment dominated, mainly due to the familiarity of Japanese enterprises with the Indonesian textile industry since war reparations had included much textile machinery from Japan.

Nevertheless, in the event the volume of Japanese investment in a quite new textile industry was staggering and caused associations of Indonesian entrepreneurs to demonstrate in protest. However, they were fighting a losing battle. Powerful influences appeared to have already determined that Indonesia should have a modern textile industry which would be competitive with overseas industries. The

TABLE 5.12

Foreign Investment Approvals in the Textile Industry to December 1973
($ million)

	Jakarta	West Java	Central Java	East Java	Total
Japan	52.25	139.37		22.6	214.22
Hong Kong	14.35	11.96		28.25	54.56
Singapore					—
USA		20.0			20.0
Thailand		2.6			2.60
Bahamas	9.0				9.0
UK				4.93	4.93
India				5.0	5.0
New Zealand				1.1	1.1
Netherlands			7.3		7.3
Total	75.60	173.93	7.3	61.88	318.71

Source: Foreign Investment Board, Jakarta.
N.B. These data omit the periods July to December 1972 and July to September 1973.

prone state of the domestic industry was taken as adequate evidence that it could not recover. By January 1970, 39 new foreign textile firms had had applications for investments totalling $117 million approved, against 45 domestic firms for Rupiah 11·6 billion (about $28 million).

The new investment was overwhelmingly concentrated in Jakarta and West Java. Table 5.12 shows that approximately three quarters of the investment was in Jakarta and West Java. (Data on approvals of foreign investment were unavailable for July to December 1972, July to September 1973 and all of 1974). Two thirds of the total was undertaken by Japanese enterprises, alone or in joint ventures. Japanese and Hong Kong enterprises accounted for five-sixths of the total new capacity. The biggest increase in the sum approved came in 1973 (a 50 per cent increase), indicating an acceleration of interest at that time.

That the handloom industry, which was so important for mass income, would suffer was a foregone conclusion. When in 1971 textile output rose to a record 732 million metres (8 per cent above the target) it was reported that 70 per cent of handlooms in the West Java textile centre of Madjalaya were still inoperative. (McCawley, 1972). Not much, if any, of the new investment could have been in production then and the figure suggests that the capacity of the existing mechanised section should have been at near full capacity. In 1974 output, at over 900 million metres, exceeded the target for textile production set out in the first Five Year Plan. The Second Plan target is for 1,500 million metres by 1979. Given continued Japanese interest in the textile industry it is likely to be achieved. But, as has already been demonstrated in this chapter, employment creation has by no means been promoted by this greater output.

One of the great dreams of Indonesian planners has been the Asahan hydroelectric project in Sumatra which would feed power to an industrial complex and transform the economy of the island. First mooted by the Dutch long before the second world war it has ever since been regarded as the principal jewel in a future economy.

Soon after the present government took over in March 1966, USAID assisted in a project survey which alone cost $1 million. Then the IDA came forward with a loan of $4 million (50;10;0·75 per cent) to finance technical research and consultants for planning the project. At the same time eight large companies from the United States, the United Kingdom, France, Japan, the Soviet Union, Canada and the Netherlands considered a consortium to raise the estimated $420 million cost of the Asahan Electricity Centre and the Aluminium Foundry Project. Work was expected to begin at the end of 1972 to build a power station of 430,000 KW and an alumina smelter for

200,000 tons a year. However the European and Canadian interests soon faded from the scene. In September 1972, the Japanese interests were still negotiating a soft loan from their own government. Five Japanese companies as well as Alcoa (USA) and Kaiser (USA) were urging that part of the total capital be financed by a government-to-government loan.

At this stage the Indonesian government wished to see the project as one package deal of a power station, infrastructure, port, bauxite mine and smelter; all of this to be transferred free to Indonesia after 30 years. This presented something of a setback to the Japanese interests but in October 1972 representatives of the five Japanese companies arrived in Jakarta to reopen negotiations. The two American companies were to be informed of the outcome by the Japanese companies.

But there was not to be any successful outcome then and a year later confusion still reigned. In August 1973 it was announced that details were about to be given but then this statement was withdrawn. In December a basic agreement for £600 million for the seven hydroelectric power stations totalling 500 MW and the aluminium smelter for 275,000 tons was reached. The contract was expected to be signed in mid-1974. In November Alcoa and Kaiser pulled out, and in April 1975 there arose uncertainty about the soft loans from the Japanese government, promised by ex-Premier Tanaka. Moreover, the estimated cost had risen to £900 million plus, 60 per cent higher than in January 1974. The increasing militancy of the Indonesian government towards the Japanese companies followed on the oil crisis but more recently there has been a softening in its attitude because of the Pertamina crisis and the shortage of international capital.

Finally agreement came into 1976 to build the electric power station and the aluminium smelting works at a total cost of $870 million to be raised from shareholders' own capital ($260 million), loans from the Japanese government and banks ($519 million), and the Indonesian government ($91 million). The work is to be completed in 1981 and the smelter will have an output of 150,000 tons in its ninth year (Stockwin, 1976). The power station will have a capacity of 600 megawatts (compared with total electricity power in Java today of around 1,000 megawatts). Ten thousand jobs will be created at the cost of $87,000 each (McDonald, 1976f).

In 1973–4 Indonesia consumed about one million tons of steel but produced only around 150,000 tons. Self-sufficiency in steel was planned for 1980 by increasing capacity to two to three million tons (Monthly Economic Letter, April 1974). It was hoped that most of this might eventually be produced at the one steel plant in Cilegon, now known as P.T. Krakatau. The Cilegon steel works, started with Soviet aid in Sukarno's time, was scheduled (in 1969) to be completed with American aid in 1976 and to be capable of producing 800,000 tons a year. Then in 1970 P.T. Krakatau was formed on the half-erected plant as a 60:40 venture between Pertamina and the Ministry of Industry. But confusion reigned over the completion of the plant. One year later, in 1971, Soviet experts arrived to re-survey it. Then in March 1973 the Minister for Industrial Affairs stated that it was hoped that continuation of the Cilegon steel works would be undertaken on the basis of cooperation with the Netherlands and West Germany, cooperation with the Soviet Union having been decided against. But rising oil prices brought Pertamina's funding potential for a steel industry into greater prominence, and Pertamina included Krakatau in its investment portfolio. Permission was granted for Krakatau to raise $500 million on the international capital market to build an integrated steel complex on the basis of the uncompleted Cilegon steel works. This was to include steel plants (300,000 tons a year), a plant for reinforcing iron ((150,000) tons a year) and a sheet steel plant (350,000 tons a year) (Arndt, 1974).

In 1974 when Pertamina found itself unable to roll-over debts of $900 million to contractors the government gave permission to Pertamina to withhold oil revenues to help these debt payments. But later when the full story of Pertamina's financial stake was unfolded Krakatau was one of the big industrial enterprises detached from the Pertamina conglomerate. In mid-1976 Krakatau obtained credits valued at $480 million (part of the $1 billion of commercial credits agreed to by IGGI in addition to its record aid total) from a consortium of German banks to continue construction (Sinar Harapan, 25 June 1976).

The estimated final cost of the steel complex of $2,400 million, which was to have a total capacity of two million tons of steel a year, was reduced to $1,300 million after negotiations with the German contractors (Coggin, 1975).

Cement is another industry which has been affected by oil price rises, but in a different way. In 1971 Indonesia produced 500,000 metric tons and imported another 900,000 metric tons. Plans for self-sufficiency in 1978 involve creating total capacity of 2·14 million tons (McCawley, 1972). The International Finance Corporation (World Bank affiliate) is to assist in doubling the capacity of P.T. Semen Cibinong, West Java, which was established in 1970 by Kaiser Cement, Gypsum Carrier and P.T. Semen Gresik (Monthly Economic Letter, July 1974).

For a country which intends to revolutionise crop technology a guaranteed supply of fertiliser is a must. The recent rise in the price of artificial fertiliser plus the presence of a petroleum industry argues strongly for self-sufficiency, if not for an exportable surplus, of fertiliser production. It was estimated that by 1974 Indonesia would be requiring 600,000 tons of urea annually.

P.N. Pusri's big fertiliser factory at Palembang (Sriwidjaja) received a total of $68 million for its expansion from 100,000 metric tons to 480,000 metric tons by 1973. This sum was put together by the World Bank ($30 million), the Asian Development Bank ($10 million), the United States ($20 million) and Japan ($8 million). Another $19 million was to be contributed by the government (Far East Trade and Development, vol. 27, no.6). The expansion of the plant, which came into operation in August 1974, takes natural gas from Pertamina, seventy miles from its site, and turns it into urea. Another plant, of 500,000 tons, in East Kalimantan, came into operation in 1976 (Bulletin of Indonesian Economic Studies, Vol.10, No.3). Work has already begun on a second extension of the Pusri plant, this time of 570,000 tons capacity. In addition, Pertamina has undertaken a joint venture with the Japanese Ammonium Sulphate Association (a federation of Japanese chemical fertiliser companies) to build an ammonium sulphate plant at Cirebon, in West Java, to exploit natural gas in the area. Its capacity will be 500,000 tons.

The fertiliser section of new investment is one of the more successful and least damaging aspects of the new development strategy. The government's consciousness of fertiliser requirements was awakened by its commitment to raise rice productivity, but the presence of a domestic natural gas supply and the finance-raising *potential* of Pertamina have undoubtedly helped to facilitate this investment.

CONCLUSION

Foreign enterprise was able to invest faster and with larger sums than domestic enterprise between 1967 and 1971. The result was that foreign capital appropriated the obviously most lucrative sectors of timber and minerals. Because these commodities are mostly exported to the country of investment origin (often providing the means of capital repayment) the Indonesian government is likely to face resistance to its demands for processing the raw material prior to export. In particular, when one country dominates both the extractive investment and the overseas market that resistance is bound to be very great.

As foreign capital moved into the manufacturing sector it had the effect of competing with some existing capacity of a less advanced technology. On top of the protracted liquidity crisis suffered by domestic manufacturing this led to thousands of national bankrupties. Even with new technology and management it can hardly be argued that competition was encouraged. Protection from foreign and domestic competition was successfully sought from the government on some occasions because when replacing imports, which have a restricted domestic market, the case could usually be made that the minimum size of plant for breaking even required a large guaranteed share of that market. And the more advanced the technique the larger that necessary size invariably is.

After 1971 domestic investments overtook foreign investments in some sectors, and overtook the total of foreign investments in 1973. The move towards part-indigenous ownership of foreign enterprises should place share capital under national control. This move, however, is bound to encourage foreign enterprises to lodge the lowest possible equity and to supplement this with loans from international parent companies.

The geographical spread of all investments shows a concentration in Kalimantan, West Java and Jakarta. Job creation has been correspondingly concentrated, so that direct job creation estimates over a seven-year period per 1,000 of population vary from 370 in East Kalimantan and 36 in Jakarta to 0·5 in Central Java and 0·4 in East Java. Since domestic investments have not experienced a radically different geographical spread from this it can be concluded that outside of the capital city there has been no relation between new productive investments and population centres. Jakarta may appear important to foreign visitors but it is in no way representative of the mass-based economy, the vast bulk of which has been by-passed by new investment.

It was hoped that foreign investment would accelerate development without supplanting domestic investment. This chapter has cast a great deal of doubt upon the realisation of that hope. The recent sharp decline in foreign investment is most likely to have been caused by revisions in the Foreign Investment Law, especially those pertaining to shares held by indigenous nationals. The world-wide recession and contraction of available capital have also contributed. But the cause of a simultaneous decline in domestic private investment must be largely explained by the very high interest rates on bank loans and to the fact that the even higher deposit rates make it attractive to potential domestic investors to lodge the capital they have in savings accounts. The recent upheavals in the monetary system, due to Pertamina's financial crash, are likely to postpone the time when the government can re-align bank interest rates to encourage more domestic private investment. Pertamina's problems have already led to a paring down or postponement of domestic public investment in industry.

Chapter 6

The Oil Sector

PRE-1966 DEVELOPMENTS

The oil industry of Indonesia has been long established with very large American and Dutch interests dominating before the Second World War. Output in 1938 was 7·4 million metric tons compared with around 57·4 million metric tons in 1973-4. The Dutch colonial administration had made an agreement in 1948 with the oil companies to allow them to appropriate their foreign currency earnings after company taxation, and to let them continue with their earlier concessions. The following year the Indonesian government chose to let that agreement stand. It was recognised that the oil industry could emerge as a substantial foreign exchange spinner but that it required vast sums of foreign capital and advanced technology to realise this. Thus foreign oil companies have been treated quite differently from foreign investors in other sectors.

But in 1951 it was decided that past concessions would be neither extended nor expanded until new laws on the oil industry were passed. This was not to be until 1960 so that for almost a decade the foreign oil companies existed in a sort of limbo, making *ad hoc* agreements with the government when their pre-war concessions came to an end. The first company which faced this situation was Stanvac in 1951. Under these agreements share of net profits was about 50:50 between the government and the companies. Although the companies could dispose of their foreign currency all their foreign earnings had to pass through the Foreign Exchange Fund. No new concessions were granted so that the companies had only their existing concessions.

The Petroleum and Natural Gas Mining Law of 1960 relegated foreign oil companies to working as contractors only, without usual concessional rights. All the contracts were dependent on active exploration and the investment of overseas capital which, therefore, would be carrying all exploration risks. Needless to say this Law caused dismay amongst foreign companies which pressurised for a new agreement. Finally came the 1963 Tokyo Agreement between the government and the oil companies which restored concessions and facilitated new exploration by 20-year exploitation contracts with the state oil companies. Profit-sharing was fixed at 60:40 (government:foreign company). New concessional areas could be negotiated on similar 30-year contracts. Refinery assets were to pass to Indonesian state ownership within 10 to 15 years. Domestic marketing and distribution was to be taken over immediately by the state companies.

But 1964 and 1965 were very troublesome years for the companies with daily rumours of outright expropriation, while their actual operations were placed under government supervision principally for their protection. Normal operations became impossible, and in December 1965 Shell sold out its assets (including refineries), valued at $110 million, to the government. Stanvac delayed its transfer of refineries as the post-1965 government was signalling its new economic philosophy at the time. A few months before, in July, all three companies had transferred their marketing assets to the amalgam of state enterprises called P.N. Pertamin.

The relative roles of the three foreign oil companies had changed radically. Caltex had rapidly expanded output of crude to produce 55 per cent of the total by 1963 (11·5 million metric tons). But it had no refining capacity and was shipping crude to refineries in the Philippines, Australia and Japan. It was Caltex's expansion which allowed exports to rise while domestic consumption of petroleum and its products was also making big strides. The troubles at Shell and Stanvac, on the other hand, had reduced their respective outputs to levels lower than their refining capacity so that the sale of refining assets in a very uncertain climate did not appear such a great loss.

The metamorphosis of the state oil sector occurred thus: previously P.N. Permina controlled all exploration, development and refining and P.N. Pertamin undertook domestic distribution. In August 1968 the two companies were amalgamated to form P.N. Pertamina.

The pattern of foreign investment in the oil sector since 1966 has been markedly different. The world's giant companies preferred to concentrate on their large concessions in the Middle East and elsewhere. To higher cost Indonesian oilfields came a large number of much smaller oil companies. By mid-1975 twenty companies (fifteen of them from the United States alone) were negotiating contracts.

The model for these contracts was based on the 1963 Tokyo Agreement. Leases granted were essentially management contracts under which the lessees also carried all capital risks at the exploration stage. Pertamina was the ultimate owner and controller of all equipment financed by the foreign companies. Forty per cent of production was to be retained by the foreign companies with which to cover their exploration and production costs. The profits (or revenue) of the remainder would be split 65:35 for the first 75,000 barrels per day, and then split 67·5:32·5.

When the windfall profits to the foreign oil companies following on the 1973 price increases became all too apparent Pertamina asked them to renegotiate their production-sharing contracts so that Pertamina could share more in the new profits. After a period of argument it was agreed in January 1974 that the old profit split applied to the first $5·00 per barrel only, with Pertamina taking 85 per cent of the revenue from prices above $5·00. This was believed to bring in a 250 per cent increase in state revenue from oil.

Oil prices increased again but it was only in 1976, after Pertamina's huge cash-flow problems disrupted government finance, that further renegotiation of contracts were called for. The government, in fact, left little room for argument, and quickly assumed a 'take-it-or-leave-it' posture. This time an additional levy per barrel was demanded. Caltex was the first company approached and settled on giving up to the government $1 out of its profit of $2-2·30 per barrel, or an addition of $300 million a year in revenue. But it is reputed to retain $300-400 million a year profit (McDonald, 1976c). Caltex vainly requested rights to increase production in return.

Then the government turned its attention to production-sharing contracts. Taking $2·50 per barrel from the profits made by the companies would effectively mean that the government would take more than 85 per cent of their profits, or a total of around $340 million more revenue, retroactive to 1 January 1976. To soften the blow depreciation charges were rescheduled. These oil companies were divided into three categories: those with reserves greater than 100 million barrels at 1 January 1976 (assumed to last more than seven years), those with reserves less than 100 million barrels, and those not yet in production.

The first were allowed 14 years over which to recover capital costs and the second seven years. This formula was believed to have meant an effective additional levy of $2·50 per barrel for the first group of companies and $1·50 for the second (McDonald, 1976d). A one hundred per cent write-off of exploration costs in the first year of production was offered those companies not yet in production.

It was a bitter pill for the foreign oil contractors to swallow for, in effect, past agreements had been arbitrarily torn up in order (as they were bound to see it) to bale out Pertamina from the consequences of its own blunders. It is likely that these events will influence future exploration to some extent. Because Indonesia's oilfields are small more frequent exploration is required than in the Middle East. Already in 1975 there was a significant decline in number of drillings.

Results are also regarded as poor by international standards. Given Pertamina's inability to raise capital for exploration in the forseeable future, the extra $640 million a year in government revenue might have been won at a high long-term cost.

POST-1965 EXPANSION

Offshore exploration had not been seriously undertaken prior to the change of government. But by 1967 several contractors covered nearly all the offshore areas of the Java Sea as well as large areas off East Kalimantan and some areas off Sumatra. There was some anxiety at first that these smaller companies would not be able to raise the large amounts of capital required for oil exploration. A few years later the practice of selling out part of contracts to other companies in order to raise the full sum necessary was reported. For instance in 1970 Kyushu Oil Development Company and Union Carbide Petroleum Company sold one third of their 160,000 square mile joint oil concession territory in offshore Java and Sumatra to the Erdoelversorgungs GMBH company of West Germany (Berita Yudha, 1 Oct. 1970). For that, $750,000 was paid to each of the originals and the German company agreed to invest another $2·4 million in exploration. Part of the Wendell Philips concession in Irian Jaya was also offered to Japanese companies but the latter failed to show enthusiasm.

By October 1971 there were 40 foreign contractors with Pertamina, of whom 30 were involved in offshore drilling. Only five had found oil and were in production. The total amount invested in exploration and production facilities between 1967 and late 1971 was $295 million (Far East Trade and Development, vol. 26, no. 10). The following year approximately $100 million was spent.

There were some new oil discoveries in 1972, but the earlier predictions of discoveries were now appearing uncertain. Some observers were even visualising a levelling off of oil production in the late seventies (Grenville, 1973). Events since then have strengthened this belief.

Total oil reserves were estimated in 1972 to be between 10 and 15 billion barrels; or about 2 per cent of the then estimated world reserves (Semay, 1972). At the current rate of 1·5 million barrels per day (or 547 million barrels per year) these reserves would last 20 to 30 years. By 1976 recoverable reserves were put at 15 to 17 billion barrels, and there was reputed to be a 30 per cent success rate in drilling (Jenkins, 1976b). Indonesian oilfields proved not to be as profitable as at first thought (at pre-1974 prices) and exploration risks proved very great. The move towards company consortiums was a natural development from this. But the size of some consortiums is worth noting. For example, in early 1973 six Japanese companies reached a basic agreement with two United States companies (Tasoure Petroleum and Wendell Philips) to jointly develop oil in West Irian (Sinar Harapan, 8 Feb. 1973).

In the meantime output of crude was rising at a great pace. In 1967 output was 500,000 barrels per day. Of the original three giants Caltex accounted for 360,000 barrels per day, Stanvac 55,000 barrels per day, and the ex-Shell fields (now Pertamina's) 65,000 barrels per day. Caltex's enormous output (70 per cent of the total) was helping to keep the refineries of Stanvac and Pertamina (ex-Shell) properly utilised.

By 1971 Caltex was producing around 724,000 barrels per day (or 85 per cent of Indonesian crude) and had plans to raise this to one million barrels. By 1973 its crude oil output was 1·4 million barrels a day. Within six years output had risen 175 per cent.

But oil revenues were also important to the government budget, and increasingly so. Already by 1971-2 the oil sector contributed 25 per cent of total government revenue. With the oil price increases this rose to 66 per cent in 1974-5. It came from indirect receipts from domestic sales of petroleum and its products as well as from direct receipts (taxes on foreign oil companies).

Refining capacity loomed as a major obstacle to the rationalisation of the industry as crude output expanded quickly. It was the desire of the government to acquire as much value added from further processing of crude extraction as possible and to go on to develop a petroleum complex with various lines of petroleum products. The realisation of this was to depend on Pertamina's credit standing in the overseas capital market.

DIFFICULTIES IN CONTROLLING PERTAMINA

The state oil company, Pertamina, became responsible for a wide range of functions whose individual plans depended upon their mutuality and reciprocity for effectiveness. Refining technology needed to be subject to locational theory and quality of crude, a tanker fleet required intricate programming, capacities for processing the crude up to a range of high value added products could not be planned autonomously, and the rate of overall capacity expansion had to relate to realistic predictions of the oil sector's growing wealth. It was no less a job than planning an economy in miniature. Accounting procedures for the numerous depreciation funds, investment funds and criteria for refinancing were bound to be highly complex. But one of Indonesia's chronic problems is lack of skills and good administrative personnel. Project evaluation was slow in many other fields because of necessary skilled personnel. The oil sector alone could probably have employed all the country's accountants and company lawyers had Pertamina's business dealings been conducted in a strictly accountable manner. But until 1972 Pertamina had no guidelines or constraints imposed upon it except a loose instruction to pay over foreign company taxes as well as taxes on its own domestic marketing activities. Furthermore, the expansion was conducted on the say of virtually one man, its President-Director, Ibnu Sutowo, who practised his new profession in the manner of a warlord. Without doubt he was a man of great personal resources, with an overall view not only of the oil sector but of the whole economy. A big-time promoter standing in a desert of underpaid and insecure civil servants, he struck out on his own in a very grand manner. His style was appealing to westerners who wanted to get things done in a reasonably assured and speedy way. Given the underdeveloped state of the central government bureaucracy he had one card which he could always play: who was to judge what was 'profit' in this giant, state conglomerate?

But Sutowo overplayed his hand. It became obvious that even minimal profits were not being sent to the national treasury. From 1958 to 1963 the parent company of Pertamina neither submitted its taxation notification letter nor paid its taxes. No tax declaration was made in 1964 or 1965 but $5,200 was assessed to be due and was paid in each of these years. In 1966 the official tax levy due was $1·7 million but only $1·6 million was paid. In 1967 the dues were assessed at $5·26 million but until September 1970, at least, none of it had actually been paid. Similarly, for 1968, $13 million was due in taxes, but nothing was handed over. In 1967 earnings from the 'provision of data' to foreign oil companies were estimated to be $37 million. The whole of this should have been passed to the government, but in the event less than $4 million was paid. In 1968–9 $28 million should have come from this source but nothing of it materialised in the national treasury.

In 1969 a new system was introduced whereby the taxpayer had to make his own assessment of taxes due. Pertamina did not even make this calculation for 1969. Instead, in 1970 it submitted a budget for that year incorporating a deficit of $17 million to be financed with a long-term loan. It was submitted to the Minister of Mining on 5 February 1970. Under the Law No. 19 of 1960 the budget is said to be automatically approved if, after three months following its presentation, the Minister has failed to comment on it. No comment came from the Minister during that time. On the other hand, Pertamina spent $22·3 million on investment in land and $600,000 on housing in 1969 against an authorised expenditure of only $403,500 and $132,000 respectively. Also, contrary to a 1960 Law governing state enterprises, Pertamina was creating subsidiaries of its own and was enjoying participation in other companies.

Late in 1969 the press started its campaign against what it saw as corruption in Pertamina and against what one newspaper called the conducting of a 'twin economy' (Kompas, 8 Dec. 1969).

In January 1970 President Suharto set up a four-member commission to look into problems of corruption, including those of Pertamina. The terms of reference used by the commission in evaluating Pertamina's affairs included misdirection of national development funds, pricing and contract policies, and policies on conserving reserves of oil and natural gas.

As expected Pertamina was found guilty of not paying corporation taxes, not contributing full taxes on profits to the Development Fund and not handing over foreign companies' data compensation payments. The fact that the large profits of the oil industry were not being made available to the government budget weakened the justification for promoting the oil sector to finance the development of the economy in general. In the process of its development the expansion of the oil industry was emerging as an end in itself and was distorting the original priorities of the First Five Year Plan. In addition Pertamina was found to have illegal subsidiary companies abroad and that the foreign exchange of these subsidiaries was illegally held abroad. However, Indonesian business has a long history of under-invoicing, or including two sets of invoices, and the use of overseas subsidiaries to move profits from a domestic company to an overseas deposit is standard practice.

Another charge against Pertamina was that the terms of production-sharing left Pertamina in a weak position to control the rundown of national oil resources, to impose processing clauses on contracts, and to intervene where foreign companies sold part of the concessions already granted them.

However, the Second Five Year Plan, which stipulates an 8 per cent annual increase in crude output, must be seen as official inspiration of such depletion of reserves. Indonesian officials appear very confident that current exploitation of oil resources will bring about future national economic development. Also with so much latitude granted Pertamina in arranging contracts with foreign oil companies it must be concluded that it lay in the character of Pertamina's management that processing clauses were not included. On the other hand, such clauses could be deemed to have been premature in 1970, except in the case of Caltex, because of the enormous risk capital involved in initial exploration. Until the returns to this kind of capital have been established, obligatory investment in further processing of crude can fairly be described as a deterrent to any investment. The marketing of parts of concessions is another issue which it is difficult to judge. Some of the financial problems that the smaller oil companies incurred in exploring large concessions were very likely unexpected. Exploration returns in Indonesian oilfields have proved disappointing and selling out stakes to other companies was an obvious way out.

The accusation levelled against Pertamina that its budget was not ratified by the Minister of Mining is not altogether fair. If a Minister of Mining is not prepared to comment on the budget within the statutory three months permitted, the blame can hardly be laid at the door of Pertamina. There may, of course, be an excellent case for saying three months is too short a time, or that a Minister of Mining should have the right of constant monitoring of Pertamina's budget. In fact, the Commission of Four came to such a firm conclusion and this was acted upon through legislation in 1972.

This leads on to the question of Pertamina-government relations in general. The basic confusion can be said to have arisen because of inadequate legislation governing the relationship. Pertamina's expanding role in the economy under Sutowo was not foreseen and there was little recourse that a weak and undecided Ministry had in dealing with an emerging economic warlord. To accuse Pertamina, as did the Commission of Four, of not being the commercial success that it was reputed to be in some circles was not very helpful. Compared with other nationally-run sectors the state oil company was, for a number of years, a roaring success. Profit rates on its multifarious activities were unlikely to have been equated at the margin even after allowing for the necessity of large, indivisible units of capital, and wastage of large quantities of natural gas there undoubtedly was. But until long-term marketing and technological decisions governing all fuels were taken at the highest level contradictions had to be borne. Whatever its internal economic inefficiencies the oil industry enjoyed a dynamic of its own for a period of time.

The primary criticism which loomed over all other considerations was the relation of the oil industry to the rest of the economy: its dominance by one man, its poor accountability to the overall national plan and its development as a separate economy.

The state oil company has been described as a 'state within a state'. It would be more meaningfully described as an economy within an economy, or even as a parallel economy as one observer (Bowring, 1973) put it:

> However, Pertamina itself may be the most vivid example of what some critics claim is a dangerous process towards a two-tier economy. Pertamina's belief in living up to its oil-rich image, paying high wages and fringe benefits, borrowing heavily overseas and reinvesting massively,

could be a misuse of the nation's major natural resource and fount of foreign exchange. It is the old dilemma of maximising growth or applying it as widely as possible.

Prior to its entry into the development of fertiliser, cement and other petroleum product factories Pertamina did not provide external economies to other sectors of the economy. There was no linkage between it and other industries. Since, with an inflexible technology, it could not be directed towards employment-creation the revenues extracted from it for the creation of other industries would have been its main contribution to national employment creation. If those revenues were not forthcoming the oil sector had little to do with solving the country's unemployment problem.

The Commission of Four recommended that Pertamina be subordinated not only to the Minister of Mining but also to the Minister of Finance. The 1972 Pertamina Law stated that 60 per cent of net operating profit of Pertamina should go to the central government. However, when the tax assessment for 1971–2 turned out to be only $6 million and was not expected to be as much as $9 million in 1972–3 it became apparent that Pertamina had convinced the authorities it needed its profits for reinvestment.

But by 1973 the Ministers of Mining, Finance and Planning, appointed to strutinise Pertamina's accounts had not been able to curb the company. When the company was accused of owing about $22 million in unpaid customs duties in 1973 Pertamina insisted it was all a misunderstanding about what constituted taxable revenue. The Director-General for Customs and Excise was moved to another department and the issue was shelved.

While Pertamina's corruption and autonomy were the main issues in 1970 the emphasis of criticism has shifted more recently to the company's heavy borrowings and long-term debt position. Suspicions were aroused when it became known in 1973–4 that Pertamina was having difficulty raising new loans on the international capital market.

The investments of Pertamina covered refineries, a tanker fleet, marketing apparatus, land development, housing, various processing plants, further port facilities and a host of activities with dubious connections to the oil industry.

During 1971 Pertamina, it was believed, borrowed $295 million abroad (Arndt, 1972). An Australian newspaper was quoted as reporting (National Times, 12 Feb. 1973) that Pertamina had borrowed more than $350 million during the financial year 1972–3 without the knowledge of the monetary authorities—not only in breach of domestic regulations but also in breach of IMF agreements which limited new borrowing by Indonesia to $140 million.

Together with other investments Pertamina's assets were roughly estimated to be about $2,300 million in 1972, or 25 per cent of the, then, net domestic product. But Pertamina claimed only $1,208 million worth of capital assets in 1971 and $1,264 million in 1972 (Sinar Harapan, 24 Sept. 1973). At the same time sales of oil were only $600 million a year. Clearly Pertamina was depending on a much larger turnover in the years ahead.

Amongst the most ambitious enterprises entered into by Pertamina were (i) a joint venture with foreign partners to form P. T. Krakatau, to continue the former Soviet steel project at Cilegon (North-West Java), (ii) fertiliser and other petrochemical industries, (iii) a shipbuilding venture with Mitsui and a fertiliser plant in East Kalimantan, and (iv) a 20,000 hectares rice estate in South Sumatra to produce 200,000 tons of rice a year with a capital outlay of $150 million.

But the most ambitious of all Pertamina's plans was the development of a huge oil and petrochemical complex on Batam Island in the Riau archipelago. It has been described as a service base, but was also designed to be a petroleum-based industrial estate and an operational base for the exploration and exploitation of oil and natural gas. Subsidiary plans were drawn up for service bases in West Java, East Kalimantan, and Masalembo Island in the Java Sea.

At the May 1973 IGGI meeting in Amsterdam Pertamina's borrowing came in for a great deal of criticism. It was described as 'unilateral and excessive acceptance of foreign loans' (Roeder, 1973). The IMF was concerned that the balance of payments would not be able to stand the debt consequences in future. However the reply from Pertamina was a question to the meeting whether the company's policy of accelerated expansion had been a success or a failure. Nevertheless the IGGI and the IMF continued arguing with Indonesia over what was a permissible level for Pertamina's short-term and longer term borrowings.

In late 1974 Pertamina found itself unable to pay short-term promissory notes and in the prevailing conditions of international credit it could not re-finance, or roll over, these short-term debts. In October the President gave permission to Sutowo to withhold $850 million of production-sharing contract revenues which should have been passed on to the government. The reason given at the time was that the steel complex, Krakatau, needed $900 million immediately because of cash-flow problems. A few months later Pertamina failed to re-finance in the international capital market two short-term debts amounting to $100 million. Bank Indonesia stepped in to guarantee all Pertamina's debts. The full story began to unfold fast. In March 1975 Parliament learned that Pertamina owed $3·2 billion in foreign loans and overdue payments and an additional sum equivalent to $113 million to domestic contractors (Coggin, 1975). The sudden drain on the country's foreign exchange reserves (the government itself had to borrow from the international capital market) and the alteration of the central bank's balance sheet led Bank Indonesia to suspend publication of monetary data in May 1975. By February 1976 Bank Indonesia had paid $1·6 billion to foreign creditors and the equivalent of $230 million to domestic contractors (Mc Donald, 1976).

Sukarno's foreign debt of $2·3 billion in 1965 paled into insignificance when compared with Pertamina's total debt situation. It has been difficult to piece together the components of the commonly alleged $10 billion total short, medium and long-term debt, but from four separate sources (Mc Donald, 1976a; Coggin, 1975; Mc Donald, 1976b; Kompas, 21 May 1976) the composition of most of the debt must have looked as follows:

	million
P.T. Krakatau requirements	$ 2,100
Short-term loans and letters of credit	$ 1,000
Domestic contractors	$ 1,900
TOTAL SHORT-TERM	$ 5,000
Tankers (including unknown short-term service charges)	$ 3,300
Medium and long-term loans	$ 900
Borrowing for liquefied natural gas project (probably including short-term debts)	$ 1,100
TOTAL	$10,300

As one commentator (Mc Donald, 1976a) summarised the implications the Pertamina debt of $10 billion was equal to two-and-a-half times total revenue from oil in 1976–7, or one-and-a-quarter times total government revenue (including aid), or ten times total foreign reserves, or $80 per head of population (with per capita income reputed to be only $130).

Sutowo was dismissed in March 1976, and the total debt quickly fell to $6·2 billion by a combination of repayments, detaching non-oil enterprises (including the Jatibarang fertiliser plant and Krakatau) from the Pertamina empire, and through renegotiation of debts.

Attempts to reduce the tanker debt have involved the government in protracted law suits in London, New York and Guam at least. The government is arguing that the agreements with tanker suppliers are not binding because they were not ratified by Pertamina's Supervisory Board. The tanker suppliers argue, in return, that the use of the tankers was approval enough. After a team of British lawyers was hired by Jakarta, the government also claimed that the tanker prices and charges were far above prevailing rates and that there had been a conspiracy of involved parties to defraud. One lawyer was quoted (Jenkins, 1976) as saying: 'If all this ever comes out it will make the Lockheed scandal look like the teddy bears' picnic'.

But there are other repercussions of the Pertamina fiasco. At a time when China is rapidly expanding her output of similar low sulphur oil and Japan is able to land it at $3 per barrel less than Indonesian oil, Indonesia is in a weak position to ask Japan to agree to delaying repayment of a $300 million soft loan made to Pertamina in 1973. One of the reasons for Japan's generosity was her reliance on Indonesian oil. With China's oil exports to Japan rising from $33 million in 1974 to $410 million in 1975 (Coggin, 1975a) and still rising fast, Indonesia has all but lost her special hold over Japan. The share of Indonesia's oil exports going to Japan has fallen dramatically.

IMPLICATIONS OF THE OIL PRICE INCREASES

Prior to the large rises in the price of oil it could have been said that, at the very least, Pertamina had taken enormous risks in following its development strategy. It gambled that there were enough oil reserves to make its big-time promotion pay off. These lavish reserves have not yet been discovered, but the jump in oil prices could have provided a substitute for them. They can be summarised as:

	$ per barrel
Previous to April 1973	2.96
1 April 1973	3.75
1 October 1973	4.75
1 November 1973	6.00
1 January 1974	10.80

Since January 1974 the price has risen to $12 per barrel. In addition to this, output was rising very rapidly until 1975 and it was planned to expand it by 8 per cent a year during the Second Five Year Plan.

Table 6.1 shows how the 1973 price rises would have affected the planned net foreign exchange from oil during the period of the Second Five Year Plan had the price stayed at $8 per barrel.

TABLE 6.1

Value of Planned Oil Exports, at Assumed Price of $8.00 per barrel ($ million)

	Gross	*Net**
1973/4	1,729	680
1974/5	3,727	1,470**
1975/6	4,204	1,670
1976/7	4,964	1,880
1977/8	5,830	2,190
1978/9	7,145	2,840

* Net of profit remittances by foreign companies and net of oil imports (including new investment). A comparison of this table and Table 6.3 shows that remitted foreign oil company profits are about equal to oil sector required imports and were, in 1973/4, approximately equal to 22 per cent of total *gross* oil exports.

** Assuming a price of $10.80 per barrel and the same profit split, the gross value in 1974–5 would be $5 billion and the net value $2 billion.

Source: Repelita II, quoted in S. Grenville, 'Survey of Recent Developments', *Bulletin of Indonesian Economic Studies,* vol. 10, no. 1, March 1974, p. 2.

In the event the balance of payments was even more revolutionised by the later price increases. From a position of having an empty coffer and debt servicing exceeding total expected export earnings in 1966, completely new trends of foreign exchange dealings were established (Table 6.2). But imports were quick to expand in approximate proportion to oil foreign exchange earnings. Therefore with the failure of non-oil export earnings to grow, the deficit balance on current account grew in spite of these windfall earnings.

In a matter of four years net oil earnings jumped almost six times, and rose from 37 per cent to 63 per cent of total export earnings. But non-oil export earnings rose only 140 per cent over the same period.

TABLE 6.2

Balance of Trade: 1965/6, 1971/2, and 1974/5—1976/7 (forecast)—in $ million

	1965/6	1971/2	1974/5	1975/6	1976/7 (forecast)
Non-oil exports (fob)	424	784	2,033	1,873	2,055
Non-oil imports (fob)	–550	–1,155	–4,341	–5,222	–5,868
Non-oil trade balance	–126	–371	–2,308	–3,349	–3,813
Services	–272	–552	–468	–775	–1,107
Debt services	n.a.	–107	–89	–93	–170
Balance on non-oil current account	–398	–1,030	–2,865	–4,217	–5,090
Oil exports	210	590	n.a.	n.a.	n.a.
Oil imports	–60	–132	n.a.	n.a.	n.a.
Balance on oil current account	150	458	2,638	3,133	3,400
Final Balance on current account	–248	–572	–227	–1,084	–1,690

Source: Arndt, H. W. (1973), 'Survey of Recent Developments', *Bulletin of Indonesian Economic Studies,* vol. 9, no. 2; and 'Statistics', *Bulletin of Indonesian Economic Studies,* vol. 4, no. 3; and Rice, R. C. and Lim, D., (1976), 'Survey of Recent Developments', *Bulletin of Indonesian Economic Studies,* vol. 12, no. 2.

The very great danger that the radically altered foreign payments position presented in 1974 was that the sense of urgency in developing smallholders' exports would be severely weakened. And with that the livelihoods of the people, as distinct from the health of the national economy (that is, of the Rupiah), would be placed in jeopardy. A similar danger of this bonanza threatened the structure of taxation through easing the need to raise (hopefully progressive) income tax. As can be seen from Table 6.3 items of government revenue other than oil company tax sharply declined in relative significance after the rise in oil prices. Even in 1972–3, before the price rises, oil company tax was accounting for 33 per cent of total government revenue from domestic resources.

TABLE 6.3

Domestic Government Revenue, 1972/3 and 1975/6 (Rupiah billion)

	1972/3	*1975/6**
Direct taxes	302.2	1,867.5
income	23.7	52.4
company	30.6	125.6
oil company	198.9	1,540.0
others	49.0	149.5
Indirect taxes	253.8	571.6
sales	34.5	109.9
import sales	27.8	88.5
excise	47.3	90.2
import duties	73.2	221.4
export duties	32.7	71.7
other oil revenue	31.6	−31.1
other	6.7	21.0
Other	34.6	57.0
Total domestic	590.6	2,496.1

* Estimate

Source McCawley, P. 'Survey of Recent Developments' *Bulletin of Indonesian Economic Studies*, vol. 9, no. 3, November 1973, and vol. 12, no. 1, March 1976.

But in 1975–6 oil company tax provided 63 per cent. The only other items of government domestic revenue that came near to rising in proportion to the total were other company tax and import duties. Income tax, on the other hand, declined from 4·1 to 2·1 per cent of the total.

With increases in the value of oil it could have been suggested that some of the other taxes were not worth collecting, given the resources that would be absorbed in that collection.

Thus we see two ways in which the oil bonanza could threaten even the existing distribution of domestic purchasing power, and possibly also endanger the earnings of the poor in absolute terms.

A further danger of this inflow of national purchasing power was inflation. There is no reason for the ruling classes, in particular the military who are neither producers nor sellers, to have felt threatened by even severe inflation. It would, however, have caused predictable hardship for small-holders and the poor everywhere.

The cash-flow problems of Pertamina in 1975 might have lifted this threat by cautioning the government against expecting the oil industry to give long-term massive support to the balance of payments and the budget, but the readiness of Indonesia's international credit consortium to bale out the government in its new debt position has terminated that likelihood.

While oil price rises have made Indonesia free, in theory, of an aid consortium, the political character and ethos of the government would suggest that continued underdevelopment is more likely than new development from so much money. Pertamina's cash problems should be resolved in something less than the next decade but, unless oil earnings are used to diversify national production to expand the number of livelihoods for the poor, the great opportunities offered by oil exploitation will have been missed when oil production starts declining after 25 years or so. The use of that breathing space of a generation is an issue to which the government has so far declined to address itself. To rush the exploitation of very limited known reserves when there are abundant leakages of returns due to lack of social control, and when reinvestment is done in a manner which contradicts the new pronounced social concern of the Second Five Year Plan, would seem a sad end to Indonesia's prime money-spinner. Furthermore, if increasing levies on the foreign oil companies' profits leave them with little inclination to undertake further exploration, and if the pricing and output policies of China and Saudi Arabia continue to weaken the efficacy of the collusive tendering of other OPEC countries such as Indonesia, the country's oil industry might not last as long as one generation as a back-stop to development.

Chapter 7

Disenchantment and Partial Rectification

It did not require the help of theoretical critiques, Marxist or otherwise, for Indonesians to become hostile to the strategy of economic development, for they saw and felt the effects all around them. From the loss of jobs in domestically-owned enterprises, through all-too-visible myriad establishments designed to cater to the privileged, to the sense of impotency and outrage, the impact of the new economic style escaped few.

The chief criticisms are listed here.

1. The new exports of timber and minerals have overtaken traditional agricultural exports (which include a large smallholder sector) and there is a danger that the latter will be neglected as they are seen to take an ever decreasing share of exports.
2. There has been an imbalance of promotional schemes within the food sector between rice, on the one hand, and other foodcrops, on the other. As a result farmers with access to good *sawah* land have been the beneficiaries of intensification programmes while productivity of other foodcrops has been neglected.
3. In manufacturing preference has been shown to large-scale investments, whereas what is required to safeguard both domestic ownership and jobs is small-scale investment. This complaint cannot be separated from that of an emphasis on capital-intensity instead of labour-intensity in new industrial investment.
4. Foreign investment has seized the most lucrative exploitation of all—that of natural resources—sometimes to the point, as in the case of timber, of raping the national heritage. It has also taken the lion's share of the most profitable import-replacement industries sometimes after persuading the authorities to protect it from other competition, both foreign and domestic.
5. Foreign investment has strengthened the economic position of the Chinese and has squeezed out the indigenous *(pribumi)* entrepreneurs. With the Chinese comprising only three per cent of the population (as against about 37 per cent in neighbouring Malaysia) the national economic power was concentrated in the hands of a

minority with cultural, religious and ethnic affinities at variance with those of the indigenous majority.

6. Closely associated with this is the complaint against the relationship between the Chinese and persons in the military-bureaucratic complex who have enriched themselves by close financial links with foreigners.

7. There is anxiety over the near exclusivity of Japanese interests in major Indonesian exports (timber and oil) and the increasing dominance of Japanese investment in parts of secondary industry. The heavy reliance on one foreign market has been the concern of those who fear monopsonistic practices or instability in exports.

8. Foreign investment and the emphasis on new exports have caused an increasing regional imbalance in economic development. Foreign investment has not been distributed according to population and those provinces which fortuitously found themselves in possession of the new emerging exports have done very well. Within Java there has been an overconcentration of industrial investment in Jakarta, leaving stagnant, or even declining, industries elsewhere.

Some of the causes of these criticisms have been weakened either by deliberate intervention (crop diversification of intensification programmes) or by external factors (the decline in relative importance of Japan's oil purchases).

Towards the end of 1973 separate criticisms were coming together in something of a crescendo. In October 1973 a petition from the students of the University of Indonesia called for a reappraisal of the whole strategy of development. Frustration and hostility erupted into the fury vented during the visit of Japanese Premier Tanaka in January 1974. It is immaterial whether the demonstrations were or were not organised; the emotions were genuinely felt. But it would be quite wrong to see the demonstrations as directed merely against Japanese investment. Hariman Siregar, President of the University of Indonesia's Students Council, described the economic development that had taken place as meaning 'the expropriation of land, forced sales of rice to the government and increasingly difficult life in the villages' (Starner, 1974). The targets of the demonstrators were the technocrats, the Presidential assistants accused of benefiting directly from foreign investment, the Chinese brokers of the generals and the foreign investors themselves.

Certainly the government recognised the demonstrations as more encompassing criticisms when it handed down a six-year sentence on Siregar and chose to arrest or place under restriction persons held in the highest repute overseas: Adnan Buyung Nasution (a prominent civil rights lawyer), Soedjatmoko (regarded by many overseas as the country's leading intellectual and a former ambassador to

Washington), Professor Sarbini (former head of the Central Bureau of Statistics), and Mochtar Lubis (Newsweek columnist and President of the Asian Press Institute).

It would also be wrong to suppose that criticisms had been amassed only in 1973. Z. E. Subchan, a leading Moslem (who died unexpectedly in Mecca in January 1972), had been a consistent advocate of encouraging national enterprise. In 1969 he had been urging that a corps of private businessmen should be developed and criticised the facilities granted foreign businessmen but not national businesses.

The disenchantment with foreign investment did not commence with the plunder of timber resources or with the displacement of national textile enterprises. Numerous Indonesians have remembered the colonial past and younger compatriots had been brought up under Sukarno's denunciation of economic dependency. Suspicion of what foreign investment would do to the economy there always was. But when in the latter half of the sixties the nation's mind was on other matters, such as the immediate control of inflation by means of foreign aid, and when the New Order government reiterated many times that foreign investment was being invited in, not to be the main engine, but merely to complement domestic investment in order to accelerate development, suspicion was tempered by a 'wait and see' attitude.

THE PROLONGED LIQUIDITY CRISIS IN DOMESTIC INDUSTRY

The first source of hostility to the government's economic strategy arose over the prolonged liquidity crisis which was still affecting (non-export oriented) domestic productive capacity when the first foreign investments were being approved.

It was claimed by the economists at the time that this effect of their stabilisation policy had been expected and unavoidable, but it was never made clear whether the devastation of the textile industry by large imports of cloth on privileged exchange rates had also been expected and unavoidable. In 1967 80 per cent of credits for all textile materials was spent on finished textile imports. Even allowing for pressure from Japan to sell the product of *its* industries it is hard to believe that economists with any courage would have had to settle for such an outrageous bargain. The truth probably lies in the fact that the economists placed little importance on the resuscitation of domestic industry at this stage, mesmerised as they were with the numbers game of quantities of aid balancing aggregate figures of demand and supply.

It is still difficult to explain satisfactorily why the liquidity crisis was allowed to continue so long. Christmas, Lebaran and Chinese

New Year consumption desires at the end of 1966 had been largely appeased. Food and textiles had arrived in sufficient quantities to meet the huge backlog of 1965-6. Shortages of course there still were, but these had been not uncommon in the history of the country. It is tempting to suggest that it was also due to the technocrats' basic contempt for productive enterprise and commerce, unless it came in the well-heeled super-technology form of foreign investment. The 'nitty-gritty' of encouraging domestic enterprise appeared to be below the economists who had been given advanced western training.

STAGNANT TRADITIONAL AGRICULTURE

Unlike secondary industry, traditional export agriculture benefited from the first phase of stabilisation because of the government's need to show willingness to boost exports while restricting imports. In order to follow the export-oriented strategy, exporters' incentives in the form of proportions of exchange earnings retained by exporters for sale at a near free market rate were quickly liberalised.

But as foreign confidence in the government grew the annual amounts of the IGGI's loans also continued to ease the foreign exchange situation considerably. The first forestry investments were committed in 1967 and there followed the rapidly emerging role of timber earnings in total foreign exchange earnings. At the same time nickel earnings continued the rapid growth started in 1963 and the fuller utilisation of the oil industry followed on the clarification of some issues therein.

The dependence for foreign exchange earnings thus shifted to non-traditional exports. But it was quickly realised that this was a boon to the administration since the foreign expertise content of the non-traditional exports relieved it of having to send in skilled personnel to cope with technical problems of agricultural rehabilitation and of having to improve the run-down infrastructural outlets of smallholders' crops.

Complaints in the press of the neglect of traditional exports increased as it became apparent that their interests no longer coincided with the interests of the government in allocating its scarce resources.

The crucial issue centred on the fact that traditional exports were a great deal more labour-intensive than the newly emerging exports, that they involved either ownership of land or direct access to land by ordinary Indonesians and that they coincided with rural concentrations of population and were therefore sources of mass livelihoods. Since the new forestry and mineral centres bore no geographical relation to the dispersion of rural populations they could not be seen as employment-creating where employment was most needed.

But time did not come to the rescue of traditional exports. On the contrary, the big rise in oil prices on top of the incredible expansion of timber exports has come perilously close to sealing the fate of any expansion, or even maintenance at the present level, of traditional exports. Given that total export earnings were running well ahead of planned increases in the import bill and that traditional exports fell from 60 per cent to 20 per cent of total export earnings between 1960 and 1973, only a forceful commitment on the part of the government to mass living standards could have seen the fielding of extension workers, land and road developers, new marketing outlets and the extension of numerous small credits necessary for greater employment in traditional exports.

SMALL-SCALE VERSUS LARGE-SCALE

The arrival of so much foreign investment and its setting the pace of high technology were bound to increase the scale of operations. But given the enormous profits from forestry it is doubtful whether the size of the single huge investments in this industry were necessary to attract foreign investment. Mineral exploration and exploitation was another matter, not only for the scale of research and exploration investment but for the high level of technology required. This was one industry where maintaining modest scale to allow domestic competition would have been self-defeating. But this was certainly not true of forestry, and some of the smaller domestic investments in forestry prove that a great deal more competition from domestic investment could have occurred had foreign investors not been permitted to lay hold of such large forest concessions.

In secondary industry large scale and capital-intensity are strongly correlated. The standardisation of production machinery, the vested interest in rapid obsolescence of former technologies and the (until recently) full employment capacities of countries in which technology and much of the capital originate, present the issue of acceptance of high technology in less developed countries as a 'take it or leave it' ultimatum. The practice of foreigners of obtaining guarantees of no competition to their product also contributes to this technological licence.

In Europe capital costs of creating additional jobs in the most advanced industries may be as high as \$30,000. This makes the Indonesian Domestic Investment Board's quote of about \$5,000 in secondary industry very modest. Even so if half the annual increment to the labour force, that is about 500,000, is to be found jobs in industry at this capital cost, the total annual investment must be \$2·5 billion.

But the protests on the Indonesian side were private rather than official even when they came from government personnel. Official action was slow in coming. Until bank credit was deliberately set aside for smaller indigenous enterprises no concrete measures were taken. By late 1973 McCawley (1973) could still write:

> Despite official statements to the contrary it is difficult to avoid the impression that the government is, for the time being, giving a low priority to the development of small industries.

Since this issue is closely tied to the *pribumi* issue the new credit facilities for small, indigenous entrepreneurs are described later.

DISENCHANTMENT WITH FOREIGN INVESTMENT

Disenchantment with foreign investment had always existed but vocal opposition was better tolerated by the government earlier on. In January 1970 meetings between concerned members of the public and leading economists were held. The meetings were called 'Kita ingin tahu' (we want to know) and they were used to debate the application of economic theory without comprehension of what was occurring in practice. Four years later when the substance of the debate was so obviously true, critics were being imprisoned.

Criticism of foreign investment was far from being confined to the left or to the young. One of the most pro-western of the elder statesmen, Moh. Hatta, a former Vice-President who resigned under Sukarno, disagreed with the extent of foreign investment and its slow utilisation of concessions (Indonesian Raya, 20 March 1970). At the very least investments should be joint ventures, but preferably Indonesians should undertake the projects on loans.

Moslem nationalists were among the most vocal critics of foreign investment. Subchan was calling in 1969 for proper recognition of potential national enterprise and a reduction in the excessive incentives being offered potential foreign investors. He shrewdly pointed out that stabilisation had brought no fundamental opportunities for a strong economy because no structural changes had occurred.

Pre-emption of investment opportunities by foreigners was bound to occur. The bitterness this caused was acute. As Bowring (1973) put it: 'to go out of business is one thing; to be forced out by alien competition quite another.' The economists' obsession with the foreign exchange market, even during a period when the IGGI was obviously committed to shoring up the balance of payments, meant that foreign investors did not even have to ask for equal rights and treatment with national businessmen; they were offered unsolicited privileges.

Even with favoured treatment foreigners were investing only in very quick return investments. One of the effects of this was that Java (outside Jakarta) and some important centres in the outer islands saw little foreign investment. Even the president took up the theme of the maldistribution of foreign investment when he told a working meeting of provincial governors in 1973 that it was a pity 'they (foreign investors) are attracted only to several cities, Jakarta in particular' (Pedoman, 18 May 1973). He added that this would eventually give rise to new problems for Jakarta itself.

After 1969-70 criticisms of foreign investment grew with every year that passed. In January 1973 so prominent a person as the Chairman of the Indonesian Chamber of Commerce and Industry called for foreign investment to be governed by the same regulations and to have only the same facilities as domestic investment (Pedoman, 10 January 1973). He went on to say that without government guidance the flow of foreign investment would not be directed to fields which hold socio-economic advantages to Indonesians.

NEW FOREIGN INVESTMENT REGULATIONS

One of the first significant signs that the government was itself resisting the blandishments of foreign investors was when President Suharto declined to meet a group of 75 big businessmen from the US, Europe and Asia, attending an International Indonesia Round Table in August-September 1972 (Kompas, 1 Sept. 1972). The President was said to have light 'flu', but nobody believed this explanation. In a message sent to the Round Table he assured the participants that the role of foreign investment was not being questioned—only its procedure.

This was not strictly true. Already there had been small steps taken to limit foreign investments. In 1970 import-export activities were closed to foreign companies. Also, tax holidays had been restricted to priority industries. But the biggest restrictions on foreign investors have been the tax on foreign employees and the closure of many industries to foreign investment.

The government was determined to press ahead with the Indonesianisation of employees of foreign companies. In the original Foreign Investment Law Indonesians were to be used wherever possible and to replace foreigners as soon as possible. In April 1974 there were 18,000 licensed foreign workers in the country, 7,000 of them in forestry. Something more pressing was needed. The means to implement this was the licensing system whereby licences are granted for a specific time on the basis of the details of the investment approval. Foreign companies are obliged to pay $100 per month per employee who stays beyond the time limit specified. This tax is paid into the Bank Indonesia account of the Department governing the relevant industry and is supposed to be used to train Indonesians. It constitutes an effective tax on those companies which do not operate successful training programmes for Indonesian replacements. Regulations on time schedules for Indonesianisation are expected to be delivered, industry by industry. In November 1974 those for forestry were issued. Mining was expected to be the next field decreed for.

The closure of industries to foreign investment has come in degrees and it is not clear how definitive, in practice, will be these restrictions. Some industries are temporarily closed or open only after no domestic investors have shown an interest. Others are permanently closed to foreign investment. A certain militancy became apparent by 1972 when the government added seven kinds of industry to a United Nations Industrial Development Organisation list of 32 recommended closures to foreign investment. In early 1972 a large number of import-replacing light manufactured products were forbidden to foreign investment. They ranged from toothpaste, toothbrushes, paint, shoe polish and some food processing to hoes, nails, screws, corrugated cardboard and cycle tyres. After the January 1974 riots there were additional restrictions. They included:

> Chemical and basic industries are still generally open to foreign capital because of the need for large amounts of capital and high technology. But the pharmaceutical industry in Java is to be closed to *all* investment in order to encourage its establishment elsewhere.
>
> Seven types of chemical industry are temporarily closed to foreign capital but open to domestic capital—gas, fertiliser, assembling of fertiliser, insecticide materials, simple rubber goods, cement, calcium carbide (Java only) and aluminium sulphate.
>
> Chemical industries completely closed to foreign capital include: carbonic acid gas (Java and Sulawesi), fertiliser and ammonium sulphate, car and truck tyres, motor cycle tyres, bottles.
>
> Basic industries completely closed to foreign capital include: steel rods for reinforcing concrete, steel pipes, accumulators, dry batteries, galvanised sheet iron, air-conditioner assembling, electric light bulbs, assembling of diesel machinery, aluminium, electric wire, iron and steel smelting, photographic equipment.
>
> Forestry products: priority is to be given to domestic capital, but if domestic capital is not capable, then foreign capital will be permitted.
>
> Estates sub-sector is now a strong priority for domestic capital; except for rice estates.
>
> Domestic capital gets priority rights in the development of coal-mining, but foreign capital is encouraged in the rehabilitation of existing coal mines.

By June 1974, the government had not decided on the role of foreign capital in special construction services, but the field of general construction services for real estate was definitely closed.

If there is a pattern in these restrictions it is that complicated basic industry is still open to foreign investment but that import-replacing assembly lines and lighter industry are at least temporarily closed to it. Also the attempt to move industry to the outer provinces appeared to be directed more to foreign than domestic investment, except in the case of the pharmaceuitcal industry.

Since 1974 there has been a shift in the pattern of investment towards processing industries but individual investments were still made on a very large scale. At the same time the overall decline in applications has disturbed the authorities. The vice-chairman of the Investment Co-ordinating Board, Ir. Suhud, was moved in 1976 to point out that the multinationals were still important because they brought in new technology and expertise as did some smaller foreign investments (Angkatan Bersendjata, 2 August 1976). He did, however, re-iterate intentions to renegotiate tax holidays, interest allowances, and import duty exemptions because of conflicts between foreign and domestic investors in particular sectors.

It is easy to draw the conclusion that official attitudes towards foreign investment were, by 1976, still neither clear nor stable.

All future foreign investment has to be in the form of joint ventures with an indigenous Indonesian partner. But even on this point there is uncertainty. One report (Arndt, 1974) stated that joint ventures could be avoided by foreign capital in special cases, for example 'foot-loose labour-intensive, electronic sub-assembling operations directed to foreign markets'.

THE SPECIAL CASE OF JAPANESE INVESTMENT

It was not only the rapacious style of Japanese investment that led to criticism. Indeed in terms of investment in some small scale enterprises and extending credit to Indonesians, the Japanese were better than other foreign investors. A major source of anxiety was the huge amount of investment coming from this single country and its effect on the degree of monopsonisation of markets for Indonesian exports. Japanese attempts to dominate shipbuilding and to manage the inter-island fleet also led to feelings that Japanese capital was penetrating the Indonesian economy to a dangerous extent.

But there were other commercial practices which caused anger in some circles. For instance, timber arriving in Japan was given a lower quality evaluation, and therefore lower price, than was specified in contracts.

Chapter 5 presented data to show that Japan progressively increased her share of total foreign investment. With the increasing need of Japan to find more sources of raw materials and to export her surplus capital away from high labour cost industries at home there is every reason to believe this trend will increase. Another disturbing feature of Japanese investment is that it is very heavily concentrated in ten giant corporations each spreading into many different industries. In July 1973 the Mitsui Group was reputed to have already invested $160 million in Indonesia, and to be planning to invest a total of $1,000 million by the end of the Second Five Year Plan (*Nusantara,* 24 July 1973). This single corporation would then have invested the equivalent of more than one quarter of all foreign investment approvals between 1967 and August 1974. One highly qualified commentator believes that Japanese investment will amount to $5,200 million by 1980 (Panglaykim, 1973). That weak, undercapitalised Indonesian enterprise should be expected to compete against this onslaught is ludicrous.

Mitsui's warning was widely circulated by the Indonesian press at the time. Concern was expressed that capital of this size might bring in high technology, a low multiplier and would utilise Japanese (instead of Indonesian) banking, shipping and insurance agencies in Indonesia to implement the investments. Although foreign companies are not supposed to trade in Indonesia, the size of the Japanese representative offices can be interpreted in only one way. Mitsui hopes to invest in all sectors, including timber in North Sulawesi, sugar plantations in South Sulawesi, and oil palm plantations elsewhere. However, Japanese investment approvals in Indonesia have declined along with other foreign approvals. From the peak year of 1973, $503 million, they fell to less than $100 million in 1975 (if the $850 million from a Japanese government-banking-private enterprise consortium is seen separately). If Japan's declining interest in Indonesian oil continues, if Japan steps in to finance Chinese technological expansion, and if mass purchasing power in Indonesia fails to grow, predictions of new massive Japanese investment in Indonesia may prove excessive.

The question arises as to why there was no attempt to supervise Japanese investment implementation. As Davies (1974) pointed out:

> The agitation against foreign capital thus lacks not only perspective but has chosen the wrong target. This should be the failure of the Indonesian authorities to regulate the foreigners' activities—to see to it that timber companies do not chop down undersized trees and strip the hillsides of double the amount specified . . . .

It is, of course, easier and certainly more congenial to negotiate new things of vast size than to set up a supervisory and investigatory apparatus which must nag and constantly 'spoil the party'. However, the Indonesian government is aware of the fact that exports of raw materials and fuel to Japan set up mutual dependence and vulnerability, and since October 1973 Indonesia has become conscious of her negotiating strength. Thus the fear of 'one country (Japan), two commodities (timber and oil)' deserves a re-assessment.

Japan has a trading surplus with all other Asian countries, but has a big deficit with Indonesia. As early as 1972 Japan exported $316 million to and imported $637 million from Indonesia—a deficit of over 100 per cent. Japan is now also a much more significant trading partner than either the US or Western Europe. Fifty-one per cent of Indonesian exports went to Japan in 1972, including 70 per cent of timber exports. Since then with the stronger emergence of minerals and maize this reliance on the Japanese market has increased. There is no doubt that Japan is becoming increasingly dependent on Indonesia for raw materials, muted only by the openly admitted desire of Japan to see Indonesia buy back the processed product of her own land, from Japan. The growing mutual dependence that occurred is illustrated in Table 7.1.

TABLE 7.1

Indonesia's Balance of Trade with Japan: 1967–1974 ($ million)

	1967	*1968*	*1969*	*1970*	*1971*	*1972*	*1973*	*1974*
Total imports	649	716	781	1,002	1,174	1,562	2,347	3,906
Imports from Japan	182	159	226	295	390	532	734	1,139
% from Japan	28	22	29	29	33	34	31	29
Total exports	665	731	854	1,161	1,247	1,778	3,211	7,449
Exports to Japan	195	180	256	452	530	902	1,707	3,955
% to Japan	29	25	30	39	42	51	53	53

Source: J. Panglaykim, 'Some Notes on Japan–Indonesia Business Relations: An Indonesian View', *Indonesian Quarterly,* vol. 1, no. 4, 1973.
1972 and 1973: *Indonesian Financial Statistics,* vol. 8, no. 1, and vol. 8, no. 3.

There is one major exception to Indonesia's growing dependence on the Japanese market. In 1973 Japan took 71 per cent of Indonesia's crude oil exports but this declined to 62 per cent in 1974 and 49 per cent in 1975. With the very rapid rate of increase of China's oil exports to Japan likely to continue it is expected that this figure will fall again.

Japan's deficit with Indonesia appears to be enlarging, mainly due to the two commodities constantly under issue—oil and timber.

Products from Japan's heavy industry account disproportionately for the strong growth of imports from Japan.

Japan is achieving today with Indonesia a great deal of the Asian co-prosperity sphere policy for which it went to war 34 years ago. It now has supplies of strategic raw materials and markets for its industrial goods. But because of the vulnerability of the Japanese economic miracle to dislocations in its raw material and fuel supplies Japan's government and business community share an intimate relationship, probably unparalleled in any other non-communist country. The Japanese government provides official credit to the huge corporations on a grand scale. Very long term natural gas deals happen to be negotiated at a time when Indonesia desperately needed rice and so Indonesia gets rice at a reasonable price. Japan goes outside the IGGI to offer credit to Indonesian entrepreneurs who are obviously expected to do business with Japanese firms. And so on. But one reason why the Bank of Japan is so active in overseas investment projects is that Japanese firms distinguish themselves by having low equity and large bank loans, a general cause of irritation to Indonesia's Foreign Investment Board. This is said to facilitate interdependence of the corporation (Panglaykim, 1973a). The Bank of Japan is ready to support a Japanese bank that has overlent. Equity in joint Indonesian-Japanese ventures is financed by bank loans at lower than international market rates. But it is believed that the Japanese half of these ventures gets this subsidy back easily by overpricing of machines and equipment and by underpricing raw materials. Japanese banks are therefore subsidising the profit accumulation of private companies. And of course profits can be shifted between different subsidiaries of the corporation for tax purposes.

In this way Japanese capital has penetrated the Indonesian economy to its great advantage, while at the same time the financial basis of Indonesian entrepreneurs has remained weak.

This theme is taken up in greater detail by, ironically, a deeply involved member of the Japan lobby, Hoemardani (1974), writing in the journal of the Centre for Strategic and International Studies in Jakarta. Hoemardani points out that if 60 per cent of Japan's $55·3 billion trade is controlled by the Big Ten (corporations), then exports from many countries and the income of millions of people in raw material producing countries are determined by the Big Ten.

> When dealing with Japan we are faced not just with the government but also with the managers of the giant corporations who are very dominant in the formulation of every foreign policy move. They are financially stronger than the Japanese government itself. So they are able to pressure the government to make policy decisions which are favourable to them . . .

> Japan is a homogeneous country. The Japanese industries outside Japan will gradually control Japan's foreign policy decisions and these decisions will be based purely on economic considerations while involving the Japanese government in providing political security.

The problem of countering this influence is made more difficult by the atomistic structure of Indonesian business—numerous small and medium enterprises. One solution which has been proposed by a group associated with General Ali Murtopo's Centre for Strategic Studies is the creation of national integrated units across industry, trade and finance. A few Indonesian banks would not be adequate to finance them so that a national financial consortium, with the active participation of the foreign exchange banks would be required. This would bring in the international financial consortiums and the international money market.

This idea of national integrated units—providing the whole with economics of scale and each with externalities and shared risk with the others—occurs in the writing of another Indonesian on the *pribumi* issue and the need for an indigenous capital-owning class, and therefore it is taken up again later in this chapter.

CORRUPTION

At once, the wrong perspective on corruption is gained if it is associated with developing countries only after independence. East Indies companies of both Dutch and British origin suffered gross corruption by their own European servants and when the rate of profit was declining this corruption hastened their demise. The Dutch in Indonesia used the local indigenous aristocracy as levy collectors, never paying them adequate salaries in the full knowledge that these collectors lived well by the *ad hoc* execution of their official duties. Even so the extent of corruption in the late colonial period was too little to compare with what happened after independence. Independence introduced a new class of practitioners—civil servants who could act as brokers over import and other licences. But widespread as corruption was during Sukarno's time, it could not match the grand larceny that has occurred since 1966 with the massive inflow of aid and foreign investment. Moreover as Mackie (1970) has pointed out the checking of inflation, the regulation of administrative procedures and the improvement of conditions in the civil service make corruption less compelling. Also, in Sukarno's time there were other more serious economic problems, but recently corruption in high places has become a main burning issue.

But the magic figure of 30 per cent, sometimes of the IGGI's aid and sometimes of the GNP itself, appears as the most popular estimate of the share that regularly disappears into private pockets.

Accurate or not, nobody is in doubt that the true amount is not a marginal surplus but a figure that would make an extremely handsome contribution to national investment. The fact that these diverted funds are not properly entered into national accounts must cast suspicion on the accuracy of a whole range of statistics from project investment to rice production.

In 1970 the Commission of Four investigated organs such as the Rice Procurement Agency (BULOG) and Pertamina. Faces changed sometimes, 'escape-proof' nets were cast, but the game went on unabated. In August 1970 President Suharto saw the solution to corruption in the success of the Five Year Plan. In 1974-5 it had to be said that either the Plan was far from a success or the President presumed wrongly. Suharto was to lead the campaign against corruption personally and he issued a decree requiring the registration of the private wealth of all senior government officials. But the varied hyperboles of the Indonesian press indicated only too clearly that the Palace stood too close to the fire for effective action to be taken.

The odd official statement would suggest that corruption is on the scale of the tropical equivalent of the gift of a fur coat. 'It is not necessary to give presents or gifts to officials of the Customs and Excise apparatus, they only make for a corrupt and bad mentality', said Director-General of Customs and Excise, Slamet Danusudirdjo, at his swearing-in (Sinar Harapan, 27 May 1972).

But it is not just bad mentalities and large subventions from national income and investment that are brought about by corruption. Corruption also erodes any rational allocation of resources there might be. Economic theory is an aid to some efficient allocation of resources within given distributions of wealth and income. If those distributions are socially unjust, economic theory will reinforce that injustice. But corruption on top of unequal distribution of wealth and income is likely to make things much more unjust. Ecological damage, dangerous methods in construction, private profit running violently contrary to social profit, short-term gains versus long-term momentum of expansion, choice of industry, price-fixing to weaken labour's return even more—all these are encouraged by corruption.

The Commission of Four, for instance, found Pertamina guilty of wasting natural gas, of price-fixing and of under-invoicing, of investing profits abroad, as well as of not paying taxes to the national treasury. In short the oil industry was conducting its business without any relation to the rest of the prevailing economy.

The Japanese apparently bribe without hesitation; or they simply pass over what is requested of them knowing they can always recoup on pricing of goods. 'When asked to under-invoice by an Indonesian importer, most (Japanese) do so without blinking an eye' (Iskandar, 1972a).

Whether Europeans find it more distasteful or too risky is not known, but the impression from conversations with foreign businessmen would suggest that business is not possible in Indonesia without bribes.

It is frequently said that corruption merely greases the wheels of commerce and helps to pay the civil service wage bill. Were it such a well-spent subsidy to the national budget it could be written off as one form of foreign aid. But it is used to buy the silence and blindness of politicians and civil servants when malpractices are cheating the national treasury. It also has its influence on the allocation of resources via the degree of competition.

To some extent the issue of corruption is driving a wedge between the generations. The public campaign against corruption has always been led in Indonesia by the youth. The January 1974 demonstrations included criticism levelled at the corrupt military-bureaucrats, together with their Chinese *cukongs,* amongst their targets. It may be that the young have not yet been offered the chance to step aboard the gravy train. But it is also true that they have not had as much time to grow cynical as their parents; and if there is one thing that is poison to an anti-corruption drive it is cynicism. The press will periodically be suspended and six-year sentences will be slapped on student leaders. But every young Indonesian will have his or her searing first encounter with corruption and collective outrage will foregather again.

THE CHINESE-PRIBUMI (INDIGENOUS INDONESIAN) ISSUE

Although the Chinese community represents no more than 3 per cent of the population it dominates the financial sector outside agriculture. From the end of the nineteenth century the Chinese were granted nearly total economic freedom and in return they acted in an intermediary role for the Dutch. During the fifties newly independent Indonesia attempted to make inroads into the economic power of the Chinese by granting *benteng* (indigenous) importers and exporters exclusive privileges, but this gave rise to partnerships known as *Ali-Baba,* whereby an Indonesian was the front for a Chinese financier. President Sukarno was mindful of the effect of anti-Chinese riots on human life as well as on the economy and awarded the state's protection to the Chinese. However, for some years after October 1965 anti-Chinese feeling gave way to murderous violence. In 1967 there was a campaign to drastically limit the fields in which the Chinese could operate and this was temporarily successful.

But the power and influence of the Chinese has been enhanced, and the practice of Chinese acting as brokers for top Indonesians greatly extended, under the influence of aid and private capital inflows. If diverted aid were to be re-invested for family fortunes the advice of the Chinese was sought since it was easily the best in the country. Foreign investors wished to have able and experienced national partners and so inevitably chose Chinese ones. A Japanese embassy official admitted in 1974 that in 70 per cent of 138 joint ventures, the Indonesian partners of Japanese investors were local Chinese (Starnar, 1974).

Even the state banks were reputed to favour Chinese borrowers (Warta Harian, 6 Nov. 1969), although this may have been on no other grounds than that they met banking credit-worthiness requirements more often. The slow expansion of state bank credit was seen by other Indonesians as encouraging Chinese in their role as *cukongs,* or as financial bankers operating as silent partners to generals and politicians behind the scenes.

The advance of the Chinese relative to the *pribumi* group was causing frustration and one fear expressed was that children of *pribumi* businessmen, seeing what was happening to their fathers, would turn their ambitions away from the business world. The *benteng* method of the fifties, granting individual indigenous businessmen special privileges, was generally rejected. In its place something like group solidarity and gains from scale were seen to be possible with syndicates or with the large integrated units which were promoted in academic and journalistic literature in 1974.

Press editorials persistently castigated national leaders for using the Chinese as their own financial backers and in return granting them protection and privileges. One newspaper (*Nusantara,* 18 Feb. 1971) put it like this:

> We have never rejected the mobilisation of funds and forces to be found in this Indonesia of ours, whether it is the forcign capital that has been operating here for a long time, or that newly coming here in the frame of the Foreign Investments Law, or the investment of capital created in Indonesia from the side of what is called domestic capital. What we object to, is what is implied in the definition of the 'cukong' financial backer, of which we gave as a typical example that the group of Chinese nationals need the protection of the Indonesian government's bureaucracy and administration . . . Similarly with the participation of some high officials, or the family of high officials and the wives of certain of them, in commercial undertakings with certain Chinese financial backers . . . Those in charge of this daily are good friends and old acquaintances of President Soeharto personally. We have made efforts to communicate with him directly, but, unfortunately, ever since this paper was republished in March 1967, almost four years ago, President Soeharto has not had time

to hold consultations, as was done by the former government of President Sukarno.

Moreover, the nature of the new investments and of the exogenous economy was leaving indigenous businessmen more out in the cold than they had ever been.

> The nature of the growth of our economy in recent times is not the same as what took place in the past . . . Other parties, who have sufficient capital, have been able to adapt themselves quickly, and have caused the position of the native businessmen to be increasingly squeezed. (Angkatan Bersendjata, 12 Feb. 1971).

The President, whose close relations with Chinese big businessmen have often been hinted at in the press, replied along the lines that not utilising Chinese capital would be a loss to the country, and at any rate the government would be able to buy non-*pribumi* shares in companies when national capital was great enough (Angkatan Bersendjata, 18 Feb. 1971). As with oil and timber exploitation and the introduction of foreign investment there is the assumption that the flow of income and goods (following from a bonanza of alien-controlled capital) will inevitably come under social control and that at some future date, when the postponed rendezvous with poverty and unemployment is finally made, 'the government' will have the capacity and the willingness to re-order economic distribution.

But another problem was emerging by 1973. Bank credit granted to *cukongs* a couple of years previously had not been returned and banks were having difficulty calling it in. There can be no doubt in anybody's mind that the Chinese would only dare to create such a situation if they were sure of their protection by influential people. One newspaper (*Nusantara,* 9 Feb. 1973) reported in February 1973:

> Amongst officials of the Bank of Indonesia a situation of mutual accusations has arisen as to who must be responsible for these credits to the 'cukong' brokers. Middle-ranking officials have stated definitely that they are not prepared to take the responsibility, because they are only the technical implementers.

Worse, since the debtors were arguing that their excuse was the disadvantageous market and consequential losses, they were granted more credits.

But the axis between the generals and the *cukongs* has been seen in another light.

> Without the Chinese and the generals, the field would be left to the foreigners. And that situation might be worse than the existing setup. (Bowring, 1973)

The chief solution to the *pribumi* issue was to be a leap-frogging over the problem of encouraging embryonic *pribumi* entrepreneurship to facilitating *pribumi* purchase of shares in established enterprises. This was confusing the exercise of commercial skills with ownership of capital. It means that anyone, with or without business acumen, can become an established businessperson overnight.

Early in 1972 Suharto announced that company shares of non-*pribumi* domestic and foreign investments would have to be part-sold to native private businessmen. The move was explained by Ali Murtopo as not constituting an attempt at nationalisation, nor a move to 'free fight liberalism'. *Pribumi* shares in companies would simply eliminate ethnic inequalities in trade and industry (Berita Yudha, 8 April 1972).

In January 1974 new regulations on share ownership and definitions of Indonesian companies were announced. They were designed to hasten the process of creating a balance between foreign, *pribumi* and non-*pribumi* capital ownership, but to act only as principles of policy. The balancing of shares between foreign and Indonesian partners of joint enterprises was to be speeded up to achieve 51 per cent ownership by Indonesians. In November 1974 it was announced that this shareout had to be achieved within 10 years of an investment permit being approved. Where the joint enterprise was between foreign and non-*pribumi* partners the non-*pribumi* Indonesian must then see to it that 50 per cent of the latter should be *pribumi*-owned as soon as possible via purchases on the Stock Exchange. What this signifies is that enterprises could end up with one large foreign shareholder and a large number of Indonesian shareholders. Likely problems of this ownership structure have not been seriously discussed, but it is bound to cause dissension over dividends and internal re-financing.

In new joint ventures with foreign capital 51 per cent of shares must immediately be owned by a *pribumi* firm. The definition of a *pribumi* firm is 75 per cent *pribumi* ownership of shares or 50 per cent *pribumi* ownership plus *pribumi* management. A non-*pribumi* domestic business which has paid up its credit must then sell its shares until at least 50 per cent is in *pribumi* hands. (This guideline is not likely to act as an incentive to return credit to banks!) This could mean 25·5 per cent (51 per cent of 50 per cent) *pribumi*-capital shares, since the Chinese can still be active in '*pribumi* firms'. Even so this cannot be at all popular with foreign investors and might well prove to be quite untenable.

The most likely result of this share division will be that *pribumi* who have accumulated funds through their influential positions will become owners of shares and that the ownership of the country's capital will be concentrated in the hands of the ruling clique. It will be a formalisation of the alliance between the *pribumi* elite and their Chinese *cukongs,* embedded in an institution such as a stock exchange which simulates a situation of economic development. The ultimate of a cargo cult! The protestations of those who called for *pribumi* entrepreneurship and business knowledge will have been ignored.

There will be exceptions to this but they will be in a category of business distinguished by small size. In April 1973, sixty-five per cent of medium-term investment credits had been successfully directed to small businesses. But in November small firms were granted new privileges: they could apply for medium-term credits of up to Rupiah 5 million plus another Rupiah 5 million for working capital. The requirement of 25 per cent self-financing could also be reduced. Since January 1974 medium-term bank investment credits were to be exclusively for *pribumi* businesses. The firm maintenance of this policy and the size of the effective demand for credit from small enterprises are difficult to predict.

DEVELOPMENT OF A CAPITAL MARKET

Chronic inflation and the lack of expansion of the industrial base led to the decline of the stock exchange in the early fifties. After 1966 there was a more determined and thorough-going approach to a new capital market. Plans were pushed ahead in 1970. A starter was Bank Indonesia Certificates to be issued every month, to be sold to the public and to companies at 96¼ per cent of their nominal value. They could be redeemed at 100 per cent of their value three months later. Thus a profit of 3½ per cent was to be made in three months; or 14 per cent a year. They were similar to the highly popular fixed deposits of varying time spans. But unlike bank deposits they could be sold freely by their holders. By 1971 these Bank Indonesian Certificates were being described in terms of 'mopping up hot money' since they were sold to government and to private banks and presumably thence to the public. They became government implements in the way that treasury bills are, but were not as popular as bank deposits.

The development of the Stock Exchange was to help modernise business practices and to provide more competition. In a developed industrial economy in which there is already an established degree of competition this would be plausible. But in the case of Indonesia with economic and financial dualisms operating and where the Stock Exchange was to serve the all-important function of an exchange of existing capital (and capacity) between ethnic groups, goals of modernising business practice and increasing competition were unrealistic. The assumption of more widespread public ownership of shares has already been questioned.

Early public interest in the Stock Exchange in Indonesia was weak in spite of foreign bonds and foreign share certificates being traded there. Much of the cause of this was the greater returns to bank time deposits.

Against the background of a great deal of foreign investment and of high bank deposit rates attracting savings, the development of the Stock Exchange is an interesting, though unconcluded story. In the more recent light of the proposed speedy transfer of shares in joint ventures it would be in the interests of foreign investors to see the development of a Stock Exchange, which would make that transfer more orderly and might provide guarantees against obligatory giveaway prices.

But the government seems to have won little active cooperation from the foreign merchant banks to establish it, and by mid-1975 there had been no real progress made. The eight merchant banks included in the plan for a Stock Exchange had made only token gestures towards facilitating the development of share issues of Indonesian companies, claiming that the high subsidised savings deposit rates were an obstacle to inducing savers to buy shares (Coggin, 1975c). Deposit earnings were neither risky nor taxed. The idea of shareholders interfering in company policy was also found to be an unwelcome innovation to national entrepreneurs who had no experience of going public before. By mid-1975 not a single Indonesian company had elected to become a public company.

The creation of a Stock Exchange is also a far cry from the creation of a *pribumi* entrepreneurial group. It can even be expected that some bank credit will be passed to the select few to help them buy paper assets; that is, credit will be used to subsidise a privileged shareholding class.

A serious issue arises from this. If an unproductive *pribumi* elite is to own shares in large-scale technologically advanced enterprises while small-scale *pribumi* businesses arise from exclusive bank credits, will there emerge a conflict between the interests of these dual sectors controlled by two separate groups of *pribumi* capital-owners? In the event of a world recession? In the event of overproduction?

In general, against a financially stable background a Stock Exchange in a developing country should be able to establish institutional links with foreign capital markets, and these links should increase the quantity of fixed capital in Indonesian firms by making it more possible to gain subscribers to additional issues. In particular, it has been suggested that the international capital market would be a source of funds for national integrated units each incorporating slices from differing sectors of the economy. The model is clearly the Japanese giant corporations. Because of the units' theoretical possibilities they are discussed briefly here.

In his proposal Joesoef (1974) begins by complaining that technology has not changed the modes of thinking of the Indonesian intelligentsia and that Indonesia cannot afford to go on like this because it lives in a world rapidly gaining in technological and business knowledge.

> This world economy is where the action is, and any nation that doesn't expend any effort to get a piece of that action or, in other words, that isolates and contains itself in autarky, is surely writing a prescription for its own economic decadence.

Setting aside the fact that China's experience compared with that of South East Asian countries stands this statement on its head, the words chosen by Joesoef reveal quite clearly that western economic growth is what must be had at all costs and that economic nationalists only question who is running the show. Since 'time is short' all the preparations to cope with foreign investment cannot be made and the multinational corporations must be let in. But to counter their influence Joesoef advocates 'national integrated units', combining government bureaucrats, technocrats and businessmen to present a countervailing 'power entity'. These NIUs would include separate small businesses covering the fields of industry, management, commerce and finance— national financial consortiums.

It would appear from Joesoef's article that the sole *raison d'être* of this amalgam is that large size attracts international money, and that shortage of investment capital is what is holding up national business. It is not stated whether size is to lower costs through integrated planning within the units or through external economies. Nor is it explained how this amalgamation overcomes basic entrepreneurial inexperience. Its contribution to an internal economic dynamic or to employment and income generation is ignored. Regrettably there seems to be no planned difference between the goals of the foreign multinationals and the proposed NIUs. Thus the idea of the NIUs is that there is to be more of the same, but this time in indigenous, inexperienced hands.

CONCLUSION

Criticisms of the strategy of development since 1966 included specific resentments and fears, on the one hand, and disagreement with resource allocation, on the other. The former covered rivalry between indigenous entrepreneurs and foreign and Chinese national investors as well as trepidation at the penetration of Japanese capital. The latter pointed to the failure of advanced technology (often forced by large scale) to generate mass employment and income, the neglect of traditional sources of employment and income and the reliance on a few not easily renewable resources.

In general the former criticisms have been articulated more successfully and, because their accommodation would support the interests of the indigenous middle class, have been partly met. But the latter criticisms have not evoked any concessions. The transfer of existing shares to indigenous operators, either privately or through the Stock Exchange, will make no difference to technology, to the wages bill, etc. There has been no discussion in the literature about how raising new capital on the Stock Exchange will bring in a new technology or new geographical spread. The small-scale investment credits granted by state banks will invariably finance operations which for one reason or another large-scale joint ventures bypassed. There can be little pretence that these credits enable *pribumi* to compete with others for the same opportunities.

The partiality of the remedial action springs from an unwillingness to oblige all investment to fit in with a pre-determined plan to develop the mass-based economy and to exploit natural resources in the service of maximising livelihoods for the poor. The opposition of national businessmen to the government's favouring of foreign and Chinese investment is well founded, but this is essentially a quarrel between segments of the top stratum of Indonesian society. That the nationally-owned 'national integrated units' are designed to live better in a world of high technology and business knowledge does not bode well for the labouring classes, or for those who earn their living as petty traders. For these latter people it offers nothing different from foreign investment practices. Were these units to be designed within a framework of technological and geographical constraint there might be something truly beneficial about them.

Had there been such an ideology of development the inflow of capital could have taken different forms. Reduced to its essentials foreign investment is a capital loan to the country—in this case a 30 year loan. Profits were large enough for all kinds of arrangements to be imposed on foreign investors, given administrative competence and rationality, without driving them away. Was it not possible to persuade Japanese investors, for instance, to fell trees under contract to the Ministry of Agriculture or to a state company, and to offer investment credits to local entrepreneurs or to collectives of workers to establish wood processing plants? To turn away foreign investors for clearly delineated reasons is not the same as driving away all international development capital.

The apparent contradictions in the criticisms of the government made by students and national businessmen arise because of the failure to separate clearly the national chauvinistic defence of an economic minority and the real interests of the majority.

It must be concluded that nothing fundamental has been done to alleviate the major weaknesses of the post-1966 course of development.

Chapter 8

Conclusion

SUCCESSES AND CONTRADICTIONS OF THE CRISIS STRATEGY

The architects of the post–1965 economic strategy are likely to defend their policies by pointing out that stabilisation and rehabilitation were prerequisites for any further development and that the first Five Year Plan was, after all, only the first of several intended plans whose goals would shift progressively towards social justice and an independent economy. They could call upon official statements that foreign investment was merely to supplement domestic enterprise and to accelerate development. They could certainly point to the power of Pertamina over foreign oil companies and to the new restrictions and capital-sharing requirements imposed on foreign companies. They could deliver the *coup de grace:* that from a position in 1965 when debt servicing was about to swallow nearly all export earnings, debt repayments could comprise only five per cent of net oil earnings in the near future.

The realisation of the First Five Year Plan, 1969–1974, was a mixed performance. The most notable characteristics are described in Table 8.1 to provide a basis for comments on the post–1965 strategy. As we have already seen oil palm was the only traditional export crop which showed clear success, but in relation to expectations it was only slightly above the target. After enormous effort in Bimas programmes rice appeared almost to make the target. The failure of other crops exposed the basic weakness of the mass economy: neglect of infrastructure and failure of incentives. Timber output has, of course, wildly exceeded expectations. Crude oil has done much better than expected and is more outstanding in this respect than tin and bauxite. But there are no surprises here.

In the industrial sector only the textile target was achieved. Cement, fertiliser (urea), and paper outputs were well behind targets.

Although the industrial items here have not indicated success in this sector there has been development in many other industries not specified in the Plan outline. Their progress is recorded in Table 8.2 The greatest expansion (or successful entry) was in the non-essential,

TABLE 8.1
Planned and Realised Production: 1969/70 and 1973/4

	Planned			Realised	
	1969/70	1973/74	Percentage increase	1969	1973
AGRICULTURE					
Rice (million tons)	10.52	15.42	46.5	12.2	14.5
Oil palm—oil (1000 tons)	172	275	59.8	189	295
—kernals (1000 tons)	41	68	65.8	42	67
Sugar (estate) (1000 tons)	677	907	33.9	723	820
Copra (million tons)	1.1	1.5	36.5	1.2	1.2
Maize (million tons)	3.37	4.23	25.5	2.29	2.90
Pulses (million tons)	0.95	1.40	47.3	0.66	0.73
INDUSTRY					
Textiles (million metres)	450	900	100.0	500	927
Fertilizer (N) (1000 tons)	46.5	403.5	767.0	35.4	118.7
Cement (1000 tons)	600	1,650	175.0	541	818
Paper (1000 tons)	16	166	941.0	18	47
MINING					*1973/74*
Crude oil (million barrels)	293	440	50.1	271	521
Tin (million tons)	16	19	19.9	17	22.7
Bauxite (1000 tons)	1,000	1,200	20.0	927	1,193

Sources: K. D. Thomas and J. Panglaykim, *op. cit.; Indonesian Financial Statistics,* vol. 7, no. 11, November 1974; *Monthly Economic Letter,* First National City Bank, Jakarta, August 1974 (quoting Department of Industry, Jakarta); *Bulletin of Indonesian Economic Studies,* vol. 10, no. 2, July 1974.

TABLE 8.2
Increases in Production of Selected Industrial Products over the First Five Year Plan

Production of:	*1969*	*1973*
assembled cars (units)	—	36,000
assembled motor cycles (units)	—	149,762
cigarettes (million units)	10.7	30.2
glass/bottles (1000 units)	12.3	37.2
radio sets (1000 units)	363.5	900
TV sets (1000 units)	4.5	60.0
car tyres (1000 units)	377.4	1,046.9
motor cycle tyres (1000 units)	—	304.5
toothpaste (1000 units)	15,000	31,800
coconut oil (1000 tons)	541.3	818.1
detergent soap (1000 tons)	4.5	100.0
frying oil (1000 tons)	4.0	6.6
washing soap (1000 tons)	132.6	110.6
weaving yarn (1000 bales)	182.0	316.2

Source: *Monthly Economic Letter,* First National City Bank, Jakarta, August 1974, quoting Department of Industry, Jakarta.

consumer durable category of product. Frying oil and washing soap, on the other hand, showed relatively poor performances.

As has already been pointed out it was in the field of traditional exports that targets were least realised. Table 8.3 gives data on export targets, divided simply into Group A strong exports (rubber, tin, copra, coffee, tea, tobacco and palm oil) and Group B (all other items, *then* including timber).

The realised sub-total of non-oil exports had exceeded its target by 1970–1 and then continued to draw away from targets increasingly, but until 1973–4 this was only due to the leap in Group B exports, or more specifically the unexpected phenomenon of timber exports. The success of Group A exports in 1970 was also due to temporary rises in the price of rubber and palm oil. The sudden spurt of Group A exports in 1973 was due to a 75 per cent increase in the rubber price and strong price increases for all the other commodities. Since then the rubber price has been approximately halved and the price of tin has fallen 25 per cent. Thus the last recorded figure for Group A exports cannot be seen as part of the secular trend. On the evidence of

TABLE 8.3

Planned and Realised Exports during the First Five Year Plan ($ million)

	1969/70	*1970/71*	*1971/2*	*1972/3*	*1973/4*
PLANNED					
Group A	447	460	474	484	503
Group B	148	166	192	230	297
Sub-total	595	626	666	714	800
Net oil	77	149	118	103	124
Total	672	775	784	817	924
REALISED	*1969*	*1970*	*1971*	*1972*	*1973*
Group A	*394*	*489*	*449*	*441*	*712*
(of which rubber)	221	260	222	196	395
Group B	*73*	*172*	*291*	*414*	*847*
(of which timber)	26	101	169	231	583
Sub-total	467	661	740	855	1559
	1969/70	*1970/71*	*1971/2*	*1972/3*	*1973/4*
Net oil	92	135	204	399	641
Total (approximate)	559	796	944	1254	2200

Sources: K. D. Thomas and J. Panglaykim, *op. cit.*; *Bulletin of Indonesian Economic Studies*, vol. 8, no. 2, July 1972; vol. 10, no. 1, March 1974; vol. 10, no. 2, July 1974; *Monthly Economic Letter*, First National City Bank, Jakarta, October 1974. These data are generally greater (sometimes considerably) than those of the *Indonesian Financial Statistics*, Central Bureau of Statistics. They are chosen for that reason.

this table traditional exports failed to reach Plan targets. But the correctness of the post-1965 strategy can only be judged in relation to the past extending back perhaps to colonial days but certainly referring to the sources of mass livelihoods of the Sukarno period. Continuity in the mass-based economy was bound to be affected by the phasing and nature of stabilisation, rehabilitation and expansion, and it has to be accepted that the policy measures behind these three stages could pull in opposite directions with negative effects being carried over into the long term. Furthermore it cannot be stressed too much that the health of the economy (ultimately hardness of the currency) and the health of the people need bear no relation to each other in a free enterprise economy such as Indonesia's. We could say more: that when an economy bears certain characteristics (such as overseas markets for unprocessed products of new growth industries and capital-deepening investment) that the health of the economy is positively enhanced by the demise of parts of the population. As it happened the highly discriminatory rehabilitation policies allowed foreign investment to move in with a highly capital-intensive industrial technology and with other investments which forced export-oriented raw material extraction. What Indonesia required for long-term development was a pattern of resource exploitation which maximised value added from the use of labour. What happened was quite the opposite.

It has been seen that the financial crisis of 1965 was not felt uniformly in all sectors. Smallholders' export crops did not noticeably suffer from inflation until around 1963 and estate exports declined largely because of political and management problems. There was a serious problem in smallholder's export crops but it was a longer term problem relating to old perennials, low quality output and the decline of extension services. Staple food production directed at the domestic market was hampered by scarcity of land where there was available labour and scarcity of labour where there was new land—a problem of demographic imbalance.

But it was in the secondary industrial sector that the full force of the financial crisis was felt as foreign exchange for imported raw materials dried up and credit was restricted.

The chosen path of price stabilisation had concentrated on external supplies of badly needed consumer products and encouraging traditional primary exports through foreign exchange bonuses. The effect of these priority goods was that domestic secondary enterprise was allowed to languish in a worsening recession.

The management of the foreign exchange market in the first years after 1965 was, on the whole, highly skilled. Though its terms of reference have been questioned in this study, within those terms it was a success. The periodic blunders were quickly redressed. There were factors which made its management particularly easy: it was one single market that could be supervised in Jakarta; its operators were roughly of the same class as the economic advisers; it was agreed that this market's rehabilitation should be promoted regardless of the consequences in other sectors; and, of course, it had the backing of increasing flows of aid. Perhaps most important of all, it was a market which resembled corresponding markets in developed countries and was therefore amenable to the western training of Indonesian economists.

Thus the exercise of stabilisation, as delineated by the government, was essentially the repair of a particular machine part with which the workmen were familiar. It was also the repair of one machine part to the exclusion of others with which the economists were unfamiliar, and worse, towards which they frequently exhibited disdain. Providing incentives to exporters was one thing. Obliging manufacturers to compete with imports at such a time was another. The neglect of the manufacturing sector and its slow recovery from a protracted liquidity crisis while foreign investment was being approved exposed the degree of partiality in the stabilisation and rehabilitation policies.

But no stabilisation could have taken place without massive aid, and it was the conflict between the theory and the reality of the role of aid that gave rise to some of the contradictions in the stabilisation and rehabilitation processes.

What was behind the theory of a massive aid programme in a short period to overcome underdevelopment? Chapter 3 referred to the antibiotic theory of pitting everything against under-development before it had a chance to gain immunity to the remedy. Or, as Chenery put it, 'the most effective way to get there (at a given growth rate or per capita income level) is to grow as fast as possible.' This, however, was only part of the new aid approach, the other being the new emphasis on programme aid (raw materials, spares, etc.) to keep *existing* capacity utilised. Chenery has perhaps exaggerated the case for programme aid (Tinbergen, Chenery *et al.*, 1967). He has pointed out that whereas donor countries have argued low capital absorptive capacity of developing countries to justify low amounts of aid, the problem has really been that aid has not been in the form in which it was needed. In the past donors set up their individual projects unrelated to each other, and the consequence of this has been that investment priorities of the recipient countries have been distorted. Moreover, the history of these aid projects has been that the projects have not been efficiently used for want of foreign exchange to import raw materials. 'So the bottleneck which the donors claim to see— the limited absorptive capacity—is one of our own making.'

This was the new theory on aid with its emphasis on priming existing pumps and establishing related priorities amongst new projects.

However, the reality for Indonesia was somewhat different. Programme aid included vast quantities of consumer goods imports. Rice was imported on aid instead of fertilisers and pesticides, contrary to Chenery's belief that it should be spent on production inputs. Cloth was imported on aid while *existing* textile capacity was standing idle for lack of cotton and yarn. When yarn was imported on programme aid it was left rotting in the godowns because of the liquidity crisis in productive enterprises. This exposed a major contradiction in the aid-stabilisation strategy. If aid would only be granted if the government put the brakes on credit how was programme aid for raw materials to be effective?

On the issue of the project aid absorptive capacity, there is one area in which the argument of limited capital absorptive capacity is resoundingly justified, and that is in the poor availability of national skills. Especially in transportation, roadbuilding and public engineering works imported skills are necessary. Of course these could be regarded as commodities and so included in programme aid but they are popularly regarded as being attached to project aid.

One observer (Anon, *Far Eastern Economic Review,* vol. 82, no. 51) wrote in 1973 on the efficacy of capital inflows:

> The government's policy on borrowing and on private capital inflow has been based on the theory that the more now, and the quicker economic development, the less the need in future. However, in view of the rather low rate of efficiency in the use of funds this policy has its limits. Perhaps the main barrier to efficient use of resources is the lack of skills at almost all levels; this will take time to cure, regardless of expenditure.

One can further question Chenery's assumption that a low capital absorptive capacity is just due to bad, or unintegrated, planning by pointing out that national entrepreneurs have preferred placing their liquid assets in national savings or bank fixed deposits rather than investing them in productive capacity. Presumably their anticipated profit rates were less than the proffered interest rates of the public banking sector. It could be rejoined, of course, that those interest rates were too high, but the government clearly did not consider them too high for the purposes of maintaining monetary stabilisation as demanded by its foreign creditors. While this contradiction in aid-for-stabilisation policies remains, project aid (for the private sector at least) must be viewed as having a limited absorptive capacity.

There is one well-known case of programme aid creating conflicts with national production incentives, and that is food aid. Public Law 480 of the USA provides surplus agricultural commodities in exchange for payment in local currency. Glassburner (1969) has argued that PL 480 rice, used for public works programmes and rice rations to the government sector, has acted as a disincentive to domestic rice output. He believes that PL 480 rice has made it more difficult to rationalise prices in the rice sector so that adequate stocks can be built. The rice intensification programme was possible because of favourable cost-benefit ratios offered farmers, but if aid in the form of rice lowers the rice price then rice production inputs have to be subsidised to maintain these ratios. Glassburner believes that incentives to farmers should be held supreme. Since greater rice production is anti-inflationary, incentives to farmers must be a priority of any stabilisation or rehabilitation policy.

There are general questions of whether aid is inflationary when it involves the release of counterpart funds. In this case the counterpart funds, obtained from the sale of programme aid, drew liquidity from the economy (largely the commercial sector) and were deposited as revenue in the budget. As a result the budget deficit in 1967 was only six per cent of total expenditure. Of course, state bank credit was more profitable for importing consumer goods than for importing raw materials and one can question whether the chosen set of national interest rates provided the most appropriate means of reducing inflation, but nobody can doubt that the government was mindful of the inflationary possibilities of counterpart funds. The more serious contradictions of foreign aid lay in its uneven effect on different sectors and, above all, in its failure to revive national secondary industry before the entry of new foreign investment.

The Foreign Investment Law was passed in early 1967 at a time when the recession in some parts of industry was even worsening, and was still felt acutely in all other parts. The advanced technology, backed by greater capital resources than Indonesian entrepreneurs had a hope of mustering, was bound to create severe competition for existing national enterprises. It is impossible to conclude that the intention of the government, that foreign investment was to supplement domestic investment and to undertake ventures which domestic entrepreneurs could not through lack of skills, was realised in secondary industry. In the textile industry, in particular, it would be farcical to suggest that intentions were realised.

The only clear bonus that came with foreign investment was the assistance it rendered the balance of payments, first with capital inflows and then with export earnings from the primary producing sectors of oil, timber and minerals. But the relationship between the health of the balance of payments and the health of the people is uncertain. Relatively little of the foreign investment was where poverty was concentrated; hardly any was seen in rural Java. In urban Java the capital-intensity of investment reduced its impact as it did also when new capacity displaced existing capacity. It has already been seen from a selection of secondary production statistics that the fastest expansion was generally in non-essentials. Thus the impact of foreign investment could hardly be said to have done anything for a basic needs approach to development, from either the employment or product viewpoint.

One of the arguments that has been made in defence of the advanced technology that foreign investment brings in is that it raises the quality of the product and also standardises it. 'The interests of the consumers simply boil down to the question of price and quality.' (Swasono, 1973). They emphatically do not, and anybody who is concerned with eradicating poverty will soon realise this. Most consumers are people who have to find a living from poorly paid employment and they can only judge whether a price is high or low in relation to their opportunities to earn income. To see the problem only as one of price and quality is to see it only from the supply side and to ignore effective demand and the employment creation it depends upon.

National entrepreneurs face another contradiction emanating from policies. In its attempts to bring savings and other sources of liquidity into the official banking system the government has fixed deposit interest rates at a very high level and, for deposits of longer than 12 months, higher than the cost of borrowing. In an economy where private investment is undertaken from internal re-financing or from bank credit instead of from share issues, entrepreneurs with liquid assets may well have preferred to invest in bank savings deposits rather than in productive capacity with an uncertain rate of profitability. This is likely to be especially true of small indigenous entrepreneurs who need a great deal of bank credit for long-term investment. Thus the high deposit rate policy is undermining those credit policies directed at the indigenisation of new investment.

The policy of indigenising foreign investment and the joint ventures is not really a substitute for a small (indigenous) investors' credit policy, because the former is unlikely to benefit the non-entrepreneurial military and bureaucratic classes who have fraternised closely with the expatriate groups and are frequently financed by Chinese businessmen. The painfully slow progress of the Stock Exchange means that it will be a long time before a wide range of Indonesian shareholders, drawn from many occupational and social classes, will emerge. Instead it can be expected that the indigenisation of enterprises based on foreign capital will be a closed shop affair involving political patronage and sources of wealth arising from corruption. The reality of the indigenisation programme is likely to be very far from its professed intentions. The foreign merchant banks which have been accused of dragging their feet on the creation of a Stock Exchange point that few Indonesian firms wish to raise capital by issuing public shares. This may be a correct assessment, but until such a practice becomes common the indigenisation programme will be half-hearted and partial. In addition, the state banking sustem will be obliged to bear a monetary burden which in other countries is shared among a range of financial institutions. While such a situation would be welcomed by a committed socialist government, it has to be pointed out that in the case of Indonesia, with a government which is massively corrupt, which has little idea how to grapple with poverty and which lacks skilled banking personnel, the country might do somewhat better with capitalistic financial institutions.

In the agricultural sector it is appropriate to separate the fortunes of the export sector from the staple food sector because they have been the recipients of quite different policies.

It has already been pointed out that if the volume of output is used as an indicator of the number of livelihoods, then there has not been a significant increase in the number of livelihoods from the major export crops above the 1960 level. Given the population increase since 1960 it has to be concluded either that many people in this sector have become workless or that livelihoods have been subdivided and shared amongst more people. Either way poverty must have worsened *en masse*. If earnings have risen this should be seen in the context of both cyclical movements in world commodity prices and the rise in prices of food and other consumer goods.

The kind of investment needed in this sector—seed research, extension services, credit and transportation to help small producers reach new, distant processing plants and evaluation studies on possible crop diversification—has been very much an afterthought in the economic policies pursued. Today the members of the IGGI are urging more project aid to be given to combatting rural poverty, but there are already disturbing reports that local projects drawn up by foreign technical assistants have been revised on the orders of Indonesian civil servants with the result that resources are not directed to the poorest groups. Unless this new concern of aid donors for the rural poor is kept on a correct course aid might just as well be terminated.

The food staple sector characterises Java's agriculture, and both because it concerns the worst areas of poverty and because it has been profoundly affected by active government policies it is assessed separately.

RURAL LIVELIHOODS IN JAVA

It is easy to view the rice intensification schemes as a massive programme of technical assistance favouring the rural sector at the expense of urban development. Some might even go further and state that together with the fertiliser subsidy the technical assistance leading to higher yields and profits effectively turned the terms of trade in favour of rural areas and against urban areas. However, continuing in this strict aggregate economic vein it can easily be pointed out that estimating the terms of trade is difficult because the domestic price has been held well below international levels and so the heavily subsidised foreign aid rice consignments were undercutting Java's farmers. Had the rice price been allowed to find its international market price, who knows whether a fertiliser subsidy to rice farmers would have been necessary? Moreover, while droughts raised the price of rice, world inflation steadily pushed up the price of urban products purchased by rural people.

But more importantly, the rapid and significant changes in production methods following on the rice intensification programmes make imperative a closer look at the rural sector to see which classes of rural residents have benefited. In Chapter 4 the effects of inflation were seen to be different for landless labourers, tenants, and for small, medium and large farmers. Also it was noted that farms below a certain size had difficulty in becoming viable operations under the new technology.

When technology is introduced it is invariably accompanied by new or expanded institutions; and so it was in the case of the several Bimas programmes, with mobile banks, fertiliser coupons and kiosks, Bimas packages, and the village-based BUUDs. All these 'institutions' provided inputs and services to 'the rural sector', but their physical location and the terms on which they offered their inputs and services meant that, amongst a differentiated clientele, there was differentiated access to them. Landless labourers, of course, could be considered as having no access at all. Tenants were bound to have more restricted access than owner-cultivators, and the confusion about what constituted collateral for credit even under the Improved Bimas (*Bimas yang Disempurnakan*) demonstrates the difference between theory and reality in official programmes. When the programmes, or more specifically the input packages, were unpopular and coercion was used (that is, access was forced on farmers) it was those farmers with least economic power or political pull who were the first victims of military intimidation.

The story of the more powerful farmers gaining privileged access to the best of government services and managing to avoid the worst of them is very familiar and is certainly not unique to Indonesia. But in the period after 1965 when the pendulum was swinging against the previous struggles for land reform, when a right-wing military was intruding upon the rural scene, and when (in spite of official protestations of promoting social justice) the government was obviously 'betting on the strong', these new institutions indulged in highly discriminatory practices.

The technology itself was a catalyst to non-technological changes. When methods of production change, resource allocation alters with them, and so also do the returns to different factors of production. Inherent in this is a new set of social relations of production between the possessors of land, credit-worthiness and labour.

As potential yield and profit improvements become apparent, owners of land use their collateral to buy into a more capital-intensive cultivation process, and the differences in credit-worthiness amongst farmers reveals itself in a further economic, and later social, differentiation amongst farmers. But credit-worthiness does not merely decline to zero. Debt-labour can usefully be viewed as negative credit-worthiness whereby the relation between the creditor and debtor allows the former to exercise a monopoly control over the latter's labour and therefore make it not worth his while to seek government credit. The social relations between creditors and debtors take on a new form in a techno-commercial revolution as it becomes in the interest of the creditor to appropriate his debtor's and his debtor's family's labour and income in new forms of repayment. The finer technological points of the new method of rice production and the synchronised use of irrigation and solar capacities means that the opportunities for staggering labour inputs on neighbouring farms is lessened and if a poor farmer cannot make his family's labour available at a certain time he might just as well not bother with the new technology.

One of the consequences of the new set of social relations of production has been that whereas it has been customary to view renters of land as the landless seeking the status of farmer, today renters of land are those who are adding more land to their own landholdings. Land renting, therefore, is a factor concentrating control over land in the hands of fewer people. This trend has been marked and has been noted in some of the results of the Agro-Economic Survey. The status of the small owner has become similar to that of a landless labourer and he is likely to suffer some form of bonded labour as well, which means the return to his labour could be something less than the rural wage rate.

To say, therefore, that 'farmers' have benefited from more profitable means of cultivation is missing the connection between changing social relations of production and poverty.

It also raises the issue of land reform. It is invariably pointed out that a re-distribution of land in Java would not solve the landless question because the average farm would be too small to be viable. While this may be true there are still some things that have to be said. First, land ownership records are village-based, and were they aggregated over much larger areas it could be seen that many acres in different villages are owned by the same person. Second, land reform can mean not only reform of land title but also of land control and land use. If the trend towards concentrating control of land is excluding more and more people from a share in the benefits of technology, a breaking up of land control could allow more and more to gain an equitable share. Following on this, it is easy to see that land reform must be accompanied by other aspects of a wider agrarian reform, notably a resolution of the private debt situation. Third, to point out that there is not enough land to go round the whole rural population is no excuse for not ensuring that it goes round as far as possible. To be concerned with poverty is to eradicate as much of it as is feasible, not to sit back until a total final solution to it is found.

It might be argued that 'betting on the strong' will bring about a technological revolution in rice cultivation much faster and that not only will rice output rise but more jobs for the landless labourers can be found because the new method is known to be more labour-intensive. Thus even if the ranks of the landless are swelled the greater labour-input *per hectare* will facilitate more jobs.

In Chapter 4 it was seen that this is a dubious proposition for Java for two reasons. On the one hand, Java's 'green revolutions' in the colonial period introduced many of the labour-intensive practices which countries like the Philippines and Malaysia have only recently introduced on a large scale, while the Agro-Economic Surveys demonstrated that on good irrigated land the amount of additional labour required up to the harvesting stage was not as great as was originally supposed. On the other hand, the new set of social relations governing harvesting practices has reduced the amount of harvesting labour required, and because this is a commercial, rather than a technological, innovation it can spread to land which has not seen the increases in labour inputs due to new seeds and more fertiliser application. The new set of social relations governing harvesting and the modes of appropriating the output appears to have accelerated the demise of the much vaunted 'shared poverty' ethic of rural Java. The mechanisation of pounding and de-husking the paddy has also led to a loss of women's jobs for which the comparatively few jobs in rice mills are poor compensation.

Indonesia has been something of a paradise for instant economic experts since 1965 but the economist's tools of analysis are generally inadequate to cope with issues of poverty. Those economists loosely termed marxist economists are better equipped to provide insight on how the poor will fare during structural changes. But even these persons cannot match the training and skills of rural sociologists in understanding how different classes of rural residents see their options through a matrix of kinship and debt relations. If the government and its foreign creditors are serious about alleviating poverty they must listen more closely to an inter-disciplinary team of investigators. If they do not then they may find themselves in future wishing it were mere poverty they were confronting and not a state of widespread indigence.

PROBLEMS OF THE SECOND FIVE YEAR PLAN (REPELITA II)

In official pronouncements it has been suggested that although the government was always hoping to combat poverty and social injustice the immediate state of the national economic accounts demanded that other priorities had to govern the First Five Year Plan, but that the employment situation would be dealt with in the Second Plan, 1974-9. For this reason it might be considered unfair to the government not to examine the potential of the latter Plan.

The overall sectoral targets are intended to increase the share of gross domestic product going to industry, transport and communications, and cause a decline in agriculture's share from 40·2 per cent to 35·6 per cent. Thus in spite of transmigration, development of the outer provinces, improved marketing systems, 'continued emphasis on agriculture', agriculture is not expected to expand as fast as any other sector. The trends in sectoral composition

TABLE 8.4

Sectoral Composition of Gross Domestic Product (at 1960 Market Prices), 1960 to 1973, and Planned Change in Sectoral Composition in the Second Five Year Plan (percentages)

	1960	1965	1970	1973	1973/4 estimates	1978/9 projected estimates
Agriculture, Forestry & Fishing	53.8	52.3	47.5	42.9	40.2	35.6
Mining	3.6	3.7	5.6	7.1	9.2	9.9
Manufacturing	7.7	8.4	8.9	8.9	9.8	12.5
Construction	2.1	1.6	2.6	3.8	3.7	4.0

Sources: Calculated on the basis of data in A. Booth and B. Glassburner, 'Survey of Recent Developments', *Bulletin of Indonesian Economic Studies,* vol. 10, no. 1, March 1975; and Repelita II, quoted in *Bulletin of Indonesian Economic Studies,* vol. 10, no. 1, March 1974.

over the previous thirteen years and the planned sectoral composition are shown in Table 8.4.

Of the decline in agriculture's share from 54 to 43 per cent between 1960 and 1973, the biggest absolute falls were in farm food crops (34·4 per cent to 27·9 per cent), smallholders non-food crops (7·2 per cent to 5·4 per cent), estate crops (3·3 per cent to 2·1 per cent), and livestock (4·9 per cent to 3·7 per cent).

The planned overall annual rate of growth of GDP of 7·5 per cent between 1973-4 and 1978-9 allows for an annual per capita growth of 5·2 per cent. With agriculture, which incorporates the overwhelming share of mass livelihoods planned to grow at a (doubtful) 4·6 per cent, the egalitarian distribution of this 5·2 per cent per capita increase is at once called into question. Assuming a population growth of 2·3 per cent (7·5 minus 5·2) a year, the planned annual per capita agricultural growth is 2·3 per cent (4·6 minus 2·3).

Agriculture and irrigation are to take 20·6 per cent of investment expenditure in Repelita II compared with 30·1 per cent in Repelita I. If continued effort is to be made in the intensification of farming and the extension of wet rice-field acreage in order to achieve rice self-sufficiency, then other parts of agriculture are likely to be in for a lean time. 'Intensification' of rice cultivation is bound to mean capital and commercial input intensification as much as labour intensification. Moreover, it is intended to invest in the resuscitation of the Javanese sugar industry with the establishment of large modern sugar mills. The income multiplier effect of this may be restricted by the same locational and transport problems faced by the crumb rubber factory development in Sumatra.

To finance the expansion under Repelita II the development budget will be four times that of Repelita I. In 1974-5 65 per cent of the budget came from domestic revenues but by 1978-9 as much as 82

TABLE 8.5

Budget Receipts from Oil (at $8 per barrel) and Total Budget Receipts (Rupiah billion)

	Direct oil receipts	Indirect oil receipts	Total domestic receipts
1969/70	48.3	17.5	243.8
1974/5	653.7	19.3	1,363.4
1975/6	801.9	18.5	1,694.1
1976/7	870.9	18.0	1,967.8
1977/8	977.0	17.0	2,355.1
1978/9	1,211.9	16.0	2,852.8

Source: Repelita II, quoted in *Bulletin of Indonesian Economic Studies,* vol. 10, no. 1, March 1974.

The planned overall balance of payments during Repelita II is shown in Table 8.6.

per cent will do so, with corresponding declines in the role of foreign aid. The expected growth of government revenue from oil is shown in Table 8.5. Indirect receipts (from domestic sales) will stay constant, but the direct receipts (taxes on foreign companies) will raise the significance of oil receipts in the budget.

The most interesting aspect is the *planned* enlarging of current account deficit to be closer by greater capital inflow. Imports will increase continuously at a rising rate of expansion. Capital goods imports will increase 200 per cent, raw materials imports 150 per cent and consumer goods imports only 13 per cent.

TABLE 8.6
Balance of Payments during the Second Five Year Plan ($ million)

	1974/5	*1975/6*	*1976/7*	*1977/8*	*1978/9*
Exports fob	3,300	3,700	4,120	4,710	5,740
oil (net)	(1,470)	(1,670)	(1,880)	(2,190)	(2,840)
non-oil	(1,830)	(2,030)	(2,240)	(2,520)	(2,900)
Imports cif	−3,900	−4,350	−4,850	−5,410	−6,110
Services	−490	−660	−755	−865	−1,090
Balance on current account	−1,090	−1,310	−1,485	−1,565	−1,460
Programme	300	250	200	150	100
Project	300	350	425	495	540
Other	70	200	50	50	50
Other capital inflow	770	880	1,110	1,195	1,125
Debt services	−150	−170	−200	−225	−255
Monetary movements	−200	−200	−100	−100	−100

Source: Repelita II, quoted by S. Grenville ('Survey of Recent Developments', *Bulletin of Indonesian Economic Studies*, vol. 10, no. 1, March 1974).

Probably the most important single item of Repelita II is the employment target. Against an enlargement of the workforce of 6·2 million, jobs created are expected to be 5·5 million. Agriculture and industry will each absorb 1·2 million; communications 300,000; services, etc., 1·3 million. It is intended to influence employment by monetary policy and interest rates (presumably on investment loans.) Measures to encourage 'appropriate technology' are to be used as well but unofficial comments in the press reveal that the government is aware that this is really not possible where foreign investment is concerned. The new restrictions on foreign investors are not likely to affect employment except in the case of skilled and managerial employees taking over from their foreign counterparts. The government may be ambitious in its target of 1·2 million new jobs in industry. In particular the anticipation of 546,000 more jobs in textiles can scarcely be supported by domestic demand projections.

New jobs in industry will have to come from other import-replacement industries. The Plan includes encouragement of industries replacing imports of raw materials and intermediate goods; although the only ones quoted in ministerial statements appear to have been the textile industry and assembling factories. However, the sharp falls in foreign and domestic investment from 1974 onwards must place some of these hopes in doubt. The target of 1·2 million more jobs in industry by 1978-9 now appears over-ambitious.

But more serious are the presumptions about employment in agriculture. The Plan is supposed to give continued emphasis to agriculture, yet if employment in this sector will expand by 1·2 millions, this averages only 240,000 a year. The aggregate statistics do not help in indicating where this agricultural employment will come from.

From the data for exports in the projected balance of payments table, it is possible to deduce that the increases in non-oil exports can easily be accounted for by timber and minerals, both with poor employment prospects. This implies that traditional exports *may actually decline,* and with this employment in traditional agriculture. The threat of this occurring looms larger when it is appreciated that new oil earnings could permit the government to neglect traditional export agriculture as far as balance of payments reasons are concerned: the painstaking administrative investment in extension work, seed breeding, marketing and transportation are no longer necessary to defend the Rupiah.

The original calculations of expectations and targets for the Second Plan have been overtaken by the Pertamina troubles, the rising price of oil, the prolonged world recession, and the declining interest of foreign investors. The set of national accounts at the end of the Plan is likely to look very different. But one problem that the government knew it would always face is the tendency for imports to rise faster than planned imports.

Over a long enough period of time the cycles of prices of primary exports and of manufactured imports can be expected to balance each other in a statistical sense. However the process of releasing and distributing additional purchasing power through higher export earnings sets off a strong impetus to import more and the domestic market quickly becomes dependent upon these imports. Nor can it be expected that the differences between planned and realised imports of the First and Second Plans will be associated with the same items. During the First Plan the largest unplanned increases were of raw materials and capital goods: for 1973-4 these were planned to be of the order of $1·3 billion but actual imports were around $1·9 billion

(Grenville, 1974). It is quite possible that the target of raw material and capital goods imports for 1978-9 will not even be met because of weakened interest of foreign and domestic investors, and because of the effect of Pertamina's cash-flow problems on investment in its formerly planned industrial empire. But at the same time investment income remitted abroad, which had risen to $360 million by 1972-3 from a mere $47 million in 1966, might be as much as $1 billion by 1978-9.

Rice imports still constitute a huge imponderable. The planned self-sufficiency of 1973-4 turned into record imports of $500 million. Much of this went to building up stocks after the 1972 drought, but droughts every four or five years will still have to be contended with. Thus the balance of payments will not be unpredictable and volatile only because of fluctuating world commodity prices, which were shown in Chapter 4 to be substantial. The changes in the structure of the economy are magnified greatly in the balance of payments, and far from sheltering the economy from trends in the world markets for capital and primary products the post-1965 strategy has exposed the balance of payments even more to these winds.

The ability of the oil industry to maintain its share of total export earnings and, more important, to increase the real value of its earnings to match imported manufactures, may be at least as important during the Second Plan as during the First Plan. For this reason the harsh new terms of contract, forced on the foreign oil companies in 1975 to raise extra revenue against Pertamina's losses, may be self-defeating in the longer term.

Anxiety and arrogance have alternated rapidly in economy policy. The drought of 1972 softened the government's attitude towards Japanese investment in oil and gas and in the Asahan project. The oil price increases in 1973 hardened that attitude. Pertamina's troubles in 1975 caused panic for a time but the swift and generous action of the IGGI has probably returned the government to its usual complacency. When Pertamina returns to a profitable basis there is every likelihood that some, at least, of Ibnu Sutowo's grandiose industrial schemes will be taken up by the government.

The Indonesian economy shows many signs of moving into a high-risk era in the foreseeable future, in which the euphoria of the last decade cannot be repeated. The postponed rendezvous with issues of poverty will bring about one set of problems. The arrogance of the government in economic matters has been reflected in its foreign policy. Its neglect of its relations with Communist Asia will have to be repaired when it sees the rapidly expanding Chinese oil industry undercutting its oil markets in Asia, and when it becomes all too obvious that Asia's future rice granaries are in Communist countries.

The disdain which the government showed towards its own allies in the Association of South East Asian Nations during their efforts to create a non-Communist common market in 1975 has been somewhat softened but it can reasonably be doubted whether the government is really willing to pull its weight in these negotiations.

Some country members of the IGGI have become impatient with the neglect of poverty issues and with the continued suppression of civil rights, not to mention their disgust at the violent absorption of former Portuguese Timor into the Republic. The new administration in Washington with its professed humanitarian concern for the poor and with suppressed political opposition might well bring its influence to bear on the World Bank and International Monetary Fund members of the IGGI. If the IGGI reduces its pledges of aid, or if it only maintains aid at the present high level, the Indonesian economy is in deep trouble. So much for the once-vaunted post-1965 'economic miracle'.

Bibliography

Anon. (1973), 'The Problems of Success', *Far Eastern Economic Review,* vol. 82, no. 51.

Arndt, H. W. (1967), 'Survey of Recent Developments', *Bulletin of Indonesian Economic Studies,* vol. 3, no. 2.

Arndt, H. W. (1967a), 'Survey of Recent Developments', *Bulletin of Indonesian Economic Studies,* vol. 3, no. 4.

Arndt, H. W. (1971), 'Survey of Recent Developments', *Bulletin of Indonesian Economic Studies,* vol. 7, no. 1.

Arndt, H. W. (1972), 'Survey of Recent Developments', *Bulletin of Indonesian Economic Studies,* vol. 8, no. 2.

Arndt, H. W. (1973), 'Survey of Recent Developments', *Bulletin of Indonesian Economic Studies,* vol. 9, no. 2.

Arndt, H. W. (1974), 'Survey of Recent Developments', *Bulletin of Indonesian Economic Studies,* vol. 10, no. 2.

Arndt, H. W. (1974a), 'Survey of Recent Developments', *Bulletin of Indonesian Economic Studies,* vol. 10, no. 1.

Arndt, H. W. (1975), 'Survey of Recent Developments', *Bulletin of Indonesian Economic Studies,* vol. 11, no. 2.

Barlow, C. (1972), 'Smallholding Rubber: A Comment', *Bulletin of Indonesian Economic Studies,* vol. 8, no. 3.

Boucherie, W. (1969), 'The Textile Industry', *Bulletin of Indonesian Economic Studies,* vol. 5, no. 3.

Bowring, P. (1973), 'Dilemma of Repelita II', *Far Eastern Economic Review,* vol. 82, no. 43.

Chenery, H. B. *et al.* (1967), 'The Effectiveness of Foreign Assistance', in *Towards a Strategy of Development,* J. Tinbergen (ed.), Rotterdam University Press, Rotterdam, pp. 11–12, 14–16.

Coggin, D. (1975), 'Tethering the Corporate Tiger', *Far Eastern Economic Review,* vol. 90, no. 45.

Coggin, D. (1975a), 'Indonesia: Moving Prices into Line', *Far Eastern Economic Review,* vol. 90, no. 43.

Coggin, D. (1975b), 'Indonesia Set to Exploit Coal', *Far Eastern Economic Review,* vol. 90, no. 46.

Coggin, D. (1975c), 'Market Development at a Snail's Pace', *Far Eastern Economic Review,* vol. 89, no. 39.

Collier, W. L. (1972), *Problems of Rubber Production and Marketing in the Provinces of South Sumatra and Riau,* Agro-Economic Survey, Bogor, Indonesia.

Collier, W. L. and Werdaja, S. T. (1972), 'Smallholder Rubber Production and Marketing', *Bulletin of Indonesian Economic Studies,* vol. 7, no. 2.

Collier, W. L. and Werdaja, S. T. (1972a), 'Smallholder Rubber: A Reply', *Bulletin of Indonesian Economic Studies,* vol. 8, no. 3.

Collier, W. L. and Sajogyo (1972), *Employment Opportunities Created by the High Yielding Variables in Several Areas of Java,* Agro-Economic Survey, Research Notes, no. 8, Bogor, Indonesia.

Dapice, D. O. (1972), Indonesia's Economy in the 1970s: an Inventory and Prospectus, *Ekonomi dan Keuangan Indonesia,* vol. 20, no. 2.

Davies, D. (1974), 'Indonesia: Looking to its Own', *Far Eastern Economic Review,* vol. 83, no. 9.

Deuster, P. R. (1971), *Rural Consequences of Indonesian Inflation: A Case Study of the Yogyakarta Region,* Ph.D. Thesis, University of Wisconsin, pp. 79–96.

Glassburner, B. (1969), 'Public Law 480 Assistance and Economic Development in Indonesia', *Ekonomi dan Keuangan Indonesia,* vol. 17.

Glassburner, B. (1971), 'Indonesian Economic Policy After Sukarno, in *The Economy of Indonesia: Selected Readings,* Glassburner, B. (ed.), Cornell University Press, Ithaca and London, p. 246.

Glassburner, B. (1971a), 'Pricing of Foreign Exchange, 1966–7', in *The Economy of Indonesia: Selected Readings,* Glassburner, B. (ed.), Cornell University Press, Ithaca and London, p. 401.

Go, P. (1971), 'Nickel: Bright Future', *Far Eastern Economic Review,* vol. 74, no. 44.

Goldstone, A. (1974), 'Indonesia: Asia's timber giant', *Far Eastern Economic Review,* vol. 85, no. 26.

Grenville, S. (1973), 'Survey of Recent Developments', *Bulletin of Indonesian Economic Studies,* vol. 9, no. 1.

Grenville, S. (1974), 'Survey of Recent Developments', *Bulletin of Indonesian Economic Studies,* vol. 10, no. 1.

Hoemardani, S. (1974), 'Indonesia-Japan Relations in the Future—A Strategic Review', *Indonesian Quarterly,* vol. 2, no. 2.

Howett, L. and Morrow, M. (1974), 'Indonesia: Looking for a new deal', *Far Eastern Economic Review,* vol. 83, no. 6.

International Labour Office (1973), *The Role of the Textile Industry in the Expansion of Employment in Developing Countries,* Textiles Committee, Ninth Session, Geneva, p. 65.

Iskandar, S. (1972), 'Indonesia: Polarized Progress', *Far Eastern Economic Review,* vol. 76, no. 14.

Iskandar, S. (1972a), 'Japan's Indonesian Inroads', *Far Eastern Economic Review,* vol. 76, no. 22.

Jenkins, D. (1976), 'Showdown over Tankers', *Far Eastern Economic Review,* vol. 94, no. 46.

Jenkins, D. (1976a), 'Few Projects on the Way', *Far Eastern Economic Review,* vol. 93, no. 44.

Jenkins, D. (1976b), 'Indonesian Explorers Grim', *Far Eastern Economic Review,* vol. 93, no. 34.

Joesoef, D. (1974), 'Knowledge Economy and World Economy', *The Indonesian Quarterly,* vol. 2, no. 2.

Jones, G. W. (1966), 'The Growth and Changing Structure of the Indonesian Labor Force, 1930–81', *Bulletin of Indonesian Economic Studies,* no. 4, quoting K. Pelzer, *Pioneer Settlement in the Asiatic Tropics.*

Lie, H. K. (1974), *Foreign Investment and Economic Development in Less Developed Countries,* M. Econ. Thesis, Mcnash University, Melbourne.

McCawley, P. (1972), 'Survey of Recent Developments', *Bulletin of Indonesian Economic Studies,* vol. 8, no. 3.

McCawley, P. (1973), 'Survey of Recent Developments', *Bulletin of Indonesian Economic Studies,* vol. 9, no. 3.

McCawley, P. (1976), 'Survey of Recent Developments', *Bulletin of Indonesian Economic Studies,* vol. 12, no. 1.

McDonald, H. (1976), 'The Pertamina Spin-Off', *Far Eastern Economic Review,* vol. 92, no. 17.

McDonald, H. (1976a), 'Indonesia: Caltex Impasse Leaves Industry Gloomy', *Far Eastern Economic Review,* vol. 92, no. 15.

McDonald, H. (1976b), 'Heads Roll at Pertamina', *Far Eastern Economic Review,* vol. 92, no. 19.

McDonald, H. (1976c), 'Indonesia Cracks the Whip', *Far Eastern Economic Review,* vol. 92, no. 18.

McDonald, H. (1976d), 'Jakarta Sets its New Oil Terms', *Far Eastern Economic Review,* vol. 93, no. 32.

McDonald, H. (1976e), 'Indonesia: A New Hope for Loggers', *Far Eastern Economic Review,* no. 92, no. 21.

McDonald, H. (1976f), 'Asahan Bolsters a Hard Year', *Far Eastern Economic Review,* vol. 92, no. 26.

Mackie, J. A. C. (1970), 'The Report of the Commission of Four', *Bulletin of Indonesian Economic Studies,* vol. 6, no. 3.

Palmer, I. (1974), *The New Rice In Monsoon Asia,* United Nations Research Institute for Social Development, Geneva, pp. 155–8.

Panglaykim, J. and Arndt, H. W. (1966), *The Indonesian Economy: Facing a New Era?,* Rotterdam University Press, Rotterdam, p.33.

Panglaykim, J. and Penny, D. H., and Thalib, D. (1968), 'Survey of Recent Developments', *Bulletin of Indonesian Economic Studies,* vol. 4, no. 1.

Panglaykim, J. and Thomas K. D. (1967), *Indonesian Exports, Performance and Prospects, 1950–70,* Rotterdam University Press, Rotterdam, p. 18.

Panglaykim, J. and Thomas, K. D. (1971), *Economic Planning Experience in Indonesia,* Occasional Paper 5, Institute of Business Studies, Nanyang University, Singapore, p. 38.

Panglaykim, J. (1973), *Foreign Aid, Direct Investment in Indonesia: Some Notes,* Conference on Asia and the Western Pacific, Australian Institute of International Affairs, Canberra.

Panglaykim, J. (1973a), 'Some Notes on Japan-Indonesia Business Relations: An Indonesian View', *Indonesian Quarterly,* vol. 1, no. 4.

Penny, D. H. and Thalib, D. (1967), 'Survey of Recent Developments', *Bulletin of Indonesian Economic Studies,* vol. 3, no. 1.

Posthumus, G. A. (1971), *The Inter-Governmental Group on Indonesia,* Rotterdam University Press, Rotterdam, pp. 21, 33, 47, 53–5.

Rice, R. C. and Lim, D. (1976), 'Survey of Recent Developments', *Bulletin of Indonesian Economic Studies,* vol. 12, no. 2.

Roeder, O. G. (1973), 'Not all Sunshine', *Far Eastern Economic Review,* vol. 80, no. 2.

Sajogyo, *Modernisation without Development,* Paper contributed to the study on changes in agrarian structures, FAO–UN, 1972–3, p. 34.

Semay, M. (1972), 'Oil and Mineral Developments', *Bulletin of Indonesian Economic Studies,* vol. 8, no. 3.

Sethuraman, S. V. (1976), *Jakarta, Urban Development and Employment,* International Labour Office, Geneva.

Sie, Kwat Soen (1968), *Prospects for Agricultural Development in Indonesia,* Centre for Agricultural Publishing and Documentation, Wageningen, The Netherlands.

Simandjuntak, D. S. (1975), 'A Look at the Economy in 1974', *The Indonesian Quarterly,* vol. 3, no. 2.

Starner, F. (1974), 'Indonesia: Much on the Mind', *Far Eastern Economic Review,* vol. 83, no. 4.

Stockwin, H. (1976), 'Asahan: Why Japan Said Yes', *Far Eastern Economic Review,* vol. 92, no. 15.

Sundrum, R. M. (1975), 'Manufacturing Employment, 1969–71', *Bulletin of Indonesian Economic Studies,* vol. 11, no. 1.

Susenas, 1963–64 and 1969–70. These are the (sampled) National Social and Economic Surveys undertaken in the periods December 1963 to January 1964 and October 1969 to April 1970. The particulars referred to here are found under Particulars on Consumption. (Bureau of Planning, Jakarta).

Swasono, Sri-Edi (1973), 'Some Notes on the Nurturing of the Indonesian Entrepreneur', *The Indonesian Quarterly,* vol. 1, no. 4.

Timmer, P. C. (1973), 'Choice of Technique in Rice Milling', *Bulletin of Indonesian Economic Studies,* vol. 9, no. 2.

Vink, G. J. (1941), *The Basis of Indonesian Farms,* H. Veenman and Sons, Wageningen, Chapter 4 and Appendices 1 and 2 (quoted in Collier, W. L. and Sajogyo (1972), *Employment Opportunities Created by the High Yielding Varieties in Several Areas of Java,* Agro-Economic Survey, Research Notes no. 8, Bogor, Indonesia.)

Journals:

Bulletin of Indonesian Economic Studies, Canberra.
Ekonomi dan Keuangan Indonesia, Jakarta.
Far East Trade and Development, London.
Far Eastern Economic Review, Hong Kong.
Monthly Economic Letter, First National City Bank, Jakarta.
The Indonesian Quarterly, Jakarta.

Indonesian Official Publications:

Bank Negara Indonesia Annual Reports.
Bank Indonesia Annual Reports.
Indonesian Financial Statistics. Bank Indonesia.

Jakarta newspapers:

Abadi.
Angkatan Bersendjata.
Berita Yudha.
El Bahar.
Harian Kami.
Indonesia Raya.
Kompas.
Nusantara.
Pedoman.
Pelita.
Sinar Harapan.
Warta Harapan.